CLOSE
TO
THE
KNIVES

CLOSE TO THE KNIVES

A Memoir of Disintegration

DAVID WOJNAROWICZ

VINTAGE BOOKS
A DIVISION OF RANDOM HOUSE, INC.
NEW YORK

Library of Congress Cataloging-in-Publication Data
Wojnarowicz, David.
    Close to the knives: a memoir of disintegration / by David
Wojnarowicz.—1st ed.
        p.   cm.
    ISBN 0-679-73227-6
    1. Wojnarowicz, David—Health. 2. AIDS (Disease)—Patients—
United States—Biography. 3. Gay men—United States—Biography.
I. Title.
RC607.A26W63 1990
362.1'969792'0092—dc20
    [B]   90-50210
                    CIP

Grateful acknowledgment is made to Keiko Bonk for permission to
reprint an excerpt from the lyrics of "67 Eyes" by Keiko Bonk. Copyright
© 1989 by Keiko Bonk. Zen Jam (BMI).

Portions of this work originally appeared, in somewhat different form, in
the following journals: Between C and D Magazine, CUZ, City Lights
Review, East Village Eye, Red Tape, Diana's Almanac, Journal of
Contemporary Art, Witnesses: Against Our Vanishing, and Tongues of
Flame.

Book design by Cathryn S. Aison

Manufactured in the United States of America
30 29 28 27 26 25 24 23

"longer than China, bigger than Berlin
I go to a far away place within
taking a journey with 67 eyes
flying through fire all over the skies"
Keiko Bonk

". . . every stinking bum should wear a crown."
Iggy Pop

PERSONAL ACKNOWLEDGMENTS

Thanks to . . .

THE LIVING: Tom Rauffenbart, Patrick McDonnel, Nan Goldin, Siobhan, John Zinsser, David Coles and Peter Weiss of Center for Constitutional Rights, Paul Marcus, Susan Pyzow, Dr. Bob Friedman, Marion Scemama, Carlo McCormack, John Olsoff, Kathryn Barrett, Jonathan Gutoff, Anita Vitale, ACT-UP, Phil Zwickler, John Carlin, Elizabeth Hess, C. Carr, Lucy Lippard, David Hirsh, Bill Rice, Larry Mitchell, Karen Finley, Willy from the West Street days, Norman Frisch, Dennis Cooper, Old Reliable, Richard Kern, Amy Scholder, Ira Silverberg, Lydia Lunch, Ben Neill, Angela Davis, Judy Glantzman, Carmela Perri, Tommy and Amy Turner, Bill Burroughs, Philip Zimmerman, Jean Foos, Doug Bressler, Brian Butterick, Mary Hayslip, Phillip Yenawine, Cee Brown, Fran Lebowitz, Lynn Davis, Barry Blinderman, Christina Nordholm, Laurie Dahlberg, Peter Spooner, Kiki Smith, Syd Stoldt, Sophie Breer, Kathy Acker, Tanya, DeFazio, Ishmael and his dark sexy work, 42nd Street Movie Houses, Ann Northrop, the drag queens along the Hudson River and their truly revolutionary states, and all the guys and girls future and past who give chaos reason and delight.

THE DEAD: Peter Hujar, Keith Davis, Iolo, Montanna, Dean Savard, Arthur Bressan, Jr., Paul Proveaux, Cookie Mueller, Paul Thek, Luis Frangella, Ethyl Eichelberger, and Vito Russo for their beautiful brush fires in the social landscape.

And special thanks to my editor, Karen Rinaldi, and her muse, Lenny Dykstra.

CONTENTS

CLOSE
TO
THE
KNIVES

SELF-PORTRAIT
IN TWENTY-THREE ROUNDS

So my heritage is a calculated fuck on some faraway sun-filled bed while the curtains are being sucked in and out of an open window by a passing breeze. I'd be lying if I were to tell you I could remember the smell of sweat as I hadn't even been born yet. Conception's just a shot in the dark. I'm supposed to be dead right now but I just woke up this dingo motherfucker having hit me across the head with a slab of marble that instead of splitting my head open laid a neat sliver of eyeglass lens through the bull's-eye center of my left eye. We were coming through this four-and-a-half-day torture of little or no sleep. That's the breaks. We were staying at this one drag queen's house but her man did her wrong by being seen by some other queen with a vicious tongue in a darkened lot on the west side fucking some cute little puerto rican boy in the face and when me and my buddy knocked on the door to try and get a mattress to lay down on she sent a bullet through the door thinking it was her man—after three days of no sleep and maybe a couple of stolen donuts my eyes start separating: one goes left and one goes right and after four days of sitting on some stoop on a side street head cradled in my arms seeing four hours of pairs of legs walking by too much traffic noise and junkies trying to rip us off and the sunlight so hot this is a new york summer I feel my brains slowly coming to a boil in whatever red-blue liquid the brains float in and looking down the street or walking around I begin to see large rats the size of shoeboxes; ya see them just outta the corner of your eyes, in the outer sphere of sight and when ya turn sharp to look at them they've just disappeared around the corner or down subway steps and I'm so sick my gums start bleedin' everytime I breathe and after the fifth day I start seeing what looks like the limbs of small kids, arms and legs in the mouths of these rats and no screaming mommies or daddies to lend proof to the image and late last night me and my buddy were walking around with two meat cleavers we stole from Macy's gourmet section stuck in between our belts and dry skin lookin' for someone to mug and some queer on the upper east side tried to pick us up but my buddy's meat cleaver dropped out the back of his pants just as the guy was opening the door to his building and clang clangalang the guy went apeshit his screams bouncing through the night off half a million windows of surrounding apartments we ran thirty blocks till we felt safe. Some nights we had so much hate for the world and each other all these stupid dreams of finding his foster parents who he tried poisoning with a box of rat poison when they let him out of the attic after keeping him locked in there for a month and a half after all dear it's summer vacation and no one will miss you here's a couple of jugs of springwater and cereal don't eat it all at once we're off on a holiday after all it's better this than we return you to that nasty kids home. His parents had sharp taste buds and my buddy spent eight years in some jail for the criminally insane even though he was just a minor. Somehow though he had this idea to find his folks and scam lots of cash off them so we could start a new life. Some nights we'd walk seven or eight hundred blocks practically the whole island of manhattan crisscrossing east and west north and south each on opposite sides of the streets picking up every wino bottle we found and throwing it ten feet into the air so it crash exploded a couple of inches away from the other's feet—on nights that called for it every pane of glass in every phone booth from here to south street would dissolve in a shower of light. We slept good after a night of this in some abandoned car boiler room rooftop or lonely drag queen's palace.

———

If I were to leave this country and never come back or see it again in films or sleep I would still remember a number of different things that sift back in some kind of tidal motion. I remember when I was eight years old I would crawl out the window of my apartment seven stories above the ground and hold on to the ledge with ten scrawny fingers and lower myself out above the sea of cars burning up eighth avenue and hang there like a stupid motherfucker for five minutes at a time testing my own strength dangling I liked the rough texture of the bricks against the tips of my sneakers and when I got tired I'd haul myself back in for a few minutes' rest and then climb back out testing testing testing how do I control this how much control do I have how much strength do I have waking up with a mouthful of soot sleeping on these shitty bird-filled rooftops waking up to hard-assed sunlight burning the tops of my eyes and I ain't had much to eat in three days except for the steak we stole from the A&P and cooked in some bum kitchen down on the lower east side the workers were friendly to us that way and we looked clean compared to the others and really I had dirt scabs behind my ears I hadn't washed in months but once in a while in the men's room of a horn and hardart's on forty-second street in between standing around hustling for some red-eyed bastard with a pink face and a wallet full of singles to come up behind me and pinch my ass murmuring something about good times and good times for me was just one fucking night of solid sleep which was impossible I mean in the boiler room of some high-rise the pipes would start clanking and hissing like machine pistons putting together a tunnel under the river from here to jersey and it's only the morning 6:00 a.m. heat piping in to all those people up above our heads and I'm looking like one of them refugees in the back of life magazine only no care packages for me they give me some tickets up at the salvation army for three meals at a soup kitchen where you get a bowl of mucus water and sip rotten potatoes while some guy down the table is losing his eye into his soup he didn't move fast enough on the line and some fucked-up wino they hired as guard popped him in the eye with a bottle and I'm so lacking in those lovely vitamins they put in wonder-bread and real family meals that when I puff one drag off my cigarette blood pours out between my teeth sopping into the nonfilter and that buddy of mine complains that he won't smoke it after me and in the horn and hardart's there's a table full of deaf mutes and they're the loudest people in the joint one of them seventy years old takes me to a nearby hotel once a month when his disability check comes in and he has me lay down on my belly and he dry humps me harder and harder and his dick is soft and banging against my ass and his arm is mashing my little face up as he goes through his routine of pretending to come and starts hollering the way only a deaf mute can holler like donkeys braying when snakes come around but somehow in the midst of all that I love him maybe it's the way he returns to his table of friends in the cafeteria a smile busted across his face and I'm the one with the secret and twenty dollars in my pocket and then there's the fetishist who one time years ago picked me up and told me this story of how he used to be in the one platoon in fort dix where they shoved all the idiots and illiterates and poor bastards that thought kinda slow and the ones with speeth spitch speeeeeeech impediments that means you talk funny he said and I nodded one of my silent yes's that I'd give as conversation to anyone with a tongue in those days and every sunday morning this sadistic sonuvabitch of a sergeant would come into the barracks and make the guys come out one by one and attempt to publicly read the sunday funnies blondie and dagwood and beetle baily and dondi, with his stupid morals I was glad when some little delinquent punched his face in one sunday and he had a shiner three sundays in a row full color till the strip couldn't get any more mileage out of it and some cop busted the delinquent and put him back in the reform school he escaped from, and all the while these poor slobs are trying to read even one line the sergeant is saying lookit this stupid sonuvabitch how the fuck do you expect to serve this country of yours and you can't even read to save your ass and he'd run around the barracks smacking all the guys in the head one after the other and make them force them to laugh at this guy tryin' to read until it was the next guy's turn, and when we got to this guy's place there was three cats pissing all over the joint crusty brown cans of opened cat food littering the floor window open so they could leave by the fire escape and he had this thing for rubber he'd dress me up in this sergeant's outfit but with a pair of rubber sneakers that they made only during world war two when it was important to do that I guess canvas was a material they needed for the war effort or something and anyway so he would have me put on these pure rubber sneakers and the sergeant's outfit and then a rubber trenchcoat and then he'd grease up his dick and he would start fucking another rubber sneaker while on his belly and I'd have to shove my sneaker's sole against his face and tell him to lick the dirt off the bottom of it and all the while cursing at him telling him how stupid he was a fuckin' dingo stupid dog ain't worth catfood where'd you get your fuckin' brains surprised they even let ya past the m.p.'s on the front gate oughta call in the trucks and have you carted off to some idiot farm and where'd you get your brains and where'd you get your brains and when he came into his rubber sneaker he'd roll over all summer sweaty and say oh that was a good load musta ate some eggs today and I'm already removing my uniform and he says he loves the way my skeleton moves underneath my skin when I bend over to retrieve one of my socks.

LOSING THE FORM IN DARKNESS

It's so simple: the man without the eye against a receding wall, the subtle deterioration of weather, of shading, of images engraved in the flaking walls. See the quiet outline of a dog's head in plaster, simple as the splash of a fish in dreaming, and then the hole in the wall farther along, framing a jagged sky swarming with glints of silver and light. So simple, the appearance of night in a room full of strangers, the maze of hallways wandered as in films, the fracturing of bodies from darkness into light, sounds of plane engines easing into the distance.

It is the appearance of a portrait, not the immediate

vision I love so much: that of the drag queen in the dive waterfront coffee shop turning toward a stranger and giving a coy seductive smile that reveals a mouth of rotted teeth, but the childlike rogue slipped out from the white-sheeted bed of Pasolini; the image of Jean Genet cut loose from the fine lines of fiction, uprooted from age and time and continent, and hung up slowly behind my back against a tin wall. It's the simple sense of turning slowly, feeling the breath of another body in a quiet room, the stillness shattered by the scraping of a fingernail against a collar line. Turning is the motion that disrupts the vision of fine red and blue lines weaving through the western skies. It is the motion that sets into trembling the subtle water movements of shadows, like lines following the disappearance of a man beneath the surface of an abandoned lake.

He was moving in with the gradual withdrawal of light, a passenger on the shadows, heat cording his forehead and arms, passion lining the folds of his shirt. A handsome guy with unruly black hair, one eye like the oceans in fading light, the other a great vacant yawn shadowed black as the image of his leather jacket, all of it moved with mirage shivers over his heavy shoulders. There is a slight red color like a bruise or a blush to his cheeks, the muscles of his face smoothing into angles: hard jaw and a nose that might have once been broken. I was losing myself in the language of his movements, the slow rise and fall of a cigarette as he lifted it to his lips and brought it back down again, each drag leaving a small spherical haze to dissipate against his face.

Outside the windows the river light turned from blues to grays to flashes of rain. A serious dark veil ran the length of the horizon; there's a texture to it, a seediness like dream darkness you can breathe in or be consumed by. It swept down bringing with it strong waves and water, sending tiny people running for cars or shelter among the warehouse walls. Headlights began appearing, rain swinging through the holes in the roofs, through the windows emptied of glass. Sounds of dull puddles spreading along the floorboards. The stranger turned on his heel in the gray light and passed into other rooms, passing through layers of evening, like a dim memory, faceless for moments, just the movements of his body across the floor, the light of doorway after doorway casting itself across the length of his legs.

The river was dirty and coming toward me in the wind. A sixteen-wheel rig parked idling near the corner of the warehouse. Through the dark windows I could see this cowboy all the way from Wyoming sitting high up in the front seat, a woman with a blond bouffant seated next to him raising a bottle of whiskey to her lips. The refrigeration motor hummed while big gauze-covered bodies of cattle swung from hooks in the interior of the truck. Out along the waterfront asphalt-strip cars were turning and circling around. Headlights like lighthouse beacons drifted over the surface of the river, brief and unobtrusive, then swinging around and illuminating the outlines of men, of strangers, people I might or might not have known because their faces were invisible, just black silhouettes, outlined suddenly as each car passes one after the other, pale interior faces turned toward the windows, then fading into distance.

Sitting in the Silver Dollar restaurant earlier in the afternoon, straddling a shining stool and ordering a small cola, I dropped a black beauty and let the capsule ride the edge of my tongue for a moment, as usual, and then swallowed it. Then the sense of regret washes over me like whenever I drop something, a sudden regret at what might be the disappearance of regular perceptions: the flat drift of sensations gathered from walking and seeing and smelling and all the associations; and that strange tremor like a ticklishness that never quite reaches the point of being unbearable. There's a slow sensation of that type coming into the body, from the temples to the abdomen to the calves, and riding with it in waves, spurred on by containers of coffee, into the marvelousness of light and motion and figures coasting along the streets. Yet somehow that feeling of beauty that comes riding off each surface and movement around me always has a slight trace of falseness about it, a slight sense of regret, felt at the occurring knowledge that it's a substance flowing in my veins that cancels out the lines of thought brought along with time and aging and serious understanding of the self.

So there was that feeling of regret, a sudden impulse to bring the pill back up, a surge of weariness with the self, then the settling back and the wait for the sensations to begin. I smoked a fast cigarette and the door opened bringing with it sunlight and wind.

Restless walks filled with coasting images of sight and sound: cars bucking over cobblestones down the quiet side streets, trucks waiting at corners with swarthy drivers leaning back in the cool shadowy seats and the windows of buildings opening and closing, figures passing within rooms, faraway sounds of voices and cries and horns roll up and funnel in like some secret earphone connecting me with the creaking movements of the living city. Old images race back and forth and I'm gathering a heat in the depths of my belly from them: flashes of a curve of arm, back, the lines of a neck glimpsed among the crowds in the train stations, one that you could write whole poems to. I'm being buoyed by these discrete pleasures, walking the familiar streets and river. The streets were familiar more because of the faraway past than the recent past—streets that I walked in those odd times while living among them in my early teens when in the company of deaf mutes and times square pederasts. These streets are seen through the same eyes but each time with periods of time separating it: each time belonging to yet an older boy until the body smoothes out and lines are etched until it is a young man recalling the movements of a complicated past. I can barely remember the senses I had when viewing these streets for the first time. There's a whole change in psyche and yet there are slight traces that cut me with the wounding nature of déjà vu, filled with old senses of desire. Each desire, each memory so small a thing, becomes a small river tracing the outlines and the drift of your arms and bare legs, dark mouth and the spoken words of strangers. All things falling from the earth and sky: small movements of the body on the docks, the moaning down among the boards and the night, car lights slanting across the distance, aeroplanes falling as if in a deep surrender to the rogue embraces. Various smiles spark from the darkening rooms, from behind car windows, and the sounds of the wind-plays along the coast sustained by distance and leveled landscapes, drifting around the bare legs and through doorways and into barrooms. Something silent that is recalled, the sense of age in a familiar place, the emptied heart and light of the eyes, the white bones of street lamps and moving autos, the press of memory turning over and over. Later, sitting over coffee and remembering the cinematic motions as if witnessed from a discreet distance, I lay the senses down one by one, writing in the winds of a red dusk, turning over slowly in sleep.

———

The tattooed man came through the sheets of rain, and swinging headlights from cars entering the riverside parking lot caught him among the fine slanting lines of wind and water. Late this evening, I was sitting by the dock's edge, sitting in the rain remembering old jersey showers as a kid and the quiet deliciousness of walking through coal-gray streets where trees leaned over and by the fields where nuns in the cool green summers would hitch up their long black skirts and toss a large white medicine ball to each other in a kind of memory slow motion.

Over the jersey coast, seen through the veils of rain, the old Maxwell House coffee cup, a five-story neon cup of white, tipped over on its magical side with two red neon drops falling from its rim and disappearing into the darkness of the brush-covered cliffs. The tattooed man came up suddenly and sat down beside me in the rain like a ceramic figurine glazed with water running down the smooth colors of his shirtless chest. Huge fish fins were riding his shoulders and tattooed scales of komodo dragons, returned from the wilds of jungular africa, twisting outlines and colors of clawed feet and tails smoothing over his aged biceps and the cool white of his head, shaved to permit tattoos of mythological beasts to lift around his neck like frescoes of faded photographs of samurai warriors: a sudden flash of Mishima's private army standing still as pillars along the sides of the river.

———

He had a tough face. It was square-jawed and barely shaven. Close-cropped hair wiry and black, handsome like some face in old boxer photographs, a cross between an aging boxer and Mayakovsky. He had a nose that might have once been broken in some dark avenue barroom in a distant city invented by some horny young kid. There was a wealth of images in that jawline, slight tension to it and curving down toward a hungry-looking mouth.

Sitting in a parked car by the river's edge, he leaned over and placed the palm of his hand along the curve of my neck and I was surprised how perfectly it fit, stroking me slowly, his arms brown as the skin of his face, like a slight tan quietly receding into a blush. He seemed shy for a moment, maybe because of what he saw in my eyes, but the heat was pumping inside the car and the waves, turned over and over by the coasting winds, barreled across the surface of the river beneath darkening clouds. Some transvestites circled down from the highway, going from car to car, leaning in the driver's windows checking for business.

He eases his hands down toward my legs and slides it back up beneath my shirt, saying, "Take it off." I reached down and lifted the sweater and the t-shirt up together and pull them over my head, dropping them to the floor where my pants are straddling my ankles. He pulls off his green naval sweater revealing a t-shirt the color of ice blue, reaches down and peels that off too. We are looking at each other from opposite sides of the car. He's got a gleaming torso, thick chest with a smooth downy covering of black hair, brick-red nipples buried inside the down. He leans and bends before me licking my body softly down my sides, one hand massaging slowly between my legs, his other hand wetted briefly against his mouth and working his cock up until it is dark and red and hard.

When he lifted away from my chest I saw his eyes, the irises the color of dark chips of stone, something like the sky

15

at dusk after a clear hot summer day, when the ships are
folding down into the distance and jet exhaust trails are
uttered from the lips of strangers. The transvestites were
back and leaning in the window refusing to go away. We
pulled our clothes back on and closed up the car, heading
toward one of the abandoned structures.

Inside one of the back ground-floor rooms there are a
couple of small offices built into the garagelike space. Paper
from old shipping lines scattered all around like bomb blasts
among wrecked pieces of furniture; three-legged desks, a
naugahyde couch of mint-green turned upside down, and
small rectangles of light and wind and river over on the far
wall.

I lean toward him, pushing him against the wall, lifting
my pale hands up beneath his sweater, finding the edge of his
tight t-shirt and peeling it upward. I placed my palms
against the hard curve of his abdomen, his chest rolling
slightly in pleasure. Moving back and forth within the
tin-covered office cubicle, old soggy couch useless on the side,
the carpet beneath our shifting feet reveals our steps with
slight pools of water. We're moving around, changing positions that allow us to bend and sway and lean forward into
each other's arms so that our tongues can meet with nothing
more than a shy hesitation. He is sucking and chewing on my
neck, pulling my body into his, and over the curve of his
shoulder, sunlight is burning through a window emptied of
glass. The frame still contains a rusted screen that reduces
shapes and colors into tiny dots like a film directed by
Seurat. Pushing and smoothing against the tides, this great
dark ship with hundreds of portholes entered the film. His
head was below my waist, opening his mouth and showing
brilliant white teeth; he's unhooking the button at the top of

my trousers. I lean down and find the neckline of his sweater and draw it back and away from the nape of his neck which I gently probe with my tongue. In loving him, I saw a cigarette between the fingers of a hand, smoke blowing backwards into the room, and sputtering planes diving low through the clouds. In loving him, I saw men encouraging each other to lay down their arms. In loving him, I saw small-town laborers creating excavations that other men spend their lives trying to fill. In loving him, I saw moving films of stone buildings; I saw a hand in prison dragging snow in from the sill. In loving him, I saw great houses being erected that would soon slide into the waiting and stirring seas. I saw him freeing me from the silences of the interior life.

Stopped in the Silver Dollar just as dusk was rolling in, paid for some takeout coffee, there's a group of ten drag queens standing outside leaning on shining car fenders, applying lipstick and powders out of tiny mirrored compacts. One young man in a tight white t-shirt, hard white arms, no more dreams, heavy beer belly, had fallen on his face moments before. A couple of his teeth having popped out, there were two vermillion streaks running down the sides of his mouth and some cops were standing over him as he lay on his back, his cheekbones glistening and arms flailing like in some stream, backstroking his way out of this world, out of this life, away from this sea of blue uniforms and white boneless faces, away from this sea of city heat and faraway motion of his eyes fluttering behind dark sunglasses. Walked onto the pier and stood with my back to the river and way over the movements of the city was what looked like a falling star, a photographic negative of one in the night: a jet streak short and vertical falling from the sky, like a falling jet with a single illuminated flame tracing the domed curve of the heavens, a scratch in the sky, a blinding light caught in the scratch from the unseen sun, and slowly changing direction and connecting the rooftops of the buildings one after the other.

In the warehouse just before dark, passed along the hallways and photographed the various graffiti on the walls, some of hermaphrodites and others of sharp-faced thugs smoking cigarettes; in passing through a series of rooms, saw this short fat man with a seedy mustache standing in a broken closet filled with old wet newspapers and excrement and piss, standing with his hands locked behind his head and with a hard-on poking out through his trousers from beneath a grimy heavy overcoat: he was doing this strange dance, undulating his hips, sweat rolling down the sides of his face, beneath dark glasses, grimacing and stabbing the air with his cock and saying in a loud whisper: ". . . come in here . . . I'll make ya feel so *goood . . . so good . . .*"

Later, about 3:00 a.m., a terrific storm swept down on the city, the waves rolling like humpbacked whales just beneath the water's surface: whole schools of them riding first toward and then away from the piers. With another coffee I stepped along the walls of the warehouse and ducked beneath the low doorway to get out of the rain. Somewhere in the darkness men stood around. I thought I could hear the shuffle of their feet, the sense of their hearts palpitating in the coolness. Dark cars outside the windows slowly covered in rain, headlights clicking on suddenly, waves slashing at the pier and huge pieces of unhooked tin, torn down by the wind, clanging and crashing against the upper walls. I thought I saw a person in a white jacket disappearing as I reached the upper hallways. Walked around sloshing hot coffee over the rim of the open cup with every few steps. Looked out the side windows into the squall, tiny motions of the wet city. Inside, for as far as the eye could see, there was darkness and waving walls of iron, rusting sounds painful and rampant, crashing sounds of glass from remaining windows, and no sign of people: I realized I was completely alone. The sense of it slightly unnerving in the cavernous space. Street lamps from the westside highway burn in the windows, throwing shadows behind staircases and burying doors and halls. Walked out on the catwalk and watched the terrific gale and tossing waves of the river from one of the side doors. Huge panoramas of factories and water tanks were silhouetted by green roof lights and cars moving down the highway seen only by the red wink of their taillights.

Walking back into the main section of the warehouse I stopped in one of the rooms facing the elevated highway. The rain had slowed down and the streets were burning with a brassai light and texture. I suddenly felt a hand on my crotch in the darkness and turned toward the dark void where the face should be, stepping back as I did so. The hand belonged to a small, dwarfish man, someone out of an old Todd Browning image. I put my hand to his shoulder and said, "Sorry . . . just walking around. . . ." And as I passed through a series of rooms, he followed from a distance, sliding along the walls and appearing unexpectedly in the doorways ahead of me, the rise and fall of his cigarette describing a clear arc, like a meteorite, then disappearing into the shadows of his face. As I left by the back stairs, he drifted out of a room over to the top of the staircase and stood silently watching me descend from view.

————

Standing in a waterfront bar, having stopped in for a beer in mid-afternoon: smoky sunlight riding in through the large plate-glass windows and a thumping roll of music beating invisibly in the air. Over by one window and side wall, a group of guys are hanging out playing pool—one of them is this chicano boy, muscular and smooth with a thin cotton shirt of olive green, black cowboy hat pushed down over his head, strong collarbones pressing out, a graceful curve of muscles in his back and a solid chest, his stomach pressed like a slightly curved washboard against the front of his shirt, muscles in the arms rising and falling effortlessly as he gesticulates with one hand, talking with some guy who's leaning into the sunlight of the window; in his other hand the poolstick is balanced against his palm, a cigarette between his fingers. He leans back and takes a drag and blows lazy smoke rings one after the other that pierce the rafts of light and dissolve within the shadows. The guy that he was talking to looked like some faraway character straight from the fields of old skittering wheat and someone I once traveled with by pickup truck with beer cans in the dusty backseat and buzz in the head from summer: dark eyes and a rosy complexion, roughly formed face made of sharp lines and his hair cut short around the sides and back of his neck. Standing there sipping from a green bottle, I could see myself taking the nape of his neck in my teeth as he turned and stared out the window at the rolling lines of traffic for a moment. Light curved around his face and the back of his head, the shaved hair produced sensations that I could feel across the palm of my hand, my sweating hand, all the way from where I stood on the other side of the room. He looked around after turning away from the windows and set his eyes on me for a moment, studying me for indiscernible reasons, and I felt myself blush: felt the movement of the bass tapping against some chord where the emotions or passions lie, tilted my head back and took another swig from the beer, a humming gathering from my stomach and rising up past my ears.

He turns away and the chicano guy leans over the pool table for a shot, his back curved and taut like a bow, arm drawing back to softly clack the balls on the table: a couple dropping into the side pocket, and for a moment the two of them were lost in the drift of men entering the bar. I move over a few feet to bring them back into view and some sort of joke developed between them. The country boy reaches into the bottom slot of the table and withdraws a shiny black eight-ball and advances toward the chicano, who drew back until his buttocks hit the low sill of the window. He giggles and leans his head back at an angle and lets a hardness come from his eyes. The country boy's face turned a slight shade of red in the light and he reached out with his hands: one hand pulling the top of the chicano's shirt out and the other deftly dropping the eight-ball into the neckline. The ball rolled down and lodged near his belly and the two of them laughed as he reached in, hand sliding down the chest and stomach retrieving the ball. I took a last swig from my beer, overcome with the sensations of touch, of my fingers and palms smoothing along some untouched body in some imagined and silent sun-filled room, overcome with the heat that had been gathering in my belly and now threatened to overpower me with a sense of dizziness. I barely managed to place the bottle upright on the nearby cigarette machine and push open the doors, into the warm avenue winds, push open the doors and release myself from the embrace of the room and the silent pockets of darkness and the illuminating lines of light thinking it was Jacques Prevert who said "why work when you have a pack of cigarettes and sunlight to play with?," and listened to the horns of ships along the river, far behind the fields of buildings and traffic, turned a corner and headed across town.

————————

Passing down a long hallway there were glimpses of frescoes, vagrant frescoes painted with rough hands on the peeling walls, huge murals of nude men painted with beige and brown colors coupling several feet above the floorboards. Some of them with half-animal bodies leaning into the room's darkness with large outlined erections poised for penetration. Other walls contain crayoned buddhas and shining gems floating above their heads in green wax. One wall where a series of black wire-strewn holes pull apart the surface, where crowbars and hammers searched out copper pipes and wires, but still filled with floating faces almost japanese with pink high-boned cheeks and multicolored eyelids, a stream of hair touched by loving or by winds, small crudely drawn lanterns serving no discernible purpose but to genie these faces from the vague surface of the plaster.

Passing doorways in slow motion, passing through shadowed walls and along hallways, seeing briefly framed in the recesses of a room a series of men in various stages of leaning. Seeing the pale flesh of the frescoes come to life: the smooth turn of hands over bodies, the taut lines of limbs and mouths, the intensity of the energy bringing others down the halls where guided by little or no sounds they pass silently over the charred floors. They appear out of nowhere and line the walls like figurines before firing squads or figures in a breadline in old times pressed into history. Stopping for a moment, I thought of the eternal sleep of statues, of marble eyes and lips and the stone wind-blown hair of the rider's horse, of illuminated arms corded with soft unbreathing veins, of the wounding curve of ancient backs stooped for frozen battles, of the ocean and the eyes in fading light, of the white stone warthog in the forest of crowfoot trees, and of the face beneath the sands of the desert still breathing.

IN THE SHADOW OF THE AMERICAN DREAM
Soon All This Will Be Picturesque Ruins

I had almost become completely abstracted. At some point I think I woke up; I think it was minutes ago or maybe hours ago in this motel room. I never felt a sensation like this before but the heavy plasticized curtains covering the three windows of my room created what I imagined a flotation tank might feel like, or a dry rug-covered terrarium with the glass painted black and fitted with an airtight lid. When my eyes first opened it took some measure of time to realize I'd stepped away from myself among the veils of sleep and with that motion my eyes had disconnected from the nerves of the brain: that area where sight flows uninterrupted. The only vision from back there was a sub-vision: the magnified abstraction of a shiny black abdomen like a motorcycle gas tank or a mirrored black globe. Straining against the contours of the room and its furniture to reach back into that area and retrieve more of its form from the shadows, I could see or feel it for moments; the soundless click of its eight legs tapping the surfaces of the walls and ceiling of my sleep.

Later, drinking watery coffee in the motel restaurant, the hot sun of the day slanted across the highway illuminating truckers climbing into their rigs. In the watery circling of shapes and textures, I saw pieces of anatomy surfacing from my sleep: the lips or cheekbones or the fingers of some man or woman speaking and there was no sound but I recalled some story about a man lying in a prison cell with no sense of time forward or past, floating in either his or someone else's interior abstractions for maybe days or years or centuries. A small window high up on the wall across from his bed allowed him on tiptoe a view of a tiny piece of landscape, the tip of a rock or the shallow hip of hillside. In this landscape he could never receive evidence of the seasons and the temperature always remained constant. One day he discovered that he could measure the distances of the landscape by lying on his back in the center of the floor and placing the soles of his bare feet against the shafts of sunlight extending diagonally through the bars. With a series of small walking motions he could trace something calendar- and distance-oriented from the lengths of light. It might have been something algebraic but I never had enough of an education to question this and that was the only way it made sense.

———

Driving a machine through the days and nights of the empty and pressured landscape eroticizes the whole world flitting in through the twin apertures of the eyes. Images in the distance that could fit in the centimeter of space between the upheld thumb and forefinger of my hand carry the compacted energy of the same image close up. Possibly more. Turning the bend in the highway suddenly reveals, a quarter mile away, a highway crew standing in a jumble of broken earth and enormous machines. In that instance I see the browned flesh of a shirtless man in shorts; I see the bare arms and ribs of a man buried in the shadows of a tractor's cab; I see the bent-over back of a man swinging a pickax with all his might; I see the pale white underarm with the accompanying dark spot of wet hair belonging to a guy up in a cherry picker among the telephone wires and I feel the fist of tension rising through my solar plexus beneath my t-shirt and the sensation grows upward, spreading like some strange fever in my chest, catching only at the throat where small pockets of sound are contained. In a moment the vehicle I'm steering passes by the scene and I'm left populating the dry plains, the buttes and the cloudless sky with the touch and taste of flesh. I fill the gullies with small but heated fictions.

There is really no difference between memory and sight, fantasy and actual vision. Vision is made of subtle fragmented movements of the eye. These fragmented pieces of the world are turned and pressed into memory before they can register in the brain. Fantasized images are actually made up of millions of disjointed observations collected and collated into the forms and textures of thought. So when I see the workers taking a rest break between the hot metal frames of the vehicles, it doesn't matter that they are all actually receding miles behind me on the side of the road. I'm already hooked into the play between vision and memory and recoding the filmic exchange between the two so that I'm without a vehicle and I have my hand flung out in a hitchhiking motion and one of the men has stopped his pickup along the stretch of barren road. Now I am seated next to his body in the front seat. We are traveling and speaking soundlessly and he eventually turns off the highway onto a series of dirt roads that end among the psychedelic patterns of the tree-filled hillsides and there are my hands before me and there is the almost inaudible click of his zipper riding down between the fingers in slow motion. There is the taste of sperm at the edge of a lake cast into shadows by the surrounding mountainsides. There is the hungry unreeling of all this in the unraveling landscape of dry scrub plains through the front windshield and the rearview mirror. And here is the solitary form of my body leaning back in the sunburned interior of my car, foot pressing on the gas pedal sending me forward toward the gray veils of rain drifting across the white a hundred miles away.

———

Like the ocean's movement where every seventh wave is higher and more furious than the others, small pieces of last night's sleep return in the eddy and flow of the day's turning. The guy in the prison recalls something of his history: he once worked in a canning plant on the edge of the coastal town, in the warehouses that were large darkened metal buildings swept with the cool chill of massive refrigerating units. Under dim ceiling bulbs he spent days and months packing cartons with unlabeled tin cans, each can containing some kind of liquid, forty-eight cans to a carton, thirty-six cartons to a wood palette and then metal strapping bands tightened around each block layer to keep them from tumbling. Each minute of the day was spent making the same gestures of the arms: lift, swing, deposit, lift swing deposit, tape lift drop and push. He gets lost in himself the same way I do at some point I forget I'm in a vehicle, much less driving. After years of this work he begins to dream of the cans sitting packed away in the vast recesses of the warehouse waiting. He slowly developed the sense that each can contained a life, each breathing in forty-eight rhythms to a carton thirty-six cartons to a palette, thousands and thousands of palettes. And the combined sounds of all that consciousness waiting and waiting in the stillness of those dim buildings woke him up some nights tangled among the bedsheets laden with sweat.

I feel that I'm caught in the invisible arms of government in a country slowly dying beyond our grasp. There is something singing of this, something in the currents of wind and breeze floating along the black electric cables lining the roads, something I can't see or touch but moves in the shape of vowels and uttered sounds like the spinning soft bodies of birds playing with the sky. I play games with the road to shake myself up, at times squeezing my eyelids closed so that I drive quarter-mile stretches without sight and it becomes a fight to open my eyes before the side of the road overtakes me. It's as if a second person is sitting within my body at the wheel. The body that holds the wheel understands the danger that mounts by the moment and the second body smiles in the dark interior of the first. When the eyes finally open, they reveal nothing new about the world except a slight shift in landscape proving that increased mortality teaches me nothing. There's no enlarged or glittering new view of the nature of things or existence. No god or angels brushing my eyelids with their wings. Hell is a place on earth. Heaven is a place in your head.

Late at night when most of the traffic on the highways had exited for motel sleep, I turned off the road and drove up a dirt hill toward a truck stop hidden for a moment in the folds of the landscape. In a series of wheel motions, a neon-outlined teepee slid into view out of the darkness. I needed some coffee because the road started becoming confused with the sky. Small rocks turned up by the wheels pinged under the car's belly. Down along the service road the prehistoric silhouettes of sixteen-wheel rigs ground their gears in the blackness to shift back out to the main road. As each cab swung by me there was a video blaze of tiny green and red ornamental cab lights framing the darkened windows containing a momentary fractured bare arm or dim face filled with the stony gaze of road life. In these moments my face travels an elongated neck out my side window and floats up into the shadows of their open windows to place its tongue in between the parted lips of each driver. I could feel their arms reaching through the breeze of our moving vehicles to embrace me from behind.

Pulling through the darkness and the swirling dust I parked in front of the building. After stepping from my car and moving across the nightsoil toward the plate-glass doors, I noticed a green beat-up chevy parked under the fluorescent drift of building lights, and behind the shadows of the driver's window, as if swimming in the depths of lantern seas, was the amazing and beautiful face of a navajo man in his early fifties. He sat hunched in the driver's seat unmoving, his face tilted as if in wait for someone familiar to exit the silent doors of the building. I stopped for an extended moment lost in his distances. He was trapped within the glassed-in diorama of his metallic-and-chrome vehicle, within the museum of his own natural history as viewed through a white boy's eyes.

———

It was a tabloid moment in time. Issuing between the static waves on the car radio as I entered a small city in the west was a news story reporting that a teenage Native American boy in a small but resilient automobile had made a wrong-way turn against the rush of oncoming traffic in order to mount a curb and run over a college student waiting for a bus. The boy's car then turned back onto the road and disappeared in the morning rush-hour confusion.

Driving around the city, it didn't take long to realize that if you didn't have a vehicle, a machine of speed, you owned poverty. It was yet another city dying of a disease whose anatomy was just beyond the inhabitants' grasp. Its origins may have been as a trading post in another time but now it had become a government war town filled with a half million workers employed in the various research centers attempting to perfect a president's dream of laser warfare from the floating veil of outerspace. Local papers were filled with patriotic hard-ons in the face of recent successes in the nearby desert where researchers were able to knock a dummy missile out of the clear blue sky with a laser discharged from a device the size of a refrigerator. Other than the clouds in the sky, an occasional bird or dog and the anonymous nomadic poor, all movement in the city was confined to the automobile. Those who owned cars, when witnessed close up in the tiled halls of shopping centers, had a vague transparency and thickness to their skin. The city during the day was bathed in a hot white sunlight; a steel-pounding heat coursed off the walls of miragelike architecture in the waves of desert wind. There was a distant energy surrounding everything like fear because there was nothing about the architecture that the eye could settle on; the eye was constantly adrift almost as if it were experiencing a small panic. It was an architecture of a population anticipating impermanence or death. It was a vacuum turned inside out, prefab materials of housing resembling the dry husks of insects halfway through their molt. All along the sidewalks were the people reduced to walking; the desperation of whole families sitting in lethargy on the curbsides lost to the sounds of automobiles; the swollen slit-eyed heads of drunks bobbing in the blue air as they staggered along the sidewalks. Owning a vehicle, you could drive by and with the pressure of your foot on the accelerator and with your eyes on the road you could pass it quickly—maybe not fast enough to overlook it completely, but fast enough so that the speed of the auto and the fear centers of the brain created a fractured marriage of light and sound. The images of poverty would lift and float and recede quickly like the gray shades of memory so that these images were in the past before you came upon them. It was the physical equivalent of the evening news.

The motor replaces the horse; the speed and the intent of the vehicle replaces the dead bows and arrows of history: the kid made the next day's newspapers. An early afternoon bicyclist reported a teenager driving a dark-colored camaro who chased him down a one-way street. The cyclist narrowly avoided being run over by abandoning his bike and scrambling on top of a row of parked cars. The bicycle was left mangled and the camaro scraped along the sides of the cars in a fury before making a U-turn and disappearing. Two middle-aged women came forward with a story of having been menaced in the previous week while crossing an inter-section not far from the state campus. Other sightings of the kid were reported in the next twenty-four hours. One woman told of being grazed by a dark-colored auto that purposefully accelerated and swung toward her as she got into her own car. A slow private history was beginning to reveal itself. The hotel I stayed in was an ex-prostitution hotel with a nonfunctioning swimming pool in a former skid-row section of town. It was in the general striking area of the camaro. Every time I walked down the street or got out of my car I thought of a body stripped of flesh turning slowly on the end of a rope, I thought of the wind reeling through the red skulls of flowers, I thought of the face of our current president floating disembodied and ten stories tall over the midnight buildings. I wondered why any of these things, like the kid in his camaro, are a surprise. Why weren't more of us doing this?

There were times in my teens when I was living on the streets and selling my body to anyone interested. I hung around a neighborhood that was so crowded with homeless people that I can't even remember what the architecture of the blocks looked like. Whereas I could at least spread my legs and gain a roof over my head, all those people down in those streets had reached the point where the commodity of their bodies and souls meant nothing more to anyone but themselves. I remember times getting picked up by some gentle and repressed fag living in a high-rise apartment filled with priceless north american indian artifacts and twentieth-century art who was paying me ten bucks to suck on my dick. As I studied his head bobbing against my belly while seated on a leather couch, I marveled at how simple it would be to lift the carved stone fish from the glass coffee table and smack the top of this head in and live on easy street for a while. I thought of the hundreds of times standing in a moving subway car, a cop standing with his back to me, his holster within easy reach and me undoing the gun restraint with my eyes over and over. I thought of the neo-nazis posing as politicians and religious leaders and I thought of my genuine fantasies of murder and wondered why I never crossed the line. It's not that I'm a *good* person or even that I am afraid of containment in jail; it may be more that I can't escape the ropes of my own body, my own flesh, and bottom line in the pyramids of power and confinement one demon gets replaced by another in a moment's notice and no one gesture can erase it *all* that easily.

In the last evening in the motel room, falling to sleep amid the sounds of splintering glass from a fight in another room, I found myself walking in this rural section of the country. It was dirt roads and a thick strangling brush and woods appearing over the tops of brambles that lined the road. There were groves of beautiful firs and leafy oaks and some beech trees. I came into this area where the road turned triangular. The triangle had a stretch of sidewalk with small-town stores. There was a coffee shop, a ma and pa–type restaurant with formica counter and shining stools and a gallon bottle of hard-boiled eggs in vinegar and maybe some containers of beef jerky. I stepped up onto the sidewalk which was built like a slightly raised boardwalk of slatted wood and in the shadows of a wall there's this fourteen- or fifteen-year-old kid with long black hair and a denim jacket with cigarettes in the top pocket. He's standing outside this open screen door of the coffee shop with one leg folded beneath him the sole of his foot flat against the wall of the building and hands in pockets. As I pass the doorway of the shop, I glance inside out of the corner of my eyes and see three or four teenage guys playing a couple of pinball machines, riding the flippers and machines with bucking hip motions and thrusts and they're actually in the process of breaking open the machines to get the money. I flinch a little in that moment, realizing there is danger and I don't know where I am. I'm a stranger in these parts. My body is in motion as I take all this in and the kid leaning outside the door says what the fuck you lookin at? and before I can answer he whips out this long knife. It's about nine inches of thin steel blade and with a flick of his wrist slashes my bare arm open from wrist to elbow. I look down in slight shock and step back waving my hands in front of me saying, "Nothing man . . . nothing . . . sorry." He seems satisfied and lets me pass on down the sidewalk. I'm holding my arm to keep the wound as closed up as possible and when I reach a section of the sidewalk where there's an alley I step inside to lean shakily against a wall. I notice two other guys about my age all cut up on the arms, legs and bellies. I stumble out of the alley and suddenly this policeman shows up. He's wearing tan pants, shirt and cap and black boots and he's holding a whip about a yard long. The kid spots him coming and starts running down the road in the direction I came from. The officer starts chasing him and I run after the two of them to see what happens to the kid. The kid is in the distance and the officer stops in the middle of the road. The kid turns while running to see where we are just as the officer snaps his arm and the whip elongates into the distance and wraps around the kids head bringing him to a halt—his hands come up to his face completely wrapped in leather thong. The officer runs the distance and catches up to the kid and hog-ties him like a rodeo calf. By the time I reach them the officer steps back a few feet and pulls out a shotgun taking aim on the kid. I'm thinking, "Oh man ... he ain't gonna shoot him—he wouldn't do that." And as I'm thinking that, the officer pulls the trigger and blows a hole open in the kid's side. The kid's side is gaping open near the waist showing pulsating intestines and stomach. I'm crouching near the kid's head looking into his eyes as the officer comes up and squats down next to me. The kid is no longer a kid; he's some kind of stray dog with bristly black fur and frightened eyes. The officer takes the kid's knife from the ground and with the other hand carefully parts the flesh of the wound until the organ that seems to be the stomach is revealed, its delicate pink grayish bloat quivering like a lung puffing in and out. The officer delicately cuts it open and clear liquid pours out. I look into the dog's eyes and watch the terror and pain change into an opiumlike daze. A sensual pleasure passes beneath their surface, a strange state of grace in the flight behind the eyes speeding up, the fading of life into the pale glaze of death.

———

Americans can't deal with death unless they own it. If they own it, they will celebrate it, like in the air force base museum of the atomic bomb, where whole families of camera-toting tourists gather after the required i.d. security checks. In the gray-carpeted rooms, they walk the mazes of portable screens and platforms and enlarged photographs of death and incineration as seen from a discreet distance. The distance is far enough so you can't see the bodies, only the architecture. The tour in this museum is led by an ancient matronly type who explains various levels of the bombs invention with all the glad bearings of a parent who has just given birth to her first child. I couldn't deal with the clouds of perfume and the decaying personalities of the crowd so I wandered off by myself to walk the maze. There were machines that clicked on, set off merely by my presence and I'm walking through a paranoid blur of mechanical men's voices crawling out of hidden speakers and image after image floating and shifting into fragments of large grainy black-and-white blow-ups of sullen men standing half conscious with pride next to sinister fat canisters looking like overturned pot-bellied stoves. The voices have all the tone and texture of high school film soundtracks explaining the abstract motions of the sperm entering the side of the egg and fertilizing it, or the hunger and desire implicit in the tiny snake swallowing the egg ten times the size of its own head.

Outside the shedlike buildings are the constant shrill vibrating sounds of jets taking off into the afternoon heat. Through a back window that overlooks the concrete edges of the runways I see a playground with defunct miniature jets and spare broken engines from spacecraft of the past decades. It is a playground for the kids and at that moment there is a family gathering among the hulls of bomber planes and world war two relics for a photo op. Standing in the shadow of a late-model bomber cabled to the asphalt surface of the ground a grandmotherly type gathers three kids in close to her body, fitting them in the frame of their parents' camera shutter. It's three generations of a family and everything is so clean and abstract that I'm feeling dizzy. I'm watching all this surrounded by two screens showing speeded up videos of a nuclear reactor being built by men the size of ants. They build and rebuild the reactors in twenty seconds flat. I'm thinking if I owned the place I'd hook the constant smell of rotting flesh into the air-conditioning unit and have all the screens filled with speeded-up films of rotting corpses and the family outside the window is moving to the next plane for the next photo. A man steps out from behind a doorway I hadn't noticed before and offers me his hand in greeting, asking if I'd like a cup of coffee. He looks like the kind of guy who'd one day end up in an alcohol detox center studying snakes and insects. I turn away without a word; I'll never shake the hand of someone I might be fighting against in wartime.

———

We are born into a preinvented existence within a tribal nation of zombies and in that illusion of a one-tribe nation there are real tribes. Some of the tribes are in the business of sucker-punching peoples psyches in the form of maintaining the day-to-day job of government—they sell the masses a pile of green-tainted meat; i.e., a corrupted and false history as well as a corrupted and false future, and although that meat stinks of rot and pus and blood, this particular tribe extols these foul emissions as if they were virtues made of glorious sensitivities: "Raise Ole Glory while we do it to them again . . ."

Then there are other tribes which work hand in hand with the government, offering slices of meat in the form of doubletalk; or *hope*—hope as a chain of submission. Then there are the tribes that suckle at the breast of telecommunications every evening after work and are fatally lulled into society's deep sleep. Day after day they experience waking nightmares but they've either bought the con of language from the tribe that offers hope, or they're too fucking exhausted or fearful to break through the illusion and examine the structures of their world.

There are other tribes that experience the X ray of Civilization every time they leave the house or turn on the tv or radio or pick up a newspaper or when they suddenly realize their legs have automatically come to a halt before a changing traffic light. A civil war and a national trial for the "leaders" of this country, as well as certain individuals in organized religions, is the soundtrack that plays and replays in the heads of members of that tribe. Some members of the tribe understand the meaning of language. They also understand what *freedom* truly is and if the other tribes want to hand them the illusion of *hope* in the form of the *leash*—in the form of *language*—like all stray dogs with intelligence from experience, they know how to turn the leash into a rope to exit the jail windows or how to turn the leash into a noose to hang the jailers. But when the volume of that war reaches epic dimensions, and when the person hearing it fails to connect with another member of the same tribe who can acknowledge the sound, that person can one day find themselves at the top of a water tower in suburbia armed with a high-powered rifle firing indiscriminately at the ants crawling around below. That person can one day find himself running amok in the streets with a handgun; that person can one day find himself lobbing a grenade at the forty-car motorcade of the president; or that person can end up on a street corner, homeless hungry and wild-eyed, punching himself in the face or sticking wires through the flesh of his arms or chest.

———

I left one town and headed for another on the available interstate that led through sections of burst red earth and cables and tractors and pickup trucks and workers in dusty clothes running back and forth. It was a couple of hours before dusk and as I turned onto a lesser used road, the landscape grew more quiet and the car radio had navajo language chittering through waves of static. There were no other cars but mine and the one I was in didn't like mountains so I had to drive with the heater full blast to cool the engine down. Big goofy cactus grew in the shapes of people only green on the roadsides among burned patches of sagebrush and the occasional shock of rows of some kind of produce in long irrigated stretches.

Last night I felt unbelievably sad and sometimes it happens that way: a sensation comes out across the landscape into the cities and further into the window of the car as I'm coasting the labyrinths of the canyon streets. It feels for a moment like nothing more than wind; it's something I don't see coming and suddenly it's upon me and my eyes are blurring with tears and fragmented spills of neon and ghostly bodies of pedestrians and smokestacks and traffic lights and I'm gasping from a sense of loss and desire. I can't think of anything I am truly afraid of and I'm trying to give something unspeakable words; some of us live in big cities so we can be alone, so we can avoid ourselves, and yet by living within massive populations we can have help or love within reach if necessary.

I am fearful of something more than fear: it's something in the landscape surrounding the cities and smaller towns between here and the coast, something *out there* that feels so empty and it is not made of earth or muscle or fur; it's like a pocket of death but with no form other than the light one might cast upon its trail of fragments. For a moment I think it's just the unfamiliarity of the landscape's agenda, what it contains in the future of its emptiness. I mean, out there I am in and surrounded by a void, a "natural" counterpart to the industrial void of the cities. Out there I can feel buried under the dome of the sky and feel claustrophobic in the heat which is like a plastic cushion pressing unseen against all the surfaces of my exposed body and in all that dizzying stillness I feel like my soul and my flesh will suddenly and abruptly be consumed within the civilizational landscape or else expelled off the face of the earth. What troubles me is that I might not mind.

When I was a teenager I had a recurring fantasy that began after my first motorcycle ride. This was shortly after waking up one morning and realizing that government and god were interchangeable and that most of the people in the landscape of my birth insisted on having one or both determine the form of their lives. I recognized the fact that the landscape was slowly being chewed up and that childhood dreams of autonomy in the form of hermetic exile were quickly becoming less possible. (I was also in the threads of a childlike crush on a guy I'd met in a times square movie house who'd taken me home for twenty-four hours of sex. He was a college student who looked like he'd grown up in some part of the country like kentucky and in the angles of his chest and abdomen and face, I'd gotten him mixed up with the characters in the movie we were watching when we first noticed each other in the dark seats of the balcony. It was a movie about sexy moonshiners who walked around half naked and eventually died in a shootout with the federal authorities. After carrying on a secret affair with this guy for a number of weeks, he broke it off with the explanation that I was too young and when I got old enough I would understand the range of possibilities for different lovers and that at that abstract moment of time I would leave him.) I lay in a hotel room one night after selling my body to a customer who had gone back home to his wife and kids, and I wished I'd had a motorcycle and that I was in a faraway landscape, maybe someplace out west. I saw myself riding this machine faster and faster and faster toward the edge of a cliff until I hit the right speed that would take me off the cliff in an arcing motion. At that instant when my body and the machine cleared the edge of the cliff and hit the point in the sky where I was neither rising nor falling—somewhere in there: once my body and the motorcycle hit a point in the light and wind and loss of gravity, in that exact moment, I would suddenly disappear, and the motorcycle would continue the downward arc of gravity and explode into flames somewhere among the rocks at the bottom of the cliff. And it is in that sense of void—that marriage of body-machine and space—where one should most desire a continuance of life, that I most wish to disappear. I realized that the image of the point of marriage between body-vehicle and space was similar to the beginning of orgasm. I may be living a life that is the equivalent of a ride on an upside-down road but it is only to shake all the ropes off, even the ropes of mortality. Even in the face of something like gravity, one can jump at least three or four feet in the air and even though gravity will drag us back to the earth again, it is in the moment we are three or four feet in the air that we experience true freedom.

So what is that feeling of emptiness?

Maybe it's that the barren landscape becomes a pocket of death because of its emptiness. Maybe the enormity of the cloudless sky is a void reflecting the mirrorlike thought of myself. That to be confronted by space is to fill it like a vessel with whatever designs one carries—but it goes farther than these eyes having nothing to distract them as vision does its snake-thing and wiggles through space. There *is* something in all that emptiness—it's the shape of a particular death that got erected by tiny humans on the spare face of an enormous planet long before I ever arrived, and the continuance of it probably long after I have gone.

———

The Indian kid and his camaro got picked up by the cops in a suburban section of town and the interviewed neighbors could recall nothing more alarming about the kid than that he had an obsession with keeping his car cleaned and polished. One neighbor said that the kid loved to peel out from the gravel driveway sending cascades of stones into the air. I read all this in the local paper in the curtained hotel room just before leaving town. Outside the window of the balcony room, three Metal guys were building a new patio for the defunct pool. The pool was slowly filling with red dust carried across the roads by intermittent breezes. At some point I stood up from the table and pulled back the curtain a hair and watched the half-naked bodies of the guys climbing in and out of their truck for tools or to turn the volume of the music up. I watched them leaning for extended moments in various positions creating sexy tableaus like museum paintings, like bleached out Vermeers and Rembrandts in all that hot sunlight and shadow. I felt like a detective with only the window glass and the curtains camouflaging my desire. For a moment I was afraid the intensity of my sexual fantasies would become strangely audible; the energy of the images would become so loud that all three guys would turn simultaneously like witnesses to a nearby car crash.

―――――――

Out the side window of the car I see the thick whirling vortex of a red dust devil on the plains. I abruptly pull the car over and grab my super-8 camera to film it and it disappears. I stare at the place where I saw it, waiting for it to reappear but it doesn't so I drive on. My balls are sliding in lonesomeness. The windows are down because of the heater and the motion of the vehicle brings a false breeze onto my face and bare chest and through my scalp. For one brief moment in time no one in the world knows where I am. Not family, friends, nor members of government and that causes me to drift, gives me room to experience charges of frustrating sexuality. Turning the radio knob I come across a seductive country song. I close my eyes for periods of time as I drive on up into the mountainside, listening to the sound of the singer's voice. In fact, I turn up the volume so I can hear the reverberation of sound in the man's throat—that way I can better imagine him whispering sweet things in my ear as he fucks me, holding firm to my hips with his calloused hands. I was lost in the heat of his torso and the taste of his tongue unreeling behind my closed eyelids when I felt a bump and a pop as I knocked over a cactus on the roadside. I twisted the steering wheel in a hypnotic daze of calamity and thumped back onto the asphalt roadway leaving a scattering of surprised buzzards shifting into the air like umbrellas. The sun was slipping toward the edge of the world when I pulled over at a highway rest stop on the crest of the mountain. No one else was around so I kicked about in the red dust for a while among the various species of cactus and tumbleweeds. I took a piss behind the adobe outhouse pointing my dick in different directions so the urine formed a dark outline of a face in the dry earth. I felt sad and exhilarated simultaneously. I walked around watching the light fade over the curve of the earth, creating krazy-kat silhouettes of the cactus and scrub. Occasionally the twin beacons of light from a distant car or truck coming from the direction I was heading would float across the folds of earth and the silence would be broken by the hum of the motor. One flippy bat came out early, a baby one, wobbling through the gathering breezes under a roadside lamp, getting knocked around by the currents as it tried to catch the insects attracted by the light. Over by the drinking fountains a bunch of honey bees trying to drink water from the steel rim of the flooded basins fell in and were drowning. I spent a while picking them out one by one with a soda straw and laying them on the concrete walkway where they stumbled around in stupid circles. At the sound of each approaching car my dick grew more hard but each car continued without stopping. I wanted to run out into the dusk and throw myself headfirst onto the earth and then roll sideways for miles until the sun came back. I remembered a friend of mine dying from AIDS, and while he was visiting his family on the coast for the last time, he was seated in the grass during a picnic to which dozens of family members were invited. He looked up from his fried chicken and said, "I just want to die with a big dick in my mouth."

Sitting on the warm hood of the car as the temperature fell, a sixteen-wheel rig pulled through the distance and entered the parking strip. With a compressed hiss of brakes, the cab door swung open and a young guy swung out. He was shirtless and covered in marks of sweat and dirt. As he rounded the side of the truck he nodded: "What's up?" and proceeded to walk around the entire truck kicking each tire a couple of times while I held my breath. Then he climbed back into the cab, shifted gears and drove out of the lot, taillights blinking. Darkness had completely descended onto the landscape and I stood up and stretched my arms above my head and I wondered what it would be like if it were a perfect world. Only god knows. And he is dead.

———

I'm in a building, a high-rise building resembling the interior of an enormous ship, middle-aged sailors all around, guys that have been working on the oceans for up to twenty-five or thirty years. At times it's a building I'm standing in, at other times it becomes a ship with long rolling motions, then it becomes a building again.

I'm walking down a hallway and come to a room where this young man is standing and beginning to remove his clothes. Next to him is an open door where clouds of steam are billowing out as if a shower is running. On the floor is a newspaper with a story about the navy trying to give a dishonorable discharge to a guy because he was a homosexual. There is a photograph accompanying the story and I realize the face in the picture is the same as the guy undressing. I look up from the paper just as he drops his pants to the floor and steps out of view into the clouds of steam.

Something shifts in this sleep and I am standing in a room that has only three walls; as I turn around I realize I am in the ruins of a building, standing on a balcony. The building has different levels to it. As I walk through doorways and hallways I see that some sections are only a story tall, others are five or six stories tall and all of them belong to a dilapidated hotel. Judging by what remains of the molding on the walls and ceilings, and the chandeliers hanging from the center of each room, it was once a place for the rich maybe a century ago. Large sections of walls are missing and there is nothing but jumbles of steel rods twisted and caked with broken slabs of concrete. Off in the distance behind a line of waving palm trees, the sky is developing a dark stormy patch of gray and coal black. The funnel of a tornado is forming and I stare at it for a while before moving into the next room. There is a stranger standing in the corner of the room; he looks like a guy who would work with machines; he has dark hair, strong forearms and he's wiping his hands with a dishcloth. Behind him through the tangled rupture of broken walls, the backdrop of sky is woven through with flashes of rose and turquoise. The colors are swimming into the shape of funnels making up a couple of tornados that grow larger as I watch. The guy wiping his hands doesn't notice them or else seems unconcerned. "I think we'd better find shelter," I say as the funnels grow closer and closer. Turning from the guy, I move quickly through a series of rooms and wonder if the hotel has been through an earthquake or fire or bombings and strafing as in war. Twisted silhouettes of girders and shells of rooms with large sections of ceilings, roofs, walls and floors missing, each of them revealing different views of the tornadoes and framed horizon. The whole sky is revolving furiously and beautifully as I wake up, my eyes opening on the cool light of morning slipping between the hotel curtains.

———

The sun in the part of arizona I was traveling through was so strong it made my eyes half close and all the earth seemed like one enormous field, dry as bone. The sun was bleaching the color out of every surface and shape so my brain had to wrestle to give things form. Anything, bush, cattle, vehicle or human, immediately turned to silhouette against the bright sky. With the combination of heat and light, the air had a frail white quality. The whole sky seemed closer to the road in these parts and I could barely stand the magnesium glimmer of light burning up my lower body. My arms stretched to the steering wheel, I was skimming over the pale gray asphalt and the speedometer was measuring between eighty and ninety miles per hour. The road was so flat in stretches, or there was so little in the landscape to distract the eye, that it was impossible, without looking at the dashboard, to tell when I was speeding. It was a landscape for drifting, where time expands and contracts and vision is replaced by memories; small filmlike bursts of bodies and situations, some months ago, some years ago.

I was headed toward Meteor Crater. It's a blemish on the earth's skin where twenty-one thousand years ago a half-billion-ton chunk of iron blew through outer space and slammed into the planet leaving a hole three miles in circumference. The collision has been calculated as having had the force of a multimegaton bomb, and now, twenty-two thousand years later, some enterprising jerks charge you seven bucks to look at the hole.

———

Four miles from the service road to Meteor Crater, I pulled into the lane of a highway rest stop and coasted up a slight incline to the parking spaces. Dazed tourists in pastel clothes wandered briefly from their cars to the small building housing the toilets. Some stayed inside their cars, windows rolled up tight, air-conditioning blasting the interior. They looked like critters with hair-dos in aquariums and as I passed the line of cars they turned to look with a small panic in their eyes. It was incredibly hot and the air felt like it would burst into flames. Next to the walkway leading to the toilets was a sign: $1,000 FINE FOR DEFACING THE ROCKS, referring to a large group of sandstone boulders maybe eight feet high and fifteen yards long and wide. Maybe they were boulders that flew out of the hole three miles away when the meteor hit because they looked foreign to the landscape, as if lifted straight out of a flintstones special. Nearby was a second sign: POISONOUS SNAKES AND INSECTS INHABIT THIS AREA. On the walkway by the twin-roofed entrances to the toilets, a Native American family was seated before two blankets filled with cheap turquoise trinkets and hunger. The turquoise was actually blue plastic with mineral veins printed on it. A couple of tiny speakers above the doors to the MEN's and WOMEN's rooms spit out a steady stream of weather information that hovered in the air in a series of metallic echoes. A pretaped program offering tips on how to avoid dehydration in the concrete streets of large urban centers drifted through the men's room as the door swung shut behind me. An old white-haired man rubbed his hands under the electric dryer. I chose the second stall and opened my belt, dropped my pants and sat down on the toilet seat. To my right, about waist level on the dividing partition were two large holes peeled through the metal. An eye was peering through one of them. I leaned forward slightly and through the second hole I could see a disembodied hand pulling on a large uncircumcised dick. I bounced my own dick in the palm of my hand so the eye could see it. I waited a few minutes till the sounds of the rest room door opening and closing subsided, then stood up and pulled my pants back up and motioned toward the hole, giving the guy a signal to meet me outside.

———

I was making like the first man on the moon walking the deep creviced surfaces of the flintstones landscape. I was hoping to spot a rattler or a scorpion—after almost a decade of wandering through the southern and western states I'd never come across a rattler in the wild. Too many rattlesnake roundup jubilees and development moves have been killing them off. From the top of the boulders I also had a clear view of the bathrooms and the pathway. More cars were arriving than departing and families were going back and forth from their cars to the rest rooms. Finally the guy from the first stall stepped into the hot glare of sunlight shielding his eyes with an enormous hand. He was what some would consider a freak: a circus giant in american bloodlines and genealogies, the lumbering object of surprise and fear. Had he been of average size and carrying a machete or gun, no one would have given him a second glance. But to have a massive body and height and the two large hands broad as palm leaves caused kids and even adults to unconsciously move backward or sideways a couple of extra steps as if his height took up horizontal space along the path. His body was well proportioned to his height, slightly muscular like he'd been a farm laborer in his youth, but now he looked like a salesman: cheap cotton short-sleeved shirt and beige car-dealer pants. I found him very sexy because I love difference. An unbearably handsome face bores me unless something beneath its surface is crooked or askew: even a broken nose or one eye slightly higher than the other, or something psychological, something unfamiliar and maybe even suspect.

He looked up toward the boulders from under the roof of his hands, then crossed the pebble garden to begin climbing up. In case there were cops, I pretended not to see him and wandered out of view. State police get lots of overtime pay lurking around interstate rest stops hoping to catch some hungry queer kissing another in the loneliness of the tiled bathrooms. Some cops make it a point to step back from urinals and flash their hard dicks at a suspected queer and then arrest him when he makes a move to show he's interested. In new jersey, an undercover cop used his eighteen-year-old son who would stand at the urinals five hours at a stretch and display a hard-on to anyone entering the bathroom. In north carolina I read a newspaper story in which the columnist was worried about how the sleaze types, attracted to the highway rest stops because queers supposedly made such easy robbery targets, might accidentally beat up and and mug a family man. Funny thing was I'd seen and met family men on their knees in rest stops around the nation. The best part of the article was a map of the state that noted which rest stops had the most homosexual activity— that helped keep me from feeling lonely that day.

We met at the far end of the landscape and both acted shy, but within minutes were in our separate cars heading onto the interstate to look for a side road that would give us cover away from the eyes of the world, a place away from the trooper patrol cars where we could get to know each other. There is no such place in that part of arizona. I was tailing him when he finally pulled onto the service road leading over a small bridge and crossing the interstate in the direction of Meteor Crater. Our cars drifted down a service road in a swirl of dust and pebbles, past a low-set gas station offering free pieces of petrified wood to customers. About a quarter mile farther down the road, a mile from the crater parking lot, he pulled over onto the shoulder and stopped the engine. I pulled up behind him and walked to the passenger side of his car, opened the door and slid into the hot front seat. He was staring straight ahead out the windshield at a plume of dust that grew larger and larger because it contained a car filled with vacationers. His hands were gently smoothing over the folds in his trousers around the general area of his crotch.

———

The service road leading to the crater is made of a brown asphalt material, roped on both sides with dry red earth and plains of scrub brush and an occasional loping boulder pocked with holes made by the friction of wind-driven sand. In the distance, in any given direction, all you can see is the general curve of the earth and maybe the beginnings of mountains far away in purple tones looking like goofy cartoon hats or sideways faces. The sky is a bowl; it is like the inside curve of the eye if it were mirrored and it's filled with a dusty white blue that catches like imaginary chalk in the throat and it contains the hot disk of sun and a hot wind that buffets the sides of the car and enters over the top of the window glass. After the tourist car passed, and he could make sure of its disappearance in the rearview mirror, his face turned toward me and began the slow swim through space toward mine. His rich dark eyes set into the general outline of his face slowly obscured my view of his hand undoing the zipper of his trousers and reaching into the resulting envelope of cloth, "You ain't a cop are you?" The heat inside the car was so saunalike that I was pouring sweat down my face, under my arms and over my chest where it cooled in the slight breeze. His face was an inch from mine when he saw the answer—no—in my eyes and his tongue slipped between parted lips and entered my mouth.

Someone once said that the ancients believed that light came from within the eyes and that you cast this light upon things in the world wherever you turned. I remember wondering if the world disappeared or was cast into darkness when you closed your eyes, or, even further, if you died, did the world die also. This guy was so intensely sexy I almost couldn't look him in the eye. His body had such presence or something, I don't know what it was; perhaps his height, his large hands, the way he might look sitting in a chair with his clothes having disappeared and his legs pulled apart with me in front of him standing, his head viewed from above, or kneeling, his knees viewed from a close angle. Or maybe it's the shadows of his crotch where it meets the plastic cushion of the chair my face a camera, moving into a slow close-up of his dick, the head of it peeking from the fold of foreskin, a sexy soft-lined pink eye in a hard organ and the sense of it warm in my palms and maybe I just want to feel the sense of it sinking upward in my wet mouth; maybe it's the feeling of my moist palms running over the front of his chest through the folds of his open shirt, soon to have him more naked, his dark head tilted back and small pockets of pleasure sound escaping from the back of his throat. Maybe I just anticipate seeing that light in his eyes, that glitter of life glazing over in the heat. Or maybe it's the way his arms lift up over his head in the limited space so I can better lick the heat of his body.

If light does come from within does that make us

walking movie projectors? Are we casting form onto a dark screen? When I move my eyes very slowly from left to right while sitting still, I can feel and hear a faint clicking sensation suggesting that vision is made up of millions of tiny stills as in transparencies. Since everything is generally in movement around us, then vision is made up of millions of "photographed" and recalled pieces of information. In the seventeenth century a jesuit friar by the name of Scheiner engaged in an experiment where he peels away opaque layers at the back of the eye and revealed a faint image, a transparency of what the eye had imprinted upon it at the moment of its owner's death. Another scientist took the excised eyes of guillotined prisoners and studied them under a microscope to see if there were any legible images imprinted on them. This scientist wanted to see if an image was recorded despite the black hood placed over the guillotine victims' heads at the moment of decapitation. He reported finding one image that was fairly consistent in the eyes he examined: something like a small cloud with two tiny arms waving out from the sides.

Sometimes when I'm caught in the flow of rush-hour traffic in the tangled arteries of interstate ramps and elevated roadways that surrounded an enormous and unfamiliar city, I come to believe that I no longer exist and similarly all the forms and shapes of metal and glass that contain what appear to be human beings are also a fragment of imagination: something like a vision cast into time and space from something outside of myself. I move to a place in the back of my head and merely witness it all. I am amazed by the undefined spectacle of this vision as I pass through, waiting for the code or the anchor that reels me in, brings me through its contours and sets me down like gravity.

He was whispering behind my closed eyelids. Time had lost its strobic beat and all structures of movement and sensation and taste and sight and sound became fragmented, shifting around like particles in lakewater. I love getting lost like this. I'm trying to recall where his hands were, or how they felt under my shirt, or grasping the back of my neck while his tongue licked across my jaw, over my throat. I'm trying to recall the drift of it, trying to recall where we were. I remember sitting in his car, mine parked a few yards behind his in the side weeds. We were in the front seat of his salesman station wagon with the windows open and my door slightly ajar, the two of us jerking off and the rearview mirror adjusted so I could see the span of road behind us while he kept his eyes peeled, scanning the road in front of us, both of us looking for any signs of cop or trooper cars that might glide up silently and unannounced. But in the rearview mirror I saw nothing but empty space and earth and sky except for the lower part of one electrical stanchion—it might've been a radar tower—two grazing cows beside it and nothing else but the curve of the earth and out in front of the car through the frame of windshield: nothingness and here we are, here I am, some fugitive soul having passed through the void of the cities, skimmed across the emptiness of landforms and roadways through holes in the mountains westward to this one point in the dead road where vehicles have stopped to rest in the boiling heat and the entire landscape is silent except for the dull flat whine of insects and the dry brush. The oval stones and straw-colored vegetation and cracked red earth and everything feels dried and red except for the pale hanging color of the sky emitting a tone that matches or continues the tone of the human body in absolute stillness. And to be surrounded by this sense of displacement, as this guy's tongue pulls across my closed eyelids and down the bridge of my nose, or to be underneath all that stillness with this guy's dick in my mouth, lends a sense of fracturing. It's as if one of my eyes were hovering a few feet above the car and slowly revolving to take in the landscape and the small car with two humans inside slowly licking each other's bodies into a state of free-floating space and semiconsciousness and an eventual, small, momentary death.

Periodically a car would come. It would start as a bright spark in the distance, a glint of hot metal joining the earth and sky, and soon the unraveling shape of clouds of dust would rise beneath rear wheels, and after a long and soundless moment of this speck vibrating against the horizon, its shape would slowly become discernible and fluctuate into largeness and take on the shape of a tourist's camper or a small sedan and it would eventually gain color and the dark windshield would materialize around a face or two that were first just blank smudges and then would gain features as hot air and sound drifted by. In the moment of their approach, we would stop, rearrange our anatomies, zip up our pants and assume the body language and gaze of tourists losing themselves in the sky for an afternoon. Our hands always the hands of fear and apprehension—mixed with pleasure and frustration—until the car revealed its occupants and intentions. The momentary disengagement from the accelerations where the mind travels in sex, the multiple hands floating back and forth on the textures of trousers waiting for the vehicle to disappear so they can resume their rituals and rhythms of unfastening buckles and zippers, and our faces turn away from the hot shield of sky and burrow into the folds of each other's clothes and bodies.

A solitary tiny bird drops out of the air onto an oval-shaped blue stone and pees noiselessly onto its hot surface. The hallucinatory sensation I recall from the depths of fever is the idea that this guy and I are part of the same vascular system; he and I are two eyeballs sitting in the dark recesses of a metallic skull viewing the world through the windshield the way one's eyes would if they could proportion and transmit information independent of each other as well as recall separate private histories. The automobile is a vehicle of motion just like the human body, its motor, the brain, claiming or recalling distance and motion and passage.

My eyes are microscopes. My eyes are magnifying lenses. My face is plowing through the heat and sensations of this guy's flesh, through the waves of sweat, and in my head is the buzzing sensation of either insect or atmosphere. I see the hallucinogenic way his pores are magnified and each hair is discernible from the other and the uncircumcised dick is bouncing up against my lips as it's released from the trousers. The sensation of its thickness pulls against the surface of my tongue and rubs the walls of my throat, burying itself past the gag-reflex and then the slow slide of its withdrawal as a disembodied hand descends against the back of my neck, just barely grazing the hairline of the scalp and in the periphery of vision there's the steel-blue glaze of the steering wheel and the threads weaving themselves into the fabric of his trousers and the sound of his body bending and the cool sensation of my shirt being pulled up over my back and the shock of his tongue trailing saliva up my backbone and under my shoulder blades and I am losing the ability to breathe and feeling a dizziness descend, feeling the drift and breeze created by the whirling dervish, using the centrifugal motion of spinning and spinning and spinning to achieve that weightlessness where polar gravity no longer exists. The sounds of his breath and the echo of body movements I am no longer able to separate. The pressure of the anxiety slips closer in the shape of another vehicle or of the cops arriving, nearing the moment where the soul and the weight of flesh disappears in the fracture of orgasm: the sensation of the soul as a stone skipping across the surface of an abandoned lake, hitting blank spots of consciousness, all the whirl of daily life and civilization spiraling like a noisy funnel into my left ear, everything disintegrating, a hyper-ventilating break through the barriers of time and space and identity. And all of it mixing with the stream of semen drifting over the line of my jaw and collecting in a pool in a pocket created by the back of my neck where it meets his upper thigh and abdomen. I'm tipping over the edge in slow motion. In the moment of my orgasm, as I'm losing myself, I become vaguely aware of his hands cradling my skull and his face appearing out of the hot sky leaning in, or else he's pulling my face up close to his and I'm breaking the mental and physical barrier, I'm listening to my soul speak in sign language or barely perceptible whisperings and I'm lost in the idea that at the exact moment of the kill, the owl's eyes are always closed, and I feel his tongue burning down my throat and the car is in a seizure and he's smacking me in the face to rouse me from this sleep, leaning in close again like something on the screen of a drive-in movie, his lips forming the whispered sounds, "Where were you?" and had a cop car pulled up in that moment and had I possession of a gun, I'd have not thought twice about opening fire.

———

These are strange and dangerous times. Some of us are born with the cross hairs of a rifle scope printed on our backs or skulls. Sometimes it's a matter of thought, sometimes activity, and most times it's color. I don't receive the proper kind of paycheck to take out a seventy-year lease on my life. If I submit my gray cells to certain men and women in this country for a total overhaul and redesign I might have something called peace in my life. But what one sees if they look closely into the pupils of my eyes are a series of activities that are merely things that have occurred to me in the years of my childhood and teens. Others may be genetic, others a conditioning and response, but overall I trust myself in a way no other could. If those cops showed up in that moment I described above, I thoroughly believe that they have no right and that their laws don't reflect me. It is easy for some in this country to be vicious and murderous when they have the support of rich white men and women in power. Those people consistently abstract human life and treat minorities as nothing more than clay pigeons at a skeet-shooting range. They toss up a fake moral screen, nail it to the wall of a tv and newscaster's set and unfurl it like a movie screen. These fake moral backdrops are conceived at will and displayed like artifacts of the human sensibility as built by a caring god through millions of years.

But the very same man who orders the death of journalists off the coast of costa rica as they are uncovering a story dealing with our government's importation of cocaine and our government's use of drug profits to fund the contras is the very same man who will stand on a studio set, airfield, white house garden or convention podium and talk in the fake moral code about the humane and glorious designs he has planned for the social fabric of america if elected president. And the same man who stands before you at the altar of the church with seven television cameras pointed at his face and talks about the sanctity of the fetus is the same man who kisses the hands of dictators in central america— dictators responsible for the pillaging of an entire country dissolving in poverty, as well as the murder of hundreds of thousands of people he *perceives* as disagreeing with his power structure. The rich have interchangeable heads and their interpretations of law and religion are just as manufactured, false, interchangeable and disposable as the fake moral screen. They have an entire media system to dispense their manipulations of those scrambling for food shelter and some illusion of security. Our borders are opening and closing to refugees of the countries our government pillages, based solely on whether or not those governments toe our party line. The u.s. uses its economic blockades to starve entire populations and accelerate peoples' deaths from malnutrition or collapsed medical care systems. The bureaucratic distancing technique in washington d.c. creates poverty and mass death in another region of the hemisphere and allows officials here to proclaim that the attacked country's political system is what has made it fail. Because I am born into a created system of corruption does not mean I have to turn the other way when the fake moral screens are unfurled. I am just as capable of creating my own moral contexts. In fact, using our government's techniques, I can reinvent and redefine a screen for my own needs. Since my existence is essentially outlawed before I even come into knowledge of what my desires are or what my sensibility is, then I can only step back from the arms of government and organized religion and use similar techniques to walk from *here* to *there*. If the cops roll up in their vehicle with their shotguns cradled and bolted between the front seats, and the design of their genes and gray cells makes it possible for them to put the guns on our bodies, then I can in that moment unfurl a screen that creates a horizon and landscape that is uninfected by the letters and words of "law" and pull out my weapon and defend myself from intrusive and disruptive actions. Of course, those in power count on the fact that we are stuck inside these gravity vehicles called bodies. The pressure that gravity sustains on our bodies keeps us crawling around in this preinvented existence with the neighbors split-rail fencing preventing us from crawling out. The pressure for escape has led us from our tadpole ancestors through time till now to develop an appetite for speed. Speed of consumption, speed of physical movement, speed of transmitting and receiving information. Since speed is a luxury for those who have power and money, many of us have traded physical speed for fantasy like this mental projection: surround ourselves with enough material goods and maybe we won't see the stinking mess outside the windows, if we are lucky enough to have windows. It is no accident that every guidebook in every conceivable language contains the translated phrase: DO YOU HAVE A ROOM WITH A BETTER VIEW?

———

This morning I woke up in another part of my brain. Take the idea, for a moment, that one usually wakes up in a similar area of the brain every day of one's life. When I opened my eyes, I woke with a feeling of confusion and a sense that something indiscernible had shifted during the sleeping hours and now I was somewhere else, not in another place physically, but something similar. The "I" of *my self* had crawled through the thickness of memory and consciousness to some other place in the structure of the brain and emerged within a new gray coil. When my eyes opened, I felt I was viewing the once familiar room through a four-foot-thick piece of slightly yellowed glass. It was like being under the surface of a pond and opening one's eyes and straining to see a measure of distance to the kicking legs of one's swimming partner, only there was no one else with which to measure the dislocation. I fought the urge to lay down and return to sleep in order to regain my proper place, to shift back into a developing place where for thirty-odd years I'd been waking up. I've been moving around through the day trying to readjust within a mild sense of panic. I kept getting lost in the notion that the drift of my past and the sway of familiarity might be just a centimeter away. But in the brain, a mere centimeter can mean hundreds of miles of cranial distance. It can mean years and years, or even a whole lifetime of familiarity being dismantled by a shift within a limited physical space.

————

Two fragments of dreaming I can recall from this sleep: I was suffocating, walking through doorways or in the street just having exited from a building. There were people walking around and I felt the presence of someone I knew just over my shoulder. I felt a panic from being unable to breathe, but I couldn't speak to anyone. Finally I managed to holler and it caused my breathing to resume and the dream shifted. . . . I was in a bathroom standing in front of a mirror hanging over a sink. I saw my eyes in close-up

magnification. I saw dull brownish yellow marks on the
whites of my eyes like they were bruised or rotting from the
inside out.

————

    I feel a vague nausea stroking and tapping the lining of
my stomach. The hand holding the burning cigarette travels
sideways like a storm cloud drifting over the open desert.
How far can I reach? I'm in a car traveling the folds of the
southwest region of the country and the road is steadying out
and becoming flat and giving off an energy like a vortex
leading into the horizon line. I'm getting closer to the coast
and realize how much I hate arriving at a destination.
Transition is always a relief. Destination means death to me.
If I could figure out a way to remain forever in transition, in
the disconnected and unfamiliar, I could remain in a state of
perpetual freedom. It's the preferable sensation of arriving
at a movie fifteen minutes late and departing twenty minutes
later and retrieving an echo of *real life* as opposed to a tar pit
sensation. Destination is an entry point for the practitioners
of the fake moral screens.
    Forty miles outside of town, drifting through a section
of countryside controlled by the marine corps air station, I'm
beginning to experience the slow withdrawal from population. My body is going through slender jitters inside all the
space outside the enclosed windows of the car and I feel
something concrete slipping off a ledge back there behind my
eyes. I was up until this moment a member of the industri-
alized tribe—the illusory tribe that catapults this nation,
this society, into something thick and hallucinogenic. The
hand with the cigarette is slowly making its way back across
the hip of the horizon. Its slow-motion drift creates a dark

spot below it like a cloud shadow on the landscape that travels at the same speed. The hand with the cigarette is drifting for hours back to my waiting lips. What is it in these wrists that grab the steering wheel? What blood flows through these arms and hands? What color and sensibility in that blood? What textures and images are coded and locked into those genes, those cells, those bones that drag the world toward my eyes? What do these eyes have to do with surveillance cameras? What do the veins running through my wrists have in common with electric wiring? I'm the robotic kid with caucasian kid programming trying to short-circuit the sensory disks. I'm the robotic kid looking through digital eyes past the windshield into the pre-invented world. I'm the robotic kid gone haywire in the sudden mounds and coils of krazy-kat landscapes. I'm the robotic kid lost for a fraction of evolutionary time in the outskirts of tribal boundaries; I've slipped through the keyhole of an enormous psychic erector set of a child civilization. I'm the robotic kid lost from the blind eye of government and wandering the edges of a computerized landscape; all civilization is turning like one huge gear in my forehead. I'm seeing my hands and feet grow thousands of miles long and millions of years old and I'm experiencing the exertion it takes to move these programmed limbs. I'm the robotic kid, the human motor-works, and surveying the scene before me I wonder: What can these feet level? What can these feet pound and flatten? What can these hands raise?

BEING QUEER IN AMERICA
A Journal of Disintegration

one. I'm walking through these hallways where the windows break apart a slow dying sky and a quiet wind follows the heels of the kid as he suddenly steps through a door frame ten rooms down. A quiet and simple grace in his arms and legs as the doorways fold out to produce more doorways and it's all some barbershop vision of mirrors with the wall ending at the distance of sky: small sparks of airplanes in that late blue and yellow and these little black pills stirring like small bees in my belly. The kid passed me earlier in the street about a mile away by the black shiny fence of a church: wrought-iron spikes topped with deadly blades part zulu.

But now it's just the sun piercing the waters of a viridian sea; his eyes set in the pale white face, arms a pale shade of red—something monkey, something borneo. His eyes make him look like he's starving for food or just feeling lust or else he's got the look of one of those spiritual types that hover on street corners trying to waylay and sweet-talk some passive kid into a lifetime of psychic control.

If viewed from miles above, this place would just appear to be a small boxlike structure like thousands of others set down along the lines of the rivers in the world; the only difference being that in this one the face of the kid starts moving up the wall past a window framing the perfect hazy coastline with teeth of red factories and an incidental gas tank explosion which sends flowers of black smoke reeling up into the dusk. I could feel his lips against mine from across the room, tasting reefer or milk on them as he disappears through a square hole in the ceiling. I watch as his legs and feet leave the rungs of the metal ladder following his hips through that dark space, the soles of his sneakers floating effortlessly in the opening for a second, then shifting out of view. I followed his motions pulling myself up two rungs at a time and as my head cleared the ceiling I saw him recede farther back in the attic crawlspace. The horizontal red lines of his shirt become dark and indistinct, just the pale rose of his arms still luminous. He turned and leaned up against the wall at a point where a crack in the roof let light pass through illuminating the wall and his head like some old russian icon of a saint in mausoleum darkness. Like him I had to crouch in order to move through the narrow space, walking along the tops of spaced beams like a horizontal ladder so as not to tip and crash through the rotting tin ceiling. I bumped my head a couple of times on unseen pipes and finally reached him. His hands slid from his pockets and over the front of my trousers moving back and forth until there was swelling. My hands drifted over and repeated the actions over his crotch and like water falls from the sky I leaned in close and slid down and unsnapped his jeans button by button using only my teeth. He was wearing no underwear and I peeled back the flaps of his trousers, his dick falling neatly out to rest on my lips. It was uncircumcised, slim and warm. I passed my face underneath it, wetting it slightly, teasingly, finally taking it into my mouth and sliding my hands upward beneath his shirt; the lines of it rippling like water and I felt the downy sensation of hair beneath my palms. His chest was hard: rippling stomach, the curve of it in dim light, the brown heat of his belly against my forehead. His hands slipped softly down my collar and kneaded the muscles of my back, my neck and finally he made a rushing sound with his breath and he came. I could feel it jetting in warm streams hitting the back of my throat: warm liquid sensation. Felt good. Nothing but the energy in his hands speaking with me.

two. So I'm watching this thing move around in my environment, among friends and strangers: something invisible and abstract and scary; some connect-the-dots version of hell only it's not as simple as hell. It's got no shape yet or else maybe I'm just blind to it or we're just blind to it or else it is just invisible until all the dots are connected. Draw a line from here to there to there to here with all the dots being people you see from miles up in the air or from the ledge of a tall building or the window of a small plane but it's still not that easy, not that abstract because you can't shut out the smell of rotting. You can't shut out the sound of it: the sound of the man standing on the sidewalk trying to scream that he's going to throw himself in front of the passing automobiles because he wants to stop that slowly drawn line approaching him from the distance with all the undeniability of a slow train carrying sixteen tons of pressure; with all the measure and intent of crushing him but the guy is too weak to even get this amount of control over his life, he can't even throw a fit the proper way. You can't shut out the sights and sounds of death, the people waking up with the diseases of small birds or mammals; the people whose faces are entirely black with cancer eating health salads in the lonely seats of restaurants. Those images hurl themselves from the corners of a fast-paced city and you can't even imagine death properly enough to tell this guy you understand what he's railing against. I mean, hell, on the first day that he found out he had this certain virus he bent down to pick up a letter addressed to him that had fallen from the mailbox and he turned and said, "Even something so simple as getting a letter in the mail has an entirely different meaning."

three. I walked for hours through the streets after he died, through the gathering darkness and traffic, down into the dying section of town where bodies litter the curbsides and dogs tear apart the stinking garbage by the doorways. There was a green swell to the clouds above the buildings like a green metal retrieved from the river years ago and notions of time were retracting and extending and somewhere in the midst of this I had to take a piss. I kicked around an alleyway among the piles of dead rotting fish, buzzing flies, piles of clothing and fluttering newspapers of the past with photographs of presidents and their waving wives haloed in camera flashes and suddenly in the stench and piling of decaying fish I realized I was staring at a human hand, with the fat pale shape and color of a cherub's hand. It stirred to life and where previously there had been discarded men's suits and playing cards, a fat white man naked down to his waist suddenly materialized and sat up angrily. He had an enormous, pale belly on which was incised a terrible wound from which small white worms tumbled as he gesticulated like a marionette, shrieking, "DO YOU HAVE PERMISSION FROM THE OWNER OF THE ALLEY TO BE HERE?"

I turned and left, walking back into the gray haze of traffic and exhaust, past a skinny prostitute doing the junkie walk bent over at the waist with knuckles dragging the sidewalk. She had some kind of disease on her legs: large bloodless wounds which she attempted to disguise with makeup. Whenever she heard the sound of a car slowing down near the curb, thinking it was a potential customer, she would painfully lift her body up to reveal a delirious smile and dead eyes and a weak flailing of her arms as a sign of greeting. Kids ran back and forth on the sidewalk dragging a small kitten by a rope and a bunch of winos descended like buzzards onto the waves of cars stopped at the nearest traffic light.

My arms sometimes feel twelve feet long and I get consumed by the emptiness and void surrounding and lying beneath each and every action I witness of others and myself. Each little gesture in the movements of the planet in its canyons and arroyos, in its suburbs and cities, in the motions of wind and light, each little action continuing, helping to continue the slow death of ourselves, the slow motion approach of the unveiling of our order and disorder in its ultimate climax beginning with a spark so subtle and beautiful that to trust it is to trust our own stupidity; it sparks in the inversion of wind and then flowers out momentarily in black petals of smoke and light and then extends vertically in an enlargement of a minute vision. In the very center, if one could withstand the light, it would appear to be octopal in its appendages. Wormlike tentacles thousands of feet long vibrate stroboscopically in the bluish mist that exudes from its center. The center is something outside of what we know as visual, more a sensation: a huge fat clockwork of civilizations; the whole onward crush of the world as we know it; all the walking swastikas yap-yapping cartoon video death language; a malfunctioning cannonball filled with bone and gristle and gearwheels and knives and bullets and animals rotting with skeletal remains and pistons and smokestacks pump-pumping cinders and lightning and shreds of flesh, spewing language and motions and shit and entrails in its wake. It's all swirling in every direction simultaneously so that it's neither going forward nor backward, not from side to side, embracing stasis beyond the ordinary sense of stillness one witnesses in death, in a decaying corpse that lasts millions of years in comparison to the sense of time this thing operates within. This is the vision I see beneath the tiniest gesture of wiping one's lips after a meal or observing a traffic light.

four. I went up to see him in the hospital, it's all septic green or pale brown and yellow, hazes of light filtering in the windows, drenching the day's new flowers with color. There he is propped up in the white sheets with all the inventions of his day leading in and out of his body in the form of tubes and generators and pumps and dials and hisses and his eyes are bare slits with pearly surfaces glimmering inside them like somehow they've stopped reflecting light. Today, as yesterday, his nose is no longer the first thing I see—it's covered in the gray and white color of cancer and it looks bulbous and he said weeks ago when he was out visiting his family in the country for the last time that the little kids playing in the park thought he had the job of a clown somewhere and how he pretended he did—and, today, as yesterday, I am amazed at the fine color of his face and how as he slips closer to death his body looks more healthy. I thought of how he'd expected at least another year but in the last two days he has died twice and now he is taking his time before the third time which would be the final time. At least the doctors had finally agreed to stop jumping up and down on him if he died again and somehow through all of this I realized how much more afraid of death they were than he.

five. man on second avenue at 2:00 A.M. (N.Y.C.): "This guy I know was walking with a friend of his around West Street. They had gone into one of the bars and had a beer and after they left they were walking down the street when this car from Jersey cruised by ... kids come around all the time throwin' bottles and screamin' 'QUEER!' and then taking off—so this car cruised by them real slow and some kid leans out the window sayin', 'Suck my dick!' and my friend flipped him the finger and said something; all of a sudden the car slams on the brakes and five kids come piling outta the doors and start kicking the shit out of my friend ... for the next ten minutes about a hundred guys came outta the bars and from around the corner and surrounded these five kids beating the shit outta my friend—his friend took off right away and later my friend found out that he'd just run home, didn't bother calling the cops or nothing ... and all these guys crowding around watching five guys beat up one guy and none of them said or did a fuckin' thing ... my friend said the five kids stomped on his head and chest and broke a lot of his ribs and stomped on his legs ... at one point he could hardly feel them hitting him—they were jumping up and down on his head and arms and legs and finally he said he remembers jumping up and plowing through the crowd and running ... his face was just a puddle of blood ... the kids chased after him but he ran faster and faster and through the streets and outta the neighborhood and he kept running till he collapsed somewhere on some side street ... later he woke up in the hospital and found out that he had been unconscious for about six days ... the doctors told him that he was found by the cops unconscious on West Street surrounded by a bunch of guys who didn't do nothing; apparently he had hallucinated the whole thing of getting up and running away ... he had never gotten up ... the kids from Jersey got away before the cops even got there...."

six. In the skid-row section of town, the only movement in the streets was the automobiles cruising along the curbside and river parking lot. In the dusk they were like aquariums on wheels: amphibious stares of strangers pressed behind glass. Tall granite buildings with tiny windows speckled with fluorescent lights; gray vague shapes in the dripping alleyways and shit and garbage rattling in the wind along the flooded gutters, splashes of red and green neon sliding across the wet pavements. A skinny bum with red bare feet—once somebody's little baby—crawled into a box that once contained a refrigerator nestled in the weeds of an empty parking lot. A small black dog hurtles through the wet evening air amid a squeal of tires and thumping of glass and all civilization is at the wheel.

I pushed through the heavy glass doors and entered the place as a thin pale teenager seated at the elevated desk was yelling at the men in the back to put quarters into the machines or leave. I gave him a couple of dollars and he pumped out eight quarters from a chrome gadget on the desk. I passed through a room of enormous rubber dicks and fuck magazines and entered a moist and dark hallway. A couple of black drag queens with too much lipstick hovered in the shadows of a malfuntioning pinball machine, its flippers clacking and thrumming endlessly while the score-board revolved and whirred. A fat man with skin the color of liver sat in a booth with the door open, his mouth gaping and his tiny, perfect white hands fluttering around his open zipper.

————

He was the kind of guy I'd rob banks for, leaning against a stone wall, everyone else in the crowded street disappeared. He leaned in front of me rubbed my chest and belly like he'd known me for years—some distant relative— and I left reason behind in one of those moments where all sense of living takes a slow quiet dive into mystery and possibilities. I needed to be shook. I'd forgotten who I was and anything was welcome including the rough tight line of his neck turning in a warm shirt collar. He gave a drunken half smile and stepped inside the alleyway and began climbing the fifteen-foot-high mountain of spare tires. This was next to some gas station. I was fifteen and hungry.

———

I saw a guy in an old black leather jacket and a fishing cap half standing in the doorway of an open booth. The orange interior walls were illuminated by the metallic blue of a video monitor; over his shoulder, a sadist on a motorcycle was shoving his boots into the belly of an obviously drugged adolescent who lay naked on the gravel road. Halfway up the right wall of the booth was a large dick pushed through a hole, suspended and throbbing; it looked like it'd been hung up there like an unwanted gift.

———

I got to the top of the mountain, both of us in the cool evening wind, each footstep more like a bounce on top of all that rubber. Sounds of faraway voices and traffic circling into the alley, his cold hands started with my shirt buttons, my tongue starting with his neck and then sliding up to his mouth. Next to his left ear an enormous and luminous white ship plowed through the waters of the river.

———

A couple of quarters fished from his pockets turned on the video monitor and he flicked the stations until there was a blue image of a man's head floating across the screen. It was a forest at night and the video was badly transferred so that everything in it was translated into different shades of cobalt. An overly sensitive microphone was being used so the entire soundtrack was crickets. A blue cowboy removing his blue plaid shirt with muscled blue arms, leaning down in a blue naked haze to lick the belly of a blue shirtless bunkmate. Crickets. A close-up of an amazing blue eye floating in a blue field cut to a blue tongue coasting along the endless surface of rough blue flesh. Crickets. Blue trees at night with a luminous blue haze of light casting about their leaves. Crickets. A blue dick floating across dark blue shadows and burying itself into a waiting blue mouth. Crickets.

————

The sound of car wheels sluicing through puddles on the highway: Ah man he says as he is lowering himself onto my back one of his arms muscled and furry wrapping itself under my jaw and against the side of my face yer my babe ohh yer my babe whispering in my ear lips brushing lightly each sound a warm burst of breath ah man ... yer my babe with that roping-the-steer cowboy voice I can hear the distances in that voice and smell the gathering sweat on the surface of the tires yer my babe ahh and I'm already falling cowboy-off-the-cliff-like and he's moving his warm belly sliding it against my back taking the nape of my neck in his cold white teeth and turning my head slightly opening my eyes without my glasses and through the luminous blaze of sudden sunlight fall these shadows—the outline of thousands of leaves connected to branches that dip and bend in the wind.

————

A pair of empty cowboy boots sailing slow motion across dark blue space and bouncing lazily against a bunkhouse wall and then settling slowly into a series of geometric blue shadows. Crickets. Blue cowboy bodies amputating from blue darkness into the pale light. Crickets. Light blue semen uncoiling across a blue torso in some small fever.

seven. He's got me down on my knees and I can't even focus
on anything I have no time to understand the position of my
body or the direction of my face I see a pair of legs in rough
corduroy and the color of the pants are brown and surrounded by darkness and there's a sense of other people there
and yet I can't hear them breathe or hear their feet or
anything and his hand suddenly comes up against the back
of my head and he's got his fingers locked in my hair and he's
shoving my face forward and twisting my head almost gently
but very violent in that gentleness and I got only half a
breath in my lungs the smell of piss on the floorboards and
this fleshy bulge in his pants getting harder and harder as
my face is forced against the front of his pants the zipper
tears my lips I feel them getting bruised and all the while
he's stroking my face and tightening his fingers around the
locks of my hair and I can't focus my eyes my head being
pushed and pulled and twisted and caressed and it's as if I
have no hands I know I got hands I had hands a half hour
ago I remember lighting a cigarette with them lighting a
match and I remember how warm the flame was when I lifted
it toward my face and my knees are hurting from the floor
it's a stone floor and my knees are hurting 'cause they banged
on the floor when he dragged me down the cellar stairs I
remember a door in the darkness and the breath of a dog his
dog as it licked my hands when I reached out to stop my
headlong descent its tongue licking out at my fingers and my
face slams down and there's this electric blam inside my head
and it's as if my eyes suddenly opened on the large sun and
then went black with the switch thrown down and I'm
shocked and embarrassed and his arms swing down he's
lifting me up saying, lookin' for me?, and he buries his face in
my neck and I feel the saliva running down into the curve of

my neck and my arms are hanging loose and I can see a ceiling and a dim bulb tossing back and forth and suddenly I'm on my knees again and my face is getting mashed into his belly and sliding down across rough cloth and zippers and there's this sweet musty smell and his dick is slapping across my eyes and rubbing over my cheeks and bloody lips and suddenly it's inside my mouth and the hands twisted up in my hair and cradling my skull shove me forward and I feel his dick hit the back of my throat and I feel pain for the first time like the open pants are in focus and he's pulled his dick out of my mouth and I'm choking and he's running one hand over my face putting his fingers in my ears in my mouth dragging down my lower jaw and forcing his dick in between the fingers and the saliva and blood and shoving shoving in and out and pulling on my hair and everything goes out of focus my eyes moving around blindly the smell of basement water and sewage and mustiness and dirt and he's slapping my face like he wants to wake me up and I realize I'm crying and he tells me that he loves me and he lifts me up and puts his lips over mine and sticks his tongue in my mouth and buries his rough face down in my collar and licks and drags his tongue over my shoulder and neck and his hands are up inside my shirt and he's rubbing them back and forth across my belly and sides taking quick handfuls of flesh and twisting and rubbing and then they're inside my pants and he suddenly rips apart the opening of my pants I hear metal buttons hitting the floor and he punches me in the side of the head at the same time pulling my hair and pulling me back down to the floor and I'm on my belly I feel cold rough stone scratching my skin and he kneels down suddenly into the center of my back and it hurts and I try to yell but he's shoving my underwear into my mouth and I'm suddenly hit with such a feeling of intense claustrophobia and fear that it's hours before I realize that my hands and legs are tied together and that I'm lying on my side and the rag in my mouth is soaking wet and making small bubbling sounds each time I breathe.

eight. I saw her in mexico city after a day of walking around the outskirts of the upper-class zone of the city. A year after the big earthquake the buildings are still tumbling, great heaving cracks in their facades, thirty floors of vacant offices, burst windows, potted plastic palms and calendars flapping above dead machines. I saw her after a day filled with rich people and poor people; a day of diamond rings on lifeless fingers; a day of armless and legless men in the dawn (I saw the missing limbs for a fraction of a moment, suspended against the blue exhaust clouds of the city streets).

I saw her. She's about eight feet tall and she has the twin feet of an enormous eagle and both her arms are large serpent's heads with tongues tasting the wind and her head, they told me, had been cut off by her brother somewhere in the skies years ago in some struggle for power and now she carries her dry skull in the center of her massive belly and where her head had been were now two large serpents symbolizing the flowing of blood and around her hips she wore a skirt made entirely of snakes, dozens of them. Around her shoulders she wore a necklace of rope that was strung with human hearts and human hands and they told me she was the goddess of the earth and they told me she was the goddess of life and death and I was amazed at how seductive she was.

nine. Sometimes it's like long ago when words were slow and we were meeting beneath faraway rivers. How slowly the water shifts, how slow these stones assuming the shapes of walls and roadways, lockups and borders. When they invented the car they invented the collision and the darkness of what time leads the willing body into. It's seeing how slowly we shift position from room to room; seeing how sleep has quietly become an extension of the day; how if we take the more horrifying aspects of the world and fuse them to the unspeaking and unmoving stone lips of religious icons surely huge sections of the population will kneel before them in reverence.

Sometimes I get seized by a discrete sensation, something like a small madness where the senses reel behind the eyes. In the midst of crowds or in immense landscapes where the sense of sky is almost deafening, great big cracks in the earth like dusty photographs of lightning. I carry silence like a blood-filled egg, ready to drop it into someone's hands. When I was small and it would rain I thought it rained all over the world but now I don't think so. Riding out here over the dirt roads, the day opened up like a kid falling into sunlight; sprawling out on a green lawn tasting milk on his lips. Right this minute I could tip right down into the deep of that canyon, jump from rock to rock effortlessly, thinking bird thoughts weightless like death. Smack my face against that tree, like the bird against the front of my car. The hot sun as my witness: blind sun, blind me, blond bones, bleeding hills—put thistles and mud on the wounds, roll in the dust like a coydog, scream into those anthills, run fast without looking, close those eyes, shut those curtains, high sun, high strung, big snakes in the road, big desert, big sky, clouds zoom by . . .

ten. I walk this hallway twenty-seven times and all I can see are the cool white walls. A hand rubbing slowly across a face, but my hands are empty. Walking back and forth from room to room trailing bluish shadows I feel weak: something emotional and wild forming a crazy knot in the deep part of my stomach. On the next trip from the front of the apartment to the back, I end up in the kitchen, turn once again and suddenly sink down to the floor in a crouching position against the wall and side of the stove in a blaze of wintery sunlight. It's blinding me as my fingers trace small circles through the hair on the sides of my temples, and I've had little sleep having woken up a number of times slightly shocked at the sense of another guy's warm skin and my hands, independent of me in sleep, were tracing the lines of his arms and belly and hips and side. How the world is so much like dream sleep with my glasses hidden somewhere along the windowsill above the bed; there's a slow stir of measured breath from next to me and through the 6:00 a.m. windowpanes I see what appears to be a dim forest of trees in the distance, leafless and shivering, but it's just some old summer plants in a window box gone to sleep for the season. I think of these trees and how they look like the winter forests of my childhood and how they were always places of refuge: endless hours spent among them creating small myths of myself alone or living in hollowed-out trees or sleeping in nests twenty times larger than crows' nests made of sticks instead of twigs. I realized then how I always tend to mythologize the people, things, landscapes I love, always wanting them to somehow extend forever through time and motion. It's a similar sense I have for lovers, wanting somehow to have some degree of permanence in my contact with them but it never really goes that way. So here I am heading out into the cold winds of the canyon streets, walking down and across avenue c toward my home with the smell and taste of him wrapped around my neck and jaw like a scarf. It follows me in and out of restaurants and past cops and early morning children and past bakery windows filled with brides and grooms on rows of wedding cakes and across fields of brick and mortar. Small traces of memory fold and slip back to where he and I are sitting in his place late evening playing games of poker. I had never really played before in my life and suddenly after losing a sock and a shirt I became an expert. We're laughing about it and I don't stop for the smaller articles of clothing. I tell him I have to get it while I can, having won my first game and I motion toward his pants and in the evening stillness there's a slight rustle of clothing. Coins spill freely to the ground and my hands are animated and drifting soundlessly up his calves, up his thighs and he tells me he learned this game years ago with some kid across the street after school in some town outside atlantic city. When their clothes were gone the loser had to suck the other guy's dick, only they put saranwrap around each other's dick after all you couldn't possibly touch your tongue to flesh.

. . . Through his memories I recall hours on end sitting in the weeds in the backyard next to the lawn chair where my uncle lay in shorts and a wedding ring, his body hardened and brown from days of skin diving in faraway oceans filled with the mysterious fish and creatures he described. I stared and stared and sometimes played with his arms for hours and I remember feeling a slight dizziness that years later I came to see first as a curse and then as a tool: a wedge that I might successfully drive between me and a world that was rapidly becoming more and more insane.

eleven. A number of months ago I read in the newspaper that there was a supreme court ruling which states that homosexuals in america have no constitutional rights against the government's invasion of their privacy. The paper stated that homosexuality is traditionally condemned in america and only people who are heterosexual or married or who have families can expect these constitutional rights. There were no editorials. Nothing. Just flat cold type in the morning paper informing people of this. In most areas of the u.s.a. it is possible to murder a man and when one is brought to trial one has only to say that the victim was a queer and that he tried to touch you and the courts will set you free. When I read the newspaper article I felt something stirring in my hands; I felt a sensation like seeing oneself from miles above the earth or like looking at one's reflection in a mirror through the wrong end of a telescope. Realizing that I have nothing left to lose in my actions I let my hands become weapons, my teeth become weapons, every bone and muscle and fiber and ounce of blood become weapons, and I feel prepared for the rest of my life.

In my dreams I crawl across freshly clipped front lawns, past statues and dogs and cars containing your guardians. I enter your houses through the smallest cracks in the bricks that keep you feeling comfortable and safe. I cross your living rooms and go up your staircases and into your bedrooms where you lie sleeping. I wake you up and tell you a story about when I was ten years old and walking around times square looking for the weight of some man to lie across me to replace the nonexistent hugs and kisses from my mom and dad. I got picked up by some guy who took me to a remote area of the waterfront in his car and proceeded to beat the shit out of me because he was so afraid of the impulses of heat stirring in his belly. I would have strangled him but my hands were too small to fit around his neck. I will wake you up and welcome you to your bad dream.

twelve. There were so many days of waiting for him to die the third and final time and we'd been talking to him daily because they say hearing is the last sense to go. Sometimes alone with him, the nurse outside the room, I'd take his hands and bend over whispering in his ears: hey, I don't know what you're seeing but if there's light move toward it; if there's warmth move toward it; if you see nothing then try to imagine that one period of calm in the midst of that sky just where it reaches the ocean. That one place I've always seen as a point of time and space where everything is possible, where I could dream myself anywhere in any position and I said move into that, become that, merge with it. Death. I don't necessarily believe that it's part of some cycle that repeats in other lifetimes and what difference does it make anyway? Are you supposed to save all your living for the next life? I just tend to see it as some final moment where all the energy of my body will disperse. So now it's day three or four or five, I can't remember, and his parents and two sisters are visiting the empire state building; me and philip and betty, one of his other sisters, are standing in the room. The doctor comes in and removes him from the pumps and hisses of hoses and he leaves the room immediately afterward. There's this cloudy kind of sunlight moving about the room. The guy on the bed takes two breaths and arches his back almost imperceptibly, his lips slightly parted. I have hold of one leg and his sister one hand philip another hand or part of his arm and we're sobbing and I'm totally amazed at how quietly he dies how beautiful everything is with us holding him down on the bed on the floor fourteen stories above the earth and the light and wind scattering outside the windows and his folks at this moment standing somewhere on the observation deck of the empire state building hundreds of stories up in the clouds and light and how perfect that is to me how the whole world is still turning and somewhere it's raining and somewhere it's snowing and somewhere forest fires rage and somewhere else something moves beneath dark waters and somewhere blood appears in the hallway of the home of some old couple who aren't bleeding and somewhere someone else spontaneously self-combusts and somehow all the mysteries of this world as I know it offer me comfort and I don't know beans about heaven and hell and somehow all that stuff is no longer an issue and at the moment I'm a sixteen-foot-tall five-hundred-and-forty-eight-pound man inside this six-foot body and all I can feel is the pressure all I can feel is the pressure and the need for release.

LIVING CLOSE TO THE KNIVES

I'm sitting in his hospital room so high in the upper reaches of the building that when I walk the halls or sit in the room or wander to the waiting room to have a cigarette, it's the gradual turn of earth outside the windows, the distant plains filled with buildings that have a look of fiction because from this perspective they flatten out against one another into the distance until there are thousands of windows (each one containing at least one human being that shows no sign of life) looking like small models of a train set against postcard-perfect reproductions of late winter skies and sunsets; the yellowing of sparse clouds and miniature water tanks. Leaning against the glass of the window of his room I see dizzily down into the street and wonder what it is to fall such distances. I'm afraid he's really dying. When we brought him in here it was just for some routine tests because he wasn't pissing for days and the slightest movement of an arm or leg brought nausea. He was expected to stay for only two or three days; it's been a week now and he barely opens his eyes for more than a few seconds. I came into the room this morning, the door swinging open to pale light and that steady figure outlining the sheets. His breath was coming in rapid-fire bursts like a machine gun. I turn from the silence and the window and look at him and an iris appears beneath one half-lifted eyelid and its strength bores right through me. I turn away almost embarrassed having as much life in me as he hasn't. The iris was the size of the room; it dwarfed the winter light filling the streets outside the window; it radiated across the heavy clouds with fifty thousand windows reflecting the blue of sky through it.

———

Whales can descend to a depth of five thousand feet where they can and must sustain a pressure of one hundred and forty tons on every square foot of their bodies.

———

He seemed to wake for a moment; he drifted soundlessly for a while, then asked me in sounds that took five minutes to translate to help him into the nearby bathroom so he could shit or something. I manipulated the machinery in the structure of the bed so that his upper body rose toward me and his legs sank away. I placed my hands beneath his back, it was hot and sweaty, and I pulled him into a sitting position, took one paralyzed leg after the other pulling them over the side of the bed. Then I realized he was going nowhere. He was limp and his eyes were closed and his mouth against my arm breathing wet sounds. I felt my body thrumming with the sounds of vessels of blood and muscles contracting the sounds of aging and of disintegration—the sound of something made ridiculous with language—the sense of loving and the sense of fear. I looked into his face: the irises expanding and filling the room, the curtains of eyelids shutting down over them to lift again and again. I tried to explain that he was too weak to make the trip three feet away to the bathroom. I was suddenly scared and embarrassed again. "I'm not strong enough," I said, tilting his head back. The sounds of nurses and hospital gurneys far away in the halls but he said nothing—his dark eyes just staring and flickering back and forth from side to side in strobic motion. Was he sleeping? Was he dreaming? What thoughts lay behind them? What pictures forming? Do blind men have visual dreams, dreams of color, dreams of form?

———

After giving birth a female whale produces more than two hundred gallons of milk a day.

———

In the yellowing dusk the red bricks of the buildings go to sleep; they fade into the shadows of streets and only the uppermost windows show the slow night coming on. I can place myself out there in the sky: lie down in the texture and dream of years and years of sleep and I talk inside my head of change and of peace for this body beside me of life for this body beside me of belief in these unalterable positions in the shifting state of things; of disbelief, of need for something to suddenly and abruptly take place, like that last image of some Antonioni film where the young woman looks at the house her father built and because of her gaze it explodes not once but twice in slow motion, huge fireballs of rupturing gas lines and couches and tables and chairs splintering into waves of shards and light and glass drifting in glittering helixes and even the entire contents of the family refrigerator lovingly spilling out toward the eye in rage, a perfect rage that I was beginning to understand, seeing myself hovering in the atmosphere outside the building's walls and wanting a shout to come from my throat that would level all the buildings or else have a strength in my hands where I could rip open the earth like cheap fabric and release a windscreen of lava and heat or with the fists banging against my thighs create shockwaves that would cause all the manufacturing of the preinvented world to go tumbling down in a slow and terrifying beauty till all the earth was level or maybe just to have some water pour from my head.

First there is the World. Then there is the Other World. The Other World is where I sometimes lose my footing. In its calendar turnings, in its preinvented existence. The barrage of twists and turns where I sometimes get weary trying to keep up with it, minute by minute adapt: the world of the stoplight, the no-smoking signs, the rental world, the split-rail fencing shielding hundreds of miles of barren wilderness from the human step. A place where by virtue of having been born centuries late one is denied access to earth or space, choice or movement. The bought-up world; the owned world. The world of coded sounds: the world of language, the world of lies. The packaged world; the world of speed in metallic motion. The Other World where I've always felt like an alien. But there's the World where one adapts and stretches the boundaries of the Other World through keys of the imagination. But then again, the imagination is encoded with the invented information of the Other World. One stops before a light that turns from green to red and one grows centuries old in that moment. Someone once said that the Other World was run by a different species of humans. It is the distance of stepping back or slowing down that reveals the Other World. It's the dislocation of response that reveals it for the first time because the Other World gets into one's bloodstream with the invisibility of a lover. It slowly takes the shape of the cells and their growth, internalized until it becomes an extension of the body. Traveling into primitive cultures allows one a sudden and clear view of the Other World; how the invention of the word "nature" disassociates us from the ground we walk on. While growing up I was constantly aware of the sense of all this in the same way one experiences a vague fear yet can't distill the form of it from the table or the cup one is holding or the skies rolling beneath the window frames.

Ever since my teenage years, I've experienced the sensation of seeing myself from miles above the earth, as if from the clouds. I see the tiny human form of myself from overhead either sitting or moving through this clockwork of civilization—the huge ticking mass of it—and it all looks like something out of everyone's control. Or rather, in the control of only a few: those that made up the gears and springs of the preinvented machine or those that threw themselves from the tops of bridges and buildings. And with the appearance of AIDS and the subsequent deaths of friends and neighbors, I have the recurring sensation of seeing the streets and radius of blocks from miles above, only now instead of focusing on just the form of myself in the midst of this Other World I see everyone and everything at once. It's like pressing one's eye to a small crevice in the earth from which streams of ants utter from the shadows—and now it all looks amazing instead of just deathly.

———

By the last weeks of his life he'd lost most of the feeling in his legs and when he could get himself to his feet, he would fall endlessly forward, arms spinning like windmills until one of us would grab him and guide him. It became a routine. He'd first refuse help as a condition to accepting it; at times it seemed as if every variation of reaction and response had to pass through his brain and out his lips before he could accept certain things or acknowledge limitations.

One day over breakfast he told me he planned to go by himself to Penn Station the following weekend to take a train to see a new doctor on Long Island—earlier that week I'd seen a fifteen-second spot on the evening news about this doctor who was administering typhoid shots to people with AIDS and claiming there were some good responses. The typhoid supposedly sparked the immune system into working again. I would usually tell him of any new developments I'd heard about, if for no other reason than to give him a sense of hope, something reassuring. He'd somehow found the name and address of the doctor and made an appointment. I told him I'd be glad to drive him out there but he shook his head, no, and said he preferred going out there by himself by way of Penn Station. We all knew this was impossible; he couldn't walk across the room without falling, patterns of bruises appearing on his pale white skin. Most of his friends were concerned about whether or not his body could withstand the dosages of typhoid which apparently were expected to produce fevers of up to one hundred and seven; but we also knew that when he'd made his mind up it wasn't beyond him to drag himself to the train station. At least he'd have that much control over the illness and his life. By Saturday, three days later, he consented to let me and Anita drive him out there. The morning rolled around and it took us an hour and a half to get him dressed and down the stairs to the car, blankets bound around him to ease the cold heat dial set at full blast and still he was shivering. He'd been in a bad mood for months and this morning he was in his usual good form. He was enraged about dying and took it out on most of us. Anita had told him recently that if there was something any of us could do to make it all stop and for him to get well, some gesture we could make—a wave of a hand, a throw of a switch, something liquid or tablet we could give him—we would; but there was nothing. He softened a bit after that.

Before we even got over the Williamsburg Bridge in morning traffic he began suggesting there was a faster route. I told him I'd gone over the map and there was no faster route. He kept insisting and I missed a turn for the expressway so I stopped the car on the side of an overpass and studied the map again. There was no faster route. "There's a faster way—you just don't know it." He pulled himself deeper into the blankets looking pissed as a hornet. The traffic was worse on the expressway with cars whizzing by at eighty to eighty-five miles per hour. Somewhere out by one of the airports he announced that he had to take a piss and that I should pull over and stop the car. I was in the left lane, cars were driving at breakneck speed and a light rain was falling

and there was no shoulder to stop on. I told him I'd have to
get over to an exit. "Just pull over and stop—I have to piss."
There's nowhere I can stop; I have to reach an exit. A wave
of his bony white hand, "Pull over ... just pull over." I
looked at Anita through the rearview mirror and pulled
over, cutting off a speeding car to reach an exit that was
coming up. She grimaced back at me. We rode through the
rain-colored streets filled with used-car lots and bright
whipping banners until we found a gas station and I pulled
up to one of the pumps. I asked a cute attendant for the
bathroom but there was none. Peter insisted on getting out to
piss anyway so I went around to his side of the car and
unstrapped him from the seat belt. After pulling off his
blankets, I reached toward him to help him out. "Don't touch
me." Peter I have to touch you to help you out. "Don't touch
me it hurts." In the last few weeks his senses got hypersharp.
He could smell a piece of metal across the room and insist
that you get rid of it. Perfume or garlic banished a visitor to
a chair on the other side of the room or caused him to throw
up. The attendant was filling up the tank as Peter walked by
windmill style across the lot. Anita asked, "Are you okay?"
"If he wasn't sick I'd crack him in the teeth," I answered. The
gas tank full, I paid for it and went to find him. He was
pissing into a flowerbed that belonged to a two-story white-
frame house, his arms jerking back and forth to maintain
balance. I felt a little nervous. This didn't look like friendly
territory. When he was done I buttoned his pants back up
and led him back to the car. The attendant stared at us as I
helped him back into the seat. Then the layers of blankets. "I
don't want the seat belt on." I said, "You have to have the seat
belt on; what if there's an accident?" "I don't care." I
continued putting it on. "I don't want the seat belt on ..."

"We're not going anywhere unless it's on." He resigned himself to having the seat belt on, "Don't touch me." We were back into traffic, circling side streets, trying to find the entrance to the expressway again. He looked like some old billy goat in a cocoon, his eyes peeled for something to snap at. "I know there's a faster way."

An hour later we reached a suburban street filled with fat wet trees hanging over quiet sidewalks. The street was also lined with no-parking signs so I pulled up in front of the doctor's house, an anonymous-looking place with a high plank fence around its backyard. I let Anita and Peter off on the sidewalk. You go in and I'll be right back. I drove a few blocks and found a nursery-school parking lot, parked the car and walked back feeling relieved that the ride was over. In the distance I could see Peter staggering on the front lawn flailing about in rage. He staggered toward Anita then turned and teetered to the roadside. She stood there with her small hands clasped together, traffic whizzing by. Peter disappeared behind a big hedge—the kind they shape into hippos and elephants at kiddie parks. By the time I reached Anita, he was in the distance, a tiny speck of agitation with windmill arms. I asked her what happened. "I don't know, one minute he was complaining how long the ride took and when I said that maybe you did the best you could he went into a rage—he threatened to throw himself in front of the traffic. The saddest thing is that he's too weak to throw a proper fit. He wanted to hit me but he didn't have the strength." Where's he headed? "He said he was going to the train station to go back home." We walked after him. He was staggering alongside a chain-link fence which separated him from a group of schoolkids kicking a dented soccerball around. He turned briefly, saw us coming, tried to cross the street, changed his mind, started walking toward us, changed his mind again, turned around and started walking back toward the train station. I shouted his name and he hesitated for a moment then resumed walking. When we caught up with him he turned and started talking angrily. "Look," I said, "just forget it—none of this is important . . . we came to see the doctor. We're here, so let's go see him." He calmed down a bit and the three of us walked back to the gate and followed the path to the side door.

Up a couple of steps inside the screen door was what looked like the interior of a trailer: fake wood paneling, functional desks overflowing with papers and some rooms to the left where the patients moved in and out, and where a tall man in a white lab coat occasionally appeared to wave them in. To the right were a couple of doors lining a short hallway and beyond that a waiting room, Leave-It-to-Beaver comfortable filled mostly with men. Just next to the entrance a pale boy leaned against one of the desks waiting to pay his bill. Peter recognized him from the office of the doctor both had been seeing for most of the last year and whom both had decided to stop seeing—some scientist uptown in Manhattan. The scientist was working with nontoxic antiviral drugs he'd developed. He'd been treating cancer patients for years until the government brought a case against him for malpractice on numerous counts. He is now on a five-year probation. The fact that the government entered the scene was one of the things that convinced Peter that the doctor might be a genius. All of us hoped it was true. Over the past nine months he'd collected a drawer full of brown bottles each containing the most recent "cure" developed by this man. Some of them required injections which I administered. The deciding factor for many people to leave this doctor was a vaccine he'd developed from human shit which each person was eventually injected with. When Peter told me about this treatment I figured that because shit was one of the most dangerous corporeal substances in terms of passing disease (check the statistic on Belle Glade, Florida, where there are no adequate sewage facilities) maybe this guy figured out something in the properties of shit to develop a vaccine. After all, the bite of a rattlesnake is treated with a vaccine made of venom. But I also assumed that the doctor had at least made a vaccine for each patient out of their own shit. Later we found that one person's shit served as a base for all treatments. Almost all the patients treated with this became extremely ill. Each one who mentioned this fact was told privately that he or she was the only one who reacted badly. This turned out to be the case many times. There were regulars to this doctor's office that Peter would ask the doctor about. There was one young man in particular who everyone immediately fell in love with; the one all of them pinned their hopes on as an example of the possibility of success with the doctor's treatments. When Peter asked how this or that person was doing he was told: fine, fine. Recently he discovered this was not true at all, many were dead and buried and the young man everyone loved had died as well.

Peter talked with the pale boy inside the door for a while. The kid said he had been at the edge of death with T.B. and Kaposi's sarcoma which extended all the way down his spine and up into his ass. A couple of months after taking the typhoid treatments he was feeling better, "Just a touch of T.B. and most of the cancer has disappeared." The front door opened and an elderly gentleman who the boy had been living with in the Hamptons, came over to the desk and laid out a pile of personal checks. He proceeded to fill out and endorse each one to the scientist running the clinic. Check after check after check. After awhile a short seedy guy with lots of white teeth came over and introduced himself to us. He was the brains behind the typhoid treatment. I immediately felt uncomfortable with him. He reminded me of a guy who'd sell you dead chameleons at a circus sideshow. He told us to fill out the forms and sit in the waiting room until called. The waiting room was filled with people who recognized Peter, all former patients of the doctor in upper Manhattan. This cheered Peter up. Anita and I looked at each other in disbelief. Here was an office filled with people who were searching for "the cure." The grapevine brought them from one end of New York to the other to test out different therapies, sometimes combining them, sometimes improving for short periods of time, sometimes dying from them. What amazed us was that most of the people in this office had found this treatment independent of each other. To me, the idea that this treatment might help out with Kaposi's made a bit of sense. The introduction of a foreign element to the body sometimes sparks the immune system into momentarily working properly. Outside of New York, I'd read about some people who had done work with certain photochemicals, painting them on Kaposi's lesions which after some time dried up and fell off the skin. But in the few studies done, none of these therapies did much to stop the advancement of the more than three hundred other opportunistic infections.

One guy in his mid-thirties, a sad looking blond, asked Peter if he remembered him from fifteen or so years ago. He used to go by the name of Dorian Gray—apparently they'd had an affair back then. Peter suddenly did recognize him. "Of course I dropped the name some years ago." Peter asked

him if he was on AL7-21 and he said, "No; I just have ARC
not AIDS so I'm not worried; I don't think I'll need any of
that stuff."

The room was filled with AIDS-speak for the next half
hour. One of the guys was a sexy Italian man who'd
developed AIDS from intravenous drug use. He and his
girlfriend joined the conversation comparing different therapies and how each combined this or that treatment in
different ways. Everyone was emphatic about his or her
chemical or natural agenda. Talk swung to the typhoid
doctor and half the room tried to convince Peter he shouldn't
tell the doctor he was currently taking AZT. "He'll refuse to
treat you; he wants you to give up everything but the
typhoid shots; something about his research . . ." Finally the
brains behind the business called us into his personal office.
It looked like it had been decorated by Elvis: high lawn-
green shag carpets, K-mart paintings and Woolworth lamps.
Lots of official medical degrees with someone else's name on
them. Anita had come along to help Peter describe his
medical history because lately he was a bit slow; words came
in small clusters after much hand movements; he confused
easily. The doctor asked him how he knew he had AIDS:
"After all, you may not have it." Peter tried to describe the
last year's medical events. His description was disjointed and
unrevealing. Anita tried to step in at some point to help and
Peter waved her angrily away. The man said, "Fine, fine.
Now you must stop having sex . . ." Peter said, "I've been
celibate for two years." The man rambled on about how he
must stop having sex, or if he did, he must use rubbers. Then
he suddenly said, "Okay—go in and get your first shot." He
got up to usher us out of the office but pulled me back into
the room just as I was passing through the door. "Are you

homosexual?" "Yeah," I said. "Have you been tested for the HIV antibodies?" "Uh, no," I said, "and I haven't any plans to." "Oh," he said, "but you would be perfect for us—get the test and I'll start you on the treatments right away . . ." I cut him short, "Thanks . . . I'll think about it."

While Peter was getting his first shot Anita and I decided to ask the doctor to explain the theories behind his treatments. When we told him we want to discuss the treatment, he brought us back into his office. He immediately launched into some monologue about money: ". . . if the patient hasn't any money . . . well . . . we can work something out—I'm not in this just for the money . . . but, if they have money, they will pay. Oh, will they pay!" Anita told him we were just interested in how the typhoid treatments worked. We asked that he not spare us the medical jargon. He started off talking about how all the other doctors were quacks and how the government was trying to stop him from doing these treatments. He said he wasn't really a doctor but a research scientist with degrees in immunology. He'd hired a certified doctor to administer the shots. He went into a lengthy monologue about the immune system that made very little sense and ended up with talking about the thymus gland—only, when he gestured to his own body to indicate the location of the thymus, he pointed first to his stomach, then to his chest, then to his head saying, "Or wherever it is . . ." While we were recovering from that disturbing bit of information, he went into his research on various viruses and how he had settled on typhus as the virus that would successfully spark the immune system. When we asked him to elaborate further he took out a piece of paper and drew a series of circles on each side of a dividing line. "Say ya got a hundred army men over here; that's the T-cells . . ." We were interrupted by his assistant who told him he had to interview new patients. We left the office and looked around for Peter but he was nowhere to be found. The assistant eventually told us he was outside looking for a ride back to the city. Anita and I then realized that Peter had been in the doctor's office for merely ten minutes. We grabbed our coats and rushed out to find him standing on the sidewalk in front of the place. He looked confused. "Oh ... I thought you went home without me ..."

Before heading back to New York City we stopped at a diner along the highway and ordered food. Peter was agitated and demanded to know what we had thought of the scientist and his treatments. I explained what Anita and I had learned from the man in terms of his theories and how unsettling it all was. He looked sad and tired. He barely touched his food, staring out the window and saying, "America is such a beautiful country—don't you think so?" I was completely exhausted from the day, emotionally and physically and looking out the window at the enormous collage of high-tension wires, blinking stoplights, shredded used-car lot banners, industrial tanks and masses of humanity zipping about in automobiles just depressed me. The food we had in front of us looked like it had been fried in an electric chair. And watching my best friend dying while eating a dead hamburger left me speechless. I couldn't answer. Anita couldn't either. He got angry again, "Neither of you would know what I'm talking about ..." Finally I said, "Peter, we're just very tired. Let's go home."

On the ride back you could cut the tension in the car with a buzzsaw. Fighting late afternoon traffic, we finally arrived back on Second Avenue and just about had to carry him up the stairs. "Don't touch me, don't touch me." He staggered over to the bed and crawled in with all his clothes on, lying there with two eyes peeping from beneath the covers. "Is there anything you need? Anything we can do for you, Peter?" An angry "NO!" So we left. Later, talking on the telephone with Vince, I heard that Peter had talked with him minutes after Anita and I had left his house and Peter said, "I don't understand it, they just put me in bed and rushed out."

————

Dream. Night before Peter died. In this sleep I end up on a late-night street near a building awning like a garage port or hotel overhang and there are two thugs, street guys, tight white t-shirts, sexy thick arms and faces of possible violence: jail faces. There's a small glass box. I look through its lid and see a short fat snake with desert or jungle markings. The two guys tell me it's a pygmy rattler but there is no rattle on its tail. I lift the lid or they lift the lid and the snake jumps and fastens its teeth to the side of my nose. There is no real pain but it's there for a long time, each guy trying to pull its shiny jaws apart to free me. I'm bending over in a semicrouch waiting patiently, thinking of its poison flowing into me but no real fear of dying or anything. I'm amazed at how patient I am.

Standing in the street next to the curb, water runs like from some hydrant in the summer. There's a small blue-and-white boat like a ferry, a child's toy bobbing in the water. I crouch down to look into its tiny front windows. A voice (like from a P.A. system) says, "One of the passengers died before the ferry arrived this morning ... none of the other passengers were aware ..." The ferry suddenly becomes an enormous boat, a life-sized ferry, and it is bobbing on the ocean or river and I'm staring through the windows at what looks like a scene from an E.C. comic. The first person, alone in the front seat, stares straight ahead unmoving—obviously dead by the look in his eyes and by the shape of his skull pushing against the flesh and the almost gray-green pallor of his skin. The other passengers sit like stick dolls, some with missing teeth or hair. They're alive but not moving, staring at the back of the dead passenger's head.

———

I can't form words these past few days, sometimes thinking I've been drained of emotional content from weeping or fear. I keep doing these impulsive things like trying to make a film that records the rituals in an attempt to give grief form. It's almost winter and I drive west of New York to film myself bathing in a lake in some of the only virgin forest left on the eastern seaboard. I hold a super-8 camera in my hands and spin around and around in the woods thinking of dervishes; thinking of the intoxication of freedom witnessed in death.

Now I've driven north of New York City to the gravesite on a gray day filled with random spots of rain on a dirty windshield. All those birds' nests high in the winter trees. Everything rich and black and wet and brown, the serious rich darkness of his photographs. I'm kicking around the cemetery mud among huge lifeless tractors and the ravines they've made strewn with boulders and wet earth, talking to him; first walking around trying to find him was so difficult I started laughing nervously, "Maybe I can't find you, Peter." And these erratic pacings back and forth from his ground soil back to the car, cigarettes lit, camera retrieved from the backseat and brought back to the unmarked gravesite for a picture of Neal's flowers, "He loved flowers; loved them . . ." Months and months of illness and the house was always filled with flowers; some so big and wild they didn't even look like flowers; more like beings from some lunar slopes. All these erratic movements till finally I stopped myself, forced myself to contain my movements. Walking backward and forward at the same time, I realized how rattled I was. I was talking to him again. I get so amazingly self-conscious talking to him a thousand thoughts at once. The eye hovers in space inches from the back of my head; seeing myself seeing him, or, the surface extension of him—the wet tossed earth—and further seeing his spirit; his curled body rising invisible just above the ground; his eyes full and seeing; him behind me looking over my shoulder at himself rising over my shoulder, watching me looking at the fresh turned earth where he lies buried.

I try talking to him wondering if he knows I'm there, if he sees me. I know he sees me, he's in the wind, in the air around me. He covers the fields in a fine mist. He's in his home in the city. He's behind me. It's wet and cold but I like it like that. Like the way it numbs my fingers, makes them white and red at the knuckles. Strangers pat the earth before various stones around me; cars idle at the roadsides and long valleys and ridges on into the distance and everything is torn up and uprooted in this section—all the wet markings of the earth and the tractors, all these graves freshly developed and those birds' nests giant and wet-leaved as if they've been dropped by unseen hands into the crooks of tree limbs. I talk to him, so conscious of being alive and talking to my impressions, my memories of him, suspending all disbelief. I know he's there and I see him. I sense him in the hole down there under the surface of that earth. I see him without the covering of the plain pine box. The box no longer exists in my head, there's just a huge wide earth and grass and fields and crowfeet trees and me, my shape in the wet air and clouds like gauze like gray overlapping in fog and I tell him I'm scared and confused and I'm crying and I tell him how much I love him and how much he means to me and I tell him everything in my head, all the contradictions all fear and all love and all alone.

And his death is now as if it's printed on celluloid on the backs of my eyes. That last day when friends came to speak reassurances to him or to read letters from other friends to him or touch his hands or feet or to simply sit by his bed—there were people arriving and departing all day long—there was some point when I was sitting at the far corner of the bed in a chair thinking about leaving when I looked toward his face and his eyes moved slightly and I put two fingers up like rabbit ears behind the back of my head, a gesture, a high sign we had that we'd discreetly give when we bumped into each other at a crowded gathering in the past. I flashed him the sign and then turned away embarrassed and moments later Ethyl said, "David . . . look at Peter." We all turned to the bed and his body was completely still; and then there was a very strong and slow intake of breath and then stillness and then one more intake of breath and he was gone.

I surprised myself: I barely cried. When everyone left the room I closed the door and pulled the super-8 camera out of my bag and did a sweep of his bed: his open eye, his open mouth, that beautiful hand with the hint of gauze at the wrist that held the i.v. needle, the color of his hand like marble, the full sense of the flesh of it. Then the still camera: portraits of his amazing feet, his head, that open eye again—I kept trying to get the light I saw in that eye—and then the door flew open and a nun rushed in babbling about how he'd accepted the church and I look at this guy on the bed with his outstretched arm and I think: but he's beyond that. He's more there than the words coming from her containing these images of spirituality—I mean just the essence of death; the whole taboo structure in this culture the mystery of it the fears and joys of it the flight it contains this body of my friend on the bed this body of my brother my father my emotional link to the world this body I don't know this pure and cutting air just all the thoughts and sensations this death this event produces in bystanders contains more spirituality than any words we can manufacture.

So I asked her to leave and after closing the door again I tried to say something to him staring into that enormous eye. If in death the body's energy disperses and merges with everything around us, can it immediately know my thoughts? But I try and speak anyway and try and say something in case he's afraid or confused by his own death and maybe needs some reassurance or tool to pick up, but nothing comes from my mouth. This is the most important event of my life and my mouth can't form words and maybe I'm the one who needs words, maybe I'm the one who needs reassurance and all I can do is raise my hands from my sides in helplessness and say, "All I want is some sort of grace." And then the water comes from my eyes.

————

I go into these rages periodically that can find no real form where I end up hitting the backs of my hands against the television set instead of giving in to my real urge which is to rip the thing out of the wall and toss it blaring out the window into the traffic. Or I wake up from daydreams of tipping amazonian blowdarts in "infected blood" and spitting them at the exposed necklines of certain politicians or nazi-preachers or government health-care officials or the rabid strangers parading against AIDS clinics in the nightly news suburbs. I carry this rage in moments like some kind of panic and yes I am horrified that I feel this desire for murder but it all starts with a revolving screen of memories that mixes past and present. It contains the faces and bodies of people I loved struggling for life, people I loved and people who I thought made a real difference in the world, or at least who lent some kind of balance to those whose images and intents we get served daily through the media. It begins with the earliest memories, when sexuality first stirs beneath one's skin in an organized social structure that would kill you spiritually or physically every chance it has.

I remember when I was eight and a half, some nineteen-year-old kid brought me up the elevator to the rooftop. Under the summer night sky he placed my face against his dick and I almost lost consciousness because of the power of the unconscious desires suddenly surfacing and how for a week afterward this eight-year-old plotted murder because of fears that the guy would tell someone and I'd be locked up or institutionalized and given electroshock and how I studied my face in the mirror day after day to see if what I'd experienced was written there and the confusion I felt wondering if I'd become this hateful thing, and yet my face remained the same. For months afterward I searched the public library for information on my "condition" and found only sections of novels or manuals that described me as either a speedfreak sitting on a child's swing in a playground at dusk inventing new words for faggot—"...butterfly, wisp. . ."—or that people like me spoke with lisps and put bottles up their asses and wore dresses and had limp wrists and every novel I read that had references to queers described them as people who killed or destroyed themselves for no other reason than their realization of how terrible they were for desiring men and I felt I had no choice but to grow up and assume these shapes and characteristics. And I grew up living a schizophrenic existence in the family and in a social structure where every ad in every newspaper, tv and magazine was a promotion for heterosexual coupling sunlit muscleheads and beach bunnies. And in every playground, invariably, there's a kid who screamed, FAGGOT!, in frustration at some other kid and the sound of it resonated in my shoes, that instant solitude, that breathing glass wall no one else saw.

I hear endless news stories of murder around the nation where the defendant claims self-defense because this queer tried to touch him and the defendant being freed and I'm lying here on this bed of Peter's that was the scene of an intense illness and the channel of the tv has been turned to some show about the cost of AIDS and I'm watching a group of people die on camera because they can't afford the drugs that might extend their lives and some fella in the health-care system in texas is being interviewed—I can't even remember what he looks like because I reached through the television screen and ripped his face in half—he's saying, "If I had a dollar to spend for health care I'd rather spend it on a baby or an innocent person with some illness or defect not of their own responsibility; not some person with AIDS . . ." and I recall Philip's description of finding someone he knew almost dead on a bench in Tompkins Square Park because no hospital would take him in because he had AIDS and no health insurance and I read the newspaper stories about the politician in Arizona saying on the radio, "To solve the problem of AIDS just shoot the queers ..." and his press secretary claimed the governor just didn't know the microphone was on and besides they didn't really think this would affect his chances for reelection. And I have the memory of Peter eating alone one morning a couple of months before he died at Bruno's restaurant on Second Avenue and 12th Street and Bruno himself in the middle of the packed restaurant coming up to Peter saying, "Are you ready to pay?" And Peter saying, "Yes, but why?" And Bruno taking out a paper bag and saying, "You know why ... just put your money in here." Peter put five dollars in the bag and Bruno went behind the counter and brought back his change in another paper bag and tossed it onto the table. And what all this says in an instant. At first I wanted to go into Bruno's at rush hour and pour ten gallons of cow's blood onto the grill and simply say, "You know why." But that was something I might have done ten years ago. Instead I went in during a crowded lunch hour and screamed at Bruno demanding an explanation and every time a waitress or Bruno asked me to lower my voice I got louder and angrier until Bruno was cowering in back of the kitchen and every knife and fork in the place stopped moving. But even that wasn't enough to erase this rage. A former city government official concerned with administering AIDS policy, in a private city meeting on housing for poor people with AIDS, said, "What you want is a little place; an island where you can isolate these people so they can bang each other up with this AIDS virus ..." Statements like this are not uncommon in government meetings and the city of New York is dragging its feet on this disease just like every other city and federal agency in the country—they simply don't care—and they're allocating just enough money so it looks good on paper; not good, but at least on paper their asses are covered so in the future when the finger of responsibility points in their direction they can say, "But we did something." The government is not only withholding money, but drugs and information. People with AIDS across the country are turning themselves into human test tubes. Some of them are compiling so much information that they can call government agencies and pass themselves off as research scientists and suddenly have access to all the information that's been withheld and then they turn their tenement kitchens into laboratories, mixing up chemicals and passing them out freely to friends and strangers to help prolong lives. People are subjecting themselves to odd and sometimes dangerous alternative therapies—injections of viruses and consumption of certain chemicals used for gardening—all in order to live. And then you get these self-righteous walking swastikas claiming this is god's punishment and Buckley, in the daily newspaper, asking for a program to tattoo people with AIDS and LaRouche in California actually getting a bill up for vote that would isolate people with AIDS in camps and when I react with feelings of murder I feel horrified and tell myself that it is fascist to want to murder these people and in my horror at my feelings I attempt to rationalize them by going further saying but in this culture we accept murder as self-defense against those who try to murder us and what's going on here but public and social murder on a daily basis and it's happening in our midst and not very many people seem to say or do anything about it. There's not even an acknowledgment of this murder from most of my friends. In the evening news I'm told that violent acts against homosexuals are up forty-one percent over last year and to get away from all this I go to a cinema in the neighborhood to see a movie and it's called *Hollywood Shuffle* and it's about the plight of certain minorities in the movie industry and halfway through the movie I have to watch this stereotypic fag with a dick and designer perfume for a brain mince his way through his lines and I want to throw up because we're supposed to quietly and politely make house in this killing machine called America and pay taxes to support our own slow murder and I'm amazed that we're not running amok in the streets, and that we can still be capable of gestures of loving after lifetimes of all this.

―――――――

Previously, before leaving the city to go someplace else for a long time, the city would suddenly change. It was revealed to me as if I had let go of something that was keeping it hidden. Wonderful things tended to happen or reveal themselves in the days before departure. Life or living seemed quite an amazing spectacle. There was humanity beneath every gesture moving along the sidewalks. It was a sudden vision of the World, a transient position of the body in relation to the Other World. I came to understand that to give up one's environment was to also give up biography and all the encoded daily movements: those false reassurances of the railing outside the door. This was the beginning of a definition of the World for me. A place that might be described as interior world. The place where movement was comfortable, where boundaries were stretched or obliterated: no walls, borders, language or fear.

With the appearance of AIDS and the sense of mortality I now find everything revealing itself to me in this way.

The sense that came about in moments of departure occurs, only now I don't even have to go anywhere. It is the possibility of departure in a final sense, a sense called death that is now opening up the gates. Where once I felt acutely alien, now it's more like an immersion in a body of warm water and the water that surrounds me is air, is breathing, is life itself. I'm acutely aware of myself alive and witnessing. It's like a long-distance runner who suddenly finds himself in the solitude of distance among trees and light and the sight and sounds of friends are way back there in the distance. All behind me are the friends that have died. I'm breathing this air that they can't breathe; I'm seeing this ratty monkey in a cheap Mexican circus wearing a red-and-blue-embroidered jacket and it's collecting coins and I can reach out and touch it like they can't. Time is now compressed. I joke and say that I feel I've taken out another six-month lease on this body of mine, on this vehicle of sound and motion, and every painting or photograph or film I make, I make with the sense that it may be the last thing I do and so I try and pull everything in to the surface of that action. I work quickly now and feel there is no time for bullshit. Cut straight to the heart of the senses and map it out as clearly as tools and growth allow. In better moments I can see my friends— vague transparencies of their faces maybe over my shoulder or superimposed on the surfaces of my eyes—making me more aware of myself, seeing myself from a distance, seeing myself see others. I can almost see my own breath, see my internal organs functioning pump pumping. These days I see the edge of mortality. The edge of death and dying is around everything like a warm halo of light sometimes dim sometimes irradiated. I see myself seeing death. It's like a transparent celluloid image of myself is accompanying me everywhere I go. I see my friends and I see myself and I see breath coming from my lips and the plants are drinking it and I see breath coming from my chest and everything is fading, becoming a shadow that may disappear as the sun goes down.

POSTCARDS FROM AMERICA
X Rays from Hell

Late yesterday afternoon a friend came over unexpectedly to sit at my kitchen table and try to find some measure
of language for his state of mind. "What's left of living?" He's
been on AZT for six to eight months and his T-cells have
dropped from one hundred plus to thirty. His doctor says,
"What the hell do you want from me?" Now he's asking
himself, "What the hell do I want?" He's trying to answer this
while in the throes of agitating FEAR.

I know what he's talking about as each tense description
of his state of mind slips out across the table. The table is
filled with piles of papers and objects; a boom box, a bottle

of AZT, a jar of Advil (remember, you can't take aspirin or Tylenol while on AZT). There's an old smiley mug with pens and scissors and a bottle of Xanax for when the brain goes loopy; there's a Sony tape recorder that contains a half-used cassette of late-night sex talk, fears of gradual dying, anger, dreams and someone speaking Cantonese. In this foreign language it says: *"My mind cannot contain all that I see. I keep experiencing this sensation that my skin is too tight; civilization is expanding inside of me. Do you have a room with a better view? I am experiencing the X-ray of Civilization. The minimum speed required to break through the earth's gravitational pull is seven miles a second. Since economic conditions prevent us from gaining access to rockets or spaceships we would have to learn to run awful fast to achieve escape from where we are all heading ..."*

My friend across the table says, "There are no more people in their thirties. We're all dying out. One of my four best friends just went into the hospital yesterday and he underwent a blood transfusion and is now suddenly blind in one eye. The doctors don't know what it is ..." My eyes are still scanning the table; I know a hug or a pat on the shoulder won't answer the question mark in his voice. The AZT is kicking in with one of its little side effects: increased mental activity which in translation means I wake up these mornings with an intense claustrophobic feeling of fucking doom. It also means that one word too many can send me to the window kicking out panes of glass, or at least that's my impulse (the fact that winter is coming holds me in check). My eyes scan the surfaces of walls and tables to provide balance to the weight of words. A thirty-five millimeter camera containing the unprocessed images of red and blue and green faces in close-up profile screaming, a large postcard of a stuffed gorilla pounding its dusty chest in a museum diorama, a small bottle of hydrocortisone to keep my face from turning into a mass of peeling red and yellow flaking skin, an airline ticket to Normal, Illinois, to work on a print, a small plaster model of a generic Mexican pyramid looking like it was made in Aztec kindergarten, a tiny motorcar with a tiny Goofy driving at the wheel . . .

My friend across the table says, "The other three of my four friends are dead and I'm afraid that I won't see this friend again." My eyes settle on a six-inch-tall rubber model of Frankenstein from the Universal Pictures Tour gift shop, TM 1931: his hands are enormous and my head fills up with replaceable body parts; with seeing the guy in the hospital; seeing myself and my friend across the table in line for replaceable body parts; my wandering eyes aren't staving off the anxiety of his words; behind his words, so I say, "You know . . . he can still rally back . . . maybe . . . I mean people do come back from the edge of death . . ."

"Well," he says, "he lost thirty pounds in a few weeks . . ."

A boxed cassette of someone's interview with me in which I talk about diagnosis and how it simply underlined what I knew existed anyway. Not just the disease but the sense of death in the American landscape. How when I was out west this summer standing in the mountains of a small city in New Mexico I got a sudden and intense feeling of rage looking at those postcard-perfect slopes and clouds. For all I knew I was the only person for miles and all alone and I didn't trust that fucking mountain's serenity. I mean it was just bullshit. I couldn't buy the con of nature's beauty; all I could see was death. The rest of my life is being unwound and seen through a frame of death. And my anger is more about this culture's refusal to deal with mortality. My rage is really about the fact that WHEN I WAS TOLD THAT I'D CON-TRACTED THIS VIRUS IT DIDN'T TAKE ME LONG TO REALIZE THAT I'D CONTRACTED A DISEASED SOCIETY AS WELL.

On the table is today's newspaper with a picture of cardinal O'Connor saying he'd like to take part in operation rescue's blocking of abortion clinics but his lawyers are advising against it. This fat cannibal from that house of walking swastikas up on fifth avenue should lose his church tax-exempt status and pay taxes retroactively for the last couple of centuries. Shut down our clinics and we will shut down your "church." I believe in the death penalty for people in positions of power who commit crimes against humanity—i.e., fascism. This creep in black skirts has kept safer-sex information off the local television stations and mass transit spaces for the last eight years of the AIDS epidemic thereby helping thousands and thousands to their unnecessary deaths.

My friend across the table is talking again. "I just feel so fucking sick ... I have never felt this bad in my whole life ... I woke up this morning with such intense horror; sat upright in bed and pulled on my clothes and shoes and left the house and ran and ran and ran ..." I'm thinking maybe he got up to the speed of no more than ten miles an hour. There are times I wish we could fly; knowing that this is impossible I wish I could get a selective lobotomy and rearrange my senses so that all I could see is the color blue; no images or forms, no sounds or sensations. There are times I wish this were so. There are times that I feel so tired, so exhausted. I may have been born centuries too late. A couple of centuries ago I might have been able to be a hermit but the psychic and physical landscape today is just too fucking crowded and bought up. Last night I was invited to dinner upstairs at a neighbor's house. We got together to figure out how to stop the landlord from illegally tearing the roofs off our apartments. The buildings department had already shut the construction crew down twice and yet they have started work again. The recent rains have been slowing destroying my western wall. This landlord some time ago allowed me to stay in my apartment without a lease only after signing an agreement that if there were a cure for AIDS I would have to leave within thirty days. A guy visiting the upstairs neighbor learned that I had this virus and said he believed that although the government probably introduced the virus in the homosexual community, that homosexuals were dying en masse as a reaction to centuries of society's hatred and repression of homosexuality. All I could think of when he said this was an image of hundreds of whales that beach themselves on the coastlines in supposed protest of the ocean's being polluted. He continued, "People don't die— they choose death. Homosexuals are dying of this disease because they have internalized society's hate ..." I felt like smacking him in the head but held off momentarily, saying, "As far as your theory of homosexuals dying of AIDS as a protest against society's hatred, what about the statistics that those people contracting the disease are intravenous drug users or heterosexually inclined, and that this seems to be increasingly the case. Just look at the statistics for this area of the lower east side." "Oh," he said, "They're hated too ..." "Look," I said, "after witnessing the deaths of dozens of friends and a handful of lovers, among them some of the most authentically spiritual people I have ever known, I simply can't accept mystical answers or excuses for why so many people are dying from this disease—really it's on the shoulders of a bunch of bigoted creeps who at this point in time are in the position of power that determine where and when and for whom government funds are spent for research and medical care."

I found that, after witnessing Peter Hujar's death on November 26, 1987, and after my recent diagnosis, I tend to dismantle and discard any and all kinds of spiritual and psychic and physical words or concepts designed to make sense of the external world or designed to give momentary comfort. It's like stripping the body of flesh in order to see the skeleton, the structure. I want to know what the structure of all this is in the way only I can know it. All my notions of the machinations of the world have been built throughout my life on odd cannibalizations of different lost cultures and on intuitive mythologies. I gained comfort from the idea that people could spontaneously self-combust and from surreal excursions into nightly dream landscapes. But all that is breaking down or being severely eroded by my own brain; it's like tipping a bottle over on its side and watching the liquid contents drain out in slow motion. I suddenly resist comfort, from myself and especially from others. There is something I want to see clearly, something I want to witness in its raw state. And this need comes from my sense of mortality. There is a relief in having this sense of mortality. At least I won't arrive one day at my eightieth birthday and at the eve of my possible death and only then realize my whole life was supposed to be somewhat a preparation for the event of death and suddenly fill up with rage because instead of preparation all I had was a lifetime of adaptation to the preinvented world—do you understand what I'm saying here? I am busying myself with a process of distancing myself from you and others and my environment in order to know what I feel and what I can find. I'm trying to lift off the weight of the preinvented world so I can see what's underneath it all. I'm hungry and the preinvented world won't satisfy my hunger. I'm a prisoner of language that doesn't have a letter or a sign or gesture that approximates what I'm sensing. Rage may be one of the few things that binds or connects me to you, to our preinvented world.

———

My friend across the table says, "I don't know how much longer I can go on. . . . Maybe I should just kill myself." I looked up from the Frankenstein doll, stopped trying to twist its yellow head off and looked at him. He was looking out the window at a sexy Puerto Rican guy standing on the street below. I asked him, "If tomorrow you could take a pill that would let you die quickly and quietly, would you do it?"

"No," he said, "Not yet."

"There's too much work to do," I said.

"That's right," he said. "There's still a lot of work to do . . ."

———

I am a bundle of contradictions that shift constantly. This is a comfort to me because to contradict myself dismantles the mental/physical chains of the verbal code. I abstract the disease I have in the same way you abstract death. Sometimes I don't think about this disease for hours. This process lets me get work done, and work gives me life, or at least makes sense of living for short periods of time. Because I abstract this disease, it periodically knocks me on my ass with its relentlessness. With almost any other illness you take for granted that within a week or a month the illness will end and the wonderful part of the human body called the mind will go about its job erasing evidence of the pain and discomfort previously experienced. With AIDS or HIV infections one never gets that luxury and I find myself after a while responding to it for a fractured moment with my pre-AIDS thought processes: "All right this is enough already; it should just go away." But each day's dose of medicine, or the intermittent aerosol pentamidine treatments, or the sexy stranger nodding to you on the street corner or across the room at a party, reminds you in a clearer than clear way that at this point in history the virus' activity is forever. Outside my windows there are thousands of people without homes who are trying to deal with having AIDS. If I think *my* life at times has a nightmarish quality about it because of the society in which I live and that society's almost total inability to deal with this disease with anything other than a conservative agenda, think for a moment what it would be like to be facing winter winds and shit menus at the limited shelters, and the rampant T.B., and the rapes, muggings, stabbings in those shelters, and the overwhelmed clinics and sometimes indifferent clinic doctors, and the fact that drug trials are not open to people of color or the poor unless they have a private physician who can monitor the experimental drugs they would need to take, and they don't have those kinds of doctors in clinics because doctors in clinics are constantly rotated and intravenous drug users have to be clean of drugs for seven years before they'll be considered for experimental drug trials, and yet there are nine-month waiting periods just to get assigned to a treatment program. So picture yourself with a couple of the three hundred and fifty opportunistic infections and unable to respond physiologically to the few drugs released by the foot-dragging deal-making FDA and having to maintain a junk habit; or even having to try and kick that habit without any clinical help while keeping yourself alive seven years to get a drug that you need immediately—thank you Ed Koch; thank you Stephen Joseph; thank you Frank Young; thank you AMA.

I scratch my head at the hysteria surrounding the actions of the repulsive senator from zombieland who has been trying to dismantle the NEA for supporting the work of Andres Serrano and Robert Mapplethorpe. Although the anger sparked within the art community is certainly justified and will hopefully grow stronger, the actions by Helms and D'Amato only follow standards that have been formed and implemented by the "arts" community itself. The major museums in New York, not to mention museums around the country, are just as guilty of this kind of selective cultural support and denial. It is a standard practice to make invisible any kind of sexual imaging other than white straight male erotic fantasies. Sex in america long ago slid into a small set of generic symbols; mention the word "sex" and the general public appears to only imagine a couple of heterosexual positions on a bed—there are actual laws in parts of this country forbidding anything else even between consenting adults. So people have found it necessary to define their sexuality in images, in photographs and draw-ings and movies in order to not disappear. Collectors have for the most part failed to support work that defines a particular person's sexuality, except for a few examples such as Mapplethorpe, and thus have perpetuated the invisibility of the myriad possibilities of sexual activity. The collectors' influence on what the museum shows continues this process secretly with behind-the-scenes manipulations of curators and money. Jesse Helms, at the very least, makes public his attacks on freedom; the collectors and museums responsible for censorship make theirs at elegant private parties or from the confines of their self-created closets.

It doesn't stop at images—in a recent review of a novel in the *new york times book review*, a reviewer took outrage at the novelist's descriptions of promiscuity, saying, "In this age of AIDS, the writer should show more restraint . . ." Not only do we have to contend with bonehead newscasters and conservative members of the medical profession telling us to "just say no" to sexuality itself rather than talk about safer sex possibilities, but we have people from the thought police spilling out from the ranks with admonitions that we shouldn't *think* about anything other than monogamous or safer sex. I'm beginning to believe that one of the last frontiers left for radical gesture is the imagination. At least in my ungoverned imagination I can fuck somebody without a rubber, or I can, in the privacy of my own skull, douse Helms with a bucket of gasoline and set his putrid ass on fire or throw congressman William Dannemeyer off the empire state building. These fantasies give me distance from my outrage for a few seconds. They give me momentary comfort. Sexuality defined in images gives me comfort in a hostile world. They give me strength. I have always loved my anonymity and therein lies a contradiction because I also find comfort in seeing representations of my private experiences in the public environment. They need not be representations of my experiences—they can be the experiences of and by others that merely come close to my own or else disrupt the generic representations that have come to be the norm in the various medias outside my door. I find that when I witness diverse representations of "Reality" on a gallery wall or in a book or a movie or in the spoken word or performance, that the larger the range of representations, the more I feel there is room in the environment for my existence, that not the entire environment is hostile.

To make the *private* into something *public* is an action that has terrific repercussions in the preinvented world. The government has the job of maintaining the day-to-day illusion of the ONE-TRIBE NATION. Each public disclosure of a private reality becomes something of a magnet that can attract others with a similar frame of reference; thus each public disclosure of a fragment of private reality serves as a dismantling tool against the illusion of ONE-TRIBE NATION; it lifts the curtains for a brief peek and reveals the probable existence of literally millions of tribes. The term "general public" disintegrates. What happens next is the possibility of an X-ray of Civilization, an examination of its foundations. To turn our private grief for the loss of friends, family, lovers and strangers into something public would serve as another powerful dismantling tool. It would dispel the notion that this virus has a sexual orientation or a moral code. It would nullify the belief that the government and medical community has done very much to ease the spread or advancement of this disease.

One of the first steps in making the private grief public is the ritual of memorials. I have loved the way memorials take the absence of a human being and make them somehow physical with the use of sound. I have attended a number of memorials in the last five years and at the last one I attended I found myself suddenly experiencing something akin to rage. I realized halfway through the event that I had witnessed a good number of the same people participating in other previous memorials. What made me angry was realizing that the memorial had little reverberation outside the room it was held in. A tv commercial for handiwipes had a higher impact on the society at large. I got up and left because I didn't think I could control my urge to scream.

There is a tendency for people affected by this epidemic to police each other or prescribe what the most important gestures would be for dealing with this experience of loss. I resent that. At the same time, I worry that friends will slowly become professional pallbearers, waiting for each death, of their lovers, friends and neighbors, and polishing their funeral speeches; perfecting their rituals of death rather than a relatively simple ritual of life such as screaming in the streets. I worry because of the urgency of the situation, because of seeing death coming in from the edges of abstraction where those with the luxury of time have cast it. I imagine what it would be like if friends had a demonstration each time a lover or a friend or a stranger died of AIDS. I imagine what it would be like if, each time a lover, friend or stranger died of this disease, their friends, lovers or neighbors would take the dead body and drive with it in a car a hundred miles an hour to washington d.c. and blast through the gates of the white house and come to a screeching halt before the entrance and dump their lifeless form on the front steps. It would be comforting to see those friends, neighbors, lovers and strangers mark time and place and history in such a public way.

But, bottom line, this is my own feeling of urgency and need; bottom line, emotionally, even a tiny charcoal scratching done as a gesture to mark a person's response to this epidemic means whole worlds to me if it is hung in public; bottom line, each and every gesture carries a reverberation that is meaningful in its diversity; bottom line, we have to find our own forms of gesture and communication. You can never depend on the mass media to reflect us or our needs or our states of mind; bottom line, with enough gestures we can deafen the satellites and lift the curtains surrounding the control room.

Thanks: A.N., J.E. & R.E. (ACT-UP)

The Seven Deadly Sins
Fact Sheet

Edward Koch. Every day, new yorkers who are AIDS
workers see the human toll that their mayor's refusal to deal
with a health crisis extorts from the sick. So they have no
reason to believe the mayor has any sympathy for people
with AIDS. Koch has stalled, ranted and raved, and in
general done everything he could to avoid dealing with the
AIDS crisis.

• He has spent woefully little and at this point in time has
left 8,000–10,000 P.W.A.'s (People With AIDS) homeless in
the streets. At a recent city agency meeting city officials
heard testimony that projected 33,000 homeless people with

AIDS living on the streets of N.Y.C. by 1993. Congressmen were assured by representatives of the city that no one should worry, these people will be dying so quickly from lack of treatment that there will be no visible increase of homeless P.W.A.'s on the streets. Letting landlords warehouse apartments and letting city-owned buildings remain bricked up while he spends taxpayers' money for rat-infested welfare rooms to the tune of $1500 a month per room for those homeless who manage to get help through city agencies.

• He has done nothing for foster care or treatment, only grandstand announcements of programs that never get done (housing, etc.).

• He has come out against legislation acknowledging domestic partners.

• Even AIDS workers familiar with all of the above were aghast when the mayor earlier this year revealed the depth of his fear and loathing. In the latest installment of his autobiography (this one a co-production with the cardinal) the mayor relates a visit he made to a local ward for children with AIDS. Handing out cookies to the kids, he was so overcome with revulsion that he rushed to the nearest sink and tried to wash the experience away, in effect literalizing what he has been doing since this crisis began: Distributing sweets and washing his hands.

Cardinal John O'Connor. The world's most active liar about condoms and safer sex. No set of AIDS statistics alarms demographers more than the apparent spread of HIV infection among new york city's adolescents, many of them latino, many of them in neighborhoods dominated by the church.

• PREFERS COFFINS TO CONDOMS: At Covenant House, a supposed

safe-haven for teenage runaways who frequently have to resort to hustling and prostitution for survival while on the streets, NO condoms or safer-sex information available, although there is a high rate of recidivism. The archdiocese, which runs Covenant House, as well as keeping these children ignorant and putting them at great risk in order to maintain their "moral" code, will simply tell them it is their fault as they lay dying. NO safer-sex information or condoms talked about in parochial schools and catholic-run youth agencies.
• Archdiocese serves on the Board of Education's AIDS Advisory Committee and lobbies heavily and incessantly against teaching about safer sex and/or condoms.

• VATICAN'S POSITION ON VIOLENCE AGAINST LESBIANS AND GAYS: October 31, 1986 (after Gay Rights Bill passed) VATICAN LETTER: "Letter to the Bishops of the Catholic Church on Pastoral Care of Homosexual Persons" (issued by Vatican Congregation for the Doctrine of the Faith). Section 12 (violence):

> ". . . . when homosexual activity is consequently condoned, or when civil legislation is introduced to protect behavior to which *no one has any conceivable right*, neither the church nor society at large should be surprised when other disturbed notions and practices gain ground, and irrational and violent reactions increase.''

Cannibal?—The hierarchy of the american church appears to have dug in for the long last supper. Aside from recent harassment of people who believe in choice with regard to abortion (threats of excommunication, etc.), O'Connor, who missed his calling on soap operas, is installing a raised press platform in St. Patrick's Cathedral for television crews and reporters. His spokesman explained, "We have been planning this for a long time as a way of balancing the press's and the worshippers' needs."

Rep. William Dannemeyer (R-CA). Asked president Bush to denounce a federal study of suicide containing research by a san francisco social worker that links young gays' and lesbians' suicidal tendencies with alienation from a society largely unaware of their existence. The congressman's latest homophobic volley charged that the inquiry "adds legitimacy to the heretofore crime of child molestation."

Lesbian and gay young people who take their own lives account for 30 percent or more of all u.s. suicides, according to san francisco psychotherapist Paul Gibson. Dannemeyer called on Bush to "affirm traditional family values by denouncing the portion of the report that deals with homosexuality."

In the report, Gibson said that the root problem of gay youth suicide is a society that discriminates against and stigmatizes homosexuals while failing to recognize that a substantial number of its youth has a gay or lesbian orientation. (Contact Gregory King of the Human Rights Campaign Fund regarding a news release dated November 5, 1989, (202) 628-4160.) Dannemeyer is a longtime homophobic crazy regarded as a nut case by his congressional colleagues. Also the author of a book that declares homosexuality to be a curable illness—a position that contributes to violence against lesbians and gays.

Stephen Joseph. Shut down bathhouses in n.y.c. rather than treating them as possible places where education about AIDS and safer-sex possibilities could take place. Not long ago, in epidemiology so shoddy it shocked even the establish-

ment, his Health Department had revised its estimate of
HIV infected gay and bisexual men in n.y.c.—from 250,000
to 50,000! Why? The city's evolving party line now said the
epidemic was one of drug users and their families. The city
could not afford to recognize that, measured in the mounting
body count, the epidemic among gays was far from over. This
new ideology (and the attendant specter of funding cuts)
had required a new epidemiology. In his performance on the
witness stand Joseph had given the department's de facto
homophobia his inimitable chilly imprint.

• He uses irrelevant analogies from san francisco figures,
thereby refusing to accurately count HIV positive gay men.
Refused, as does the Centers for Disease Control, to acknowl-
edge that lesbians are at risk and have contracted AIDS.
• He hasn't pressured the Board of Education to do a real
AIDS education program in the schools.
• Hasn't insisted on declaring a state of emergency.
• Has pushed testing and contact tracing as opposed to
prevention and treatment; especially treatment.
• Wanted to outlaw anonymous testing and institute man-
datory contact tracing. Has been nothing but a stooge for
Koch. Lucky for n.y. he resigned recently.

Jesse Helms. One of the more dangerous homophobes in the
continental united states. Finds the human body, itself,
obscene. Was responsible for the original NEA flap and has
made thinly disguised racist statements detailing his reactions to certain Mapplethorpe photographs—statements concerning interracial couples. Sends out photographs of himself
to citizens and newspapers in a tireless self-enriching, self-
promoting campaign whose policies and statements contribute heavily to the murder of and violence against lesbians

and gays in this country as well as creating myths about AIDS that keep people stupid and ignorantly at risk for contracting the disease. Has introduced legislation that denies federal funding for any program that mentions homosexuality. Has succeeded in getting such legislation passed by using a campaign of intimidation that most politicians bow to. Cut out any and all AIDS education funding that relates to gays and lesbians. Introduced legislation that we must now live with that prevents any HIV positive people or PWA's from entering any border of the U.S.A. as well as deporting people with green cards forcibly tested and found to be HIV positive. Designed the New Chill that has swept through the arts community, causing institutions, artists, and curators to censor themselves rather than contest *him*. Fascists wearing conservative drag have mounted Helms and ridden him through the foundations of the Constitution. Even a true conservative would recognize the recent Frohnmayer attacks as a trampling of the First Amendment—Helms just about had a media-induced orgasm.

> "What do the anti-arts forces want? What they have always wanted in this century: political control over our culture, using moral outrage as the excuse."—Douglas Davis, artist, critic, and teacher (*Newsday*)

Under Helms, words and pictures have gained a power they haven't had in decades compared to television.

Alfonse D'Amato. More interested in lining his rich real estate friends' pockets than saving people's lives. With his eyes peeled for the camera he's made an asshole of himself ripping the Mapplethorpe catalogue into tiny pieces; clear echoes of the Nazi era. Has been so busy voting for the Helms amendments denying AIDS education that he has never had a personal meeting with a gay or lesbian organization. It seems that you must be a BIG contributor to his campaign funds before you can get a foot in the door. Despite never meeting with a representative of the lesbian and gay community, he has voted consistently against us. Dismissive of gay issues. In the 1980 election, while running against Holtzman/Javits, he was quoted as saying, "Elizabeth Holtzman is part of the Ultra-Left Gay Rights Conspiracy that is out to destroy the middle class." D'Amato clearly missed his calling; he could have increased his millions writing trash novels like Dannemeyer. If the feds ignore his wealth and move against him in the HUD scandals, seats in the courtroom will be filled to the max.

Frank Young. Has operated as a know-nothing bureaucrat who saw his job as obstruction. Young has headed a Food & Drug Administration totally unequipped to deal with the magnitude of a crisis like AIDS.

• Has refused to work actively to get treatments to people with the disease who might live and thrive.

• To him, red tape and procedure is more important than people.

• Doesn't understand issues of access for the poor, or uneducated, or communities of color.

• In classic bureaucratese, people who were dying from AIDS were told until recently that they couldn't try manageably safe, potentially effective drugs: Big Brother was protecting them from themselves. When the Commissioner finally woke up and smelled the bodies, the orders he issued might have inched the agency in the right direction. Trouble was, the bureaucracy never followed. Now that he's been dumped upstairs, will the next FDA chief in fact effect the changes that AIDS demands, or simply let the bureaucracy go back to bed?

Additional Statistics and Facts

There has been a 40 percent increase in AIDS among teenagers in just the last two years. The Centers for Disease Control did a study of blood samples and found that as many as one in one hundred teens are HIV positive in new york.

One in every twenty-five babies born in brooklyn is HIV positive.

The vatican and the catholic church ignore scientific research that shows that if latex condoms are used properly they can prevent the transmission of HIV and other diseases. They make prehistoric statements such as: "Morality is the only prevention for AIDS . . ." and "Anyone who ignores the teachings of the catholic church and contracts AIDS has only himself to blame." So, regardless of what religion you practice, you must heed the teachings of the catholic church; and if the church hires lobbyists to pressure politicians on the Hill to vote against AIDS education, and if the church is consistently allowed to be on AIDS advisory commissions in the Board of Education, somehow citizens of this country must turn a blind eye to this clear violation of the separation of church and state. We are supposed to rest assured that at least the church will take state and federal monies to house a handful of dying people who might have not contracted this disease had the church been willing to acknowledge that people do have sex, and have always had sex, and always will have sex, even in the face of centuries of the church's attempts to force us to act otherwise. Certain religious and spiritual practices in history have involved human sacrifice; the government and most citizens would rally against any form of this type of practice if they knew of it occurring in their midst— why are people silent, why are the journalists silent about the vatican's and the church's activities that amount to the same thing? Denying all people information that could protect them in an epidemic is nothing more than wholesale murder regardless of the "moral" content of those actions.

This is a country of trains, planes, and automobiles. AIDS is accelerating in small towns and small cities because the inhabitants of those places believe a number of things:

one. That this virus has a sexual orientation and a moral code.

two. That the virus obeys borders and stays within large urban centers.

three. That if the person you fuck is sweet and kind and sexy, they could not possibly have AIDS or the HIV virus.

four. That only wild or reckless people get this disease.

_____

One in every four people in the bronx is HIV positive.

_____

During the years of the Reagan administration our president was completely silent about the spread of this epidemic. It took almost eight years just to have a few public posters dealing with AIDS and these posters were only printed in english, as opposed to spanish or any other language. The small AIDS campaign effected by city governments was so unimaginative that it could only state: DON'T ASK FOR AIDS; DON'T GET IT. One doesn't get AIDS by "Asking for it." One contracts AIDS through ignorance and the denial of pertinent information that could be used by people to safeguard their sexual activities. In the next ten years, when the american public wakes up and smells the bodies collecting in their midst—when they realize their children are dying and they themselves are dying from this disease— the politicians who are supposed to be representing us will be held accountable, as will the church for its interference in policy-making decisions of government. Journalists from coast to coast have been remiss in reporting truly the extent of this epidemic, mainly because they feel the people involved are expendable and because newspaper owners and publishers have a conservative agenda in mind when dealing with news and its dissemination. In certain religions in this country a part of the spiritual practice and belief is that medicine must be refused as a possible treatment for any infections or diseases. The u.s. government has prosecuted parents for failing to allow doctors to treat their children when those children have treatable infections. Those children can and do die. If you look at *information* as a *preventative medicine*, the archdiocese and government and media have consistently withheld that information (safer-sex possibilities) and thus ensured the ultimate infection, illness, and possible deaths of millions of citizens in this country. What makes the church exempt from criticism that is extended to the religions described earlier in this paragraph?

"Bigotry is ugly, but even more so when it poses as virtue."—statement made by an individual giving testimony in support of legislation designed to protect all citizens in new york, including those of diverse sexual orientation. He was being heckled by a religious leader who didn't stop short of calling for the death of homosexuals.

Cardinal O'Connor has been stating in the press recently that citizens should have love and compassion for people with AIDS. If you follow his dangerous reasoning in regards to his stance on safer-sex information (he will only condone abstinence), he would prefer all people remain at great risk and then when they contract AIDS he will shower them with love and compassion as they lie dying. I shudder to think of him prowling the halls and rooms of the archdiocese-run AIDS residences (more aptly called warehouses of death), falling to his knees to hold the hands of the dying men, women and teenagers and rolling his eyes heavenward. The church's policies contribute to the promotion of murder and violence against lesbians and gays. Our public funds are endlessly spent tracking down serial killers; we at least know where this one lives—so why aren't public officials and local police doing something about this man?

There have been statements made in the press that seem to use the fact that I have AIDS as an excuse for the tone of my writings—for my anger at these individuals. This is insulting to me. Anybody has the right to be outraged and the right to express these things. I have been writing about these issues in this "tone" well before my diagnosis with AIDS.

We as a society have been in this political climate before. It is cyclical, and similar bigots and extremists have reared their conservative/fascist heads before in order to conduct witch hunts. (Recently, in missouri, novelist and playwright Larry Kramer experienced another example of the repressive actions of this government. In a phone call I was told by a friend that local officials in missouri apparently tried to close down a production of Kramer's play *The Normal Heart*, on the grounds that they deemed it obscene. The home of the student responsible for producing the play was later firebombed.) Years ago this kind of climate manifested itself in the public spectacle of the McCarthy hearings. McCarthy was able to conduct his deadly circus while the press and citizens witnessed the debacle in silence. McCarthy was only stopped when he was confronted by people of conscience in positions of power. Now is the time for politicians of conscience to come out on public record; now is the time for citizens of any persuasion to come out on record; now is the time for all journalists of conscience to come out on record in opposition to these men and women of politics and organized "religion" who are conducting the "moral" witch hunts and helping to insure the spread of this

AIDS epidemic through denial of pertinent safer-sex information. Now is not the time for restraint to be shown in the form of our words and gestures, for men like Helms, Dannemeyer, or O'Connor show little restraint in their zeal to trample the Constitution.

DO NOT DOUBT
THE DANGEROUSNESS
OF THE 12-INCH-TALL
POLITICIAN

(This essay was derived from talks delivered at Illinois State University at Normal, Illinois, and the University of the Arts in Philadelphia, Pennsylvania, in 1990.)

I was invited, in early 1990, to give a lecture at the University of the Arts, Philadelphia, as a "visiting photographer," which convinced me to accept the invitation because I have never called myself a "photographer." If anyone ever asked me whether I was a photographer, I would say in return: "I sometimes make photographs." I have never been comfortable calling myself anything that would label

my acts of creativity because I don't ever want to take myself
so seriously that others would then pull out their magnifying
glasses and hold me or my actions or the artifacts of those
actions up to the ART WORLD criteria of any given
medium. Anyway, I don't even know how to operate a
camera on anything other than *automatic*. That might have
something to do with the makeup of my brain because I have
a terrible time reading INSTRUCTION MANUALS. I read
the manual as far as the page that explains how to turn the
device or machine ON. Then I push and tug and shake the
machine and learn it intuitively and enough to get it to do
the things I want. After learning how to turn the damn thing
on my brain gets a little dizzy and anxious if I try to read
further. I woke up one night with the thought that the people
in this society we call *america* who can read the instruction
manuals from front to back and then follow them to the letter
are probably the people in positions of power. This is not as
silly as it sounds. The people who control the means of image
production *are* the ones who are in power. Owners of
newspapers and owners of tv stations are the ones who have
the most power.

Years ago we would not know what lay beyond the
bend in the road until we walked past it. Maybe there was an
advantage to this way of learning because we would have to
walk down the road and see things for ourselves in order to
know what was going on. Now you wake up and turn on the
television set or pick up a newspaper and suddenly you can
find yourself thirty miles beneath the ocean or behind the
front door of the WHITE HOUSE almost sitting in the
president's lap and all of us, to some extent, take it for
granted that these representations of images are in some way
an indication of *real life*. If this were true, then how come

there are so few people of color on television? How come no lesbians or homosexual men? How come we get AIDS information that is eight years old?

Less than half the people who are eligible to vote in this country even bother to do so. Tell me: What does that mean? Who does this benefit? And those who bother to vote base their decision on little pictures that come through a box we call *television*. People *trust their lives* to a little man no bigger than twelve inches tall who is transmitted from a satellite in outer space into the antennae of their tv screens. This man appears now and then to sell his image to those who go to the polling booths. Why on earth would any of us believe that this man who appears on tv is not dangerous? How on earth could we truly believe he would not do us harm once he is elected? Is it because he is only a maximum of twelve inches tall and we think we can handle him if he gets out of line? Maybe give him a little kick in the little butt if he proves to be a liar and a thief and a borderline fascist? What if the owners of tv stations and the owners of newspapers prevent that information from being shown, printed, talked about? I rarely watch tv anymore because I have a problem with believing the images that get pumped out of that little box in the corner of the room. Instead I just look out my window and pretend it's the television set or the newspaper I used to watch or read. No one can edit these images before I see them, so they tend to be more honest.

———

In the art world, photography is one of the most misunderstood mediums because the camera is accessible to almost everybody. A good portion of the population in america owns cameras. Last year Burger King was giving away a tiny plastic camera FREE WITH A PURCHASE OF TWO WHOPPERS. This camera was no larger than the roll of film that fit into it. After five rolls of film the camera fell apart. By that time you were conceivably hungry again and would go back to buy more Whoppers.

The nature of the camera's mechanisms makes it possible to never take a "bad" photograph. You can always get *something* on film and if it is blurry and out of focus or "badly" lit you only have to claim INTENT and the art world will consider it. Photography is one of the most misunderstood mediums because no one can really explain in a rational way what makes a good or bad photograph other than the artist's intent. This is why the art world will not throw billions of dollars at photography the way it has at painting; and that is what makes it an exciting medium. You can do anything or everything you want and there is no precise criteria with which the art world can dismiss it or kill it.

I used to wonder where the urge to photograph came from. I mean, there are literally billions of photographs of the eiffel tower spread all over the world by tourists with cameras. I imagine people sleep better at night having these tiny *proofs* of the existence of the eiffel tower in boxes underneath their beds.

————————

My first camera was a stolen camera. I was living on the streets of new york city and a street buddy and I were staying at some guy's house for a while. This guy was a forty-eight-year-old acid head who'd been doing the drug for five years on a daily basis. He lived on a stipend from his rich dad. He was part hippie, and he let us stay with him and didn't ask for rent. One day his dad cut off his stipend and he went into withdrawal from all the acid he'd been consuming. My buddy and I carried him to a hospital and while he was recuperating, we decided to clean his house for him. His house was a horrifying mess: ceiling to floor piles of brown newspapers and sacks of garbage and what appeared to be useless pieces of cardboard. We threw out anything that appeared to be without value or sentiment. When the guy came home from the hospital he went into a fit screaming that we had robbed him. He called the police and asked them to come and arrest us for theft. We had to run out the door before the cops got there. My buddy stole the guy's small thirty-five millimeter camera because he figured if the guy was going to call us thieves, we might as well steal something. My buddy gave the camera to me and for months afterward I'd steal rolls of film from drugstores and take photographs of the gang of ex-con transvestites we hung around with on West Street. I never had any money so I couldn't get the photographs developed. I'd put all the rolls of film in whatever bus station locker we left our meager belongings in and the first day that we forgot to put in the daily-required quarter, all our belongings were confiscated and taken to a lost and found in the outer reaches of brooklyn.

I try to think of what it meant to be engaged in the act of picture-taking. I thought at the time that it would be making pictures of the world I lived in. One that was never seen on the television sets behind the windows of electronic shops or in the pages of newspapers floating around the 5:00 A.M. streets. Or it was possibly an act of validation of our lives, something of value being implied in the preservation of our bodies.

After getting off the streets at age eighteen, I began

taking pictures with that same camera and for the first time
I was able to see what the camera saw when I pointed it at
something and snapped the shutter. I began to learn
something about representation and what that meant to me.
I learned something about defining ones impulses and
desires and ideas about the world. If you look at newspapers
you rarely see a representation of anything you believe to
be the world you inhabit. This is called information control.
This is distortion by unseen hands belonging to faceless
people. As a person who owns a camera, I am in direct
competition with the owners of television stations and
newspapers; though my gestures of communication have less
of a reverberation than a newspaper photograph has
because of the amount of copies the newspaper owner can
circulate among the populations coast to coast. The only
difference between a newspaper owner and myself is that I
believe I represent a different intention in what I point my
camera toward. I have a desire to open up certain
boundaries and release information that unties the psychic
ropes that bind the ONE-TRIBE NATION. I can speak
with photographs about many different things that the
newspaper owner is afraid to address because of agenda or
political pressure, or because of the power of advertisers
dollars. I can make photographs dealing with my sexuality
and I do because I know my sexuality is purposefully made
invisible by the owners of various media.

———

Are photographs just tiny windows looking onto the
world, frozen moments of it that lie flat and quiet without
sound or smell or movement? Susan Whatsername said
something about photographs being like small deaths which

is maybe true. Maybe not. Maybe such a statement reflects that person's fear of being photographed. Certain people in certain places for ages have felt that a photograph steals a part of your soul, so when someone aimed a camera at them they were likely to throw a spear or cut the photographers throat or shoot them, or slug the photographer on the chin and demand a fifteen percent cut of the royalties. To me, photographs are like words and I generally will place many photographs together or print them one inside the other in order to construct a free-floating sentence that speaks about the world I witness. History is made and preserved by and for particular classes of people. A camera in some hands can preserve an alternate history.

Not long ago, I had a retrospective of my paintings, photographs and sculptures in the midwest. A university professor who teaches a class on "pornography" brought his students to view my work and ask me questions. A student raised his hand and stated that he had learned from his teacher the difference between pornography and erotica but wanted to know what I considered some of my work which contained explicit sexual images. I told him that I don't think there is a separation in images of sexuality such as pornography and erotica. Some images are capable of being insulting to me because they underscore the acceptance and maintenance of straight white male fantasies, of which our museums contain many examples, while excluding the diversity of sexual possibilities. Also, what may be considered erotica by me because of its familiarity and reflection of my desire may be considered *pornography* by someone who still considers the human body a taboo subject. Consider this: as a society we had to endure the media spectacle surrounding the polyps in Ronald Reagan's asshole found during a routine examination and subsequently removed, and yet for the eight years during his presidency, he was completely silent about the AIDS epidemic. In those eight years we were denied access to any real information concerning our own bodies in the midst of this crisis. We still are. The Health and Human Services Department in 1990 finally has gotten around to printing a pamphlet explaining how to use a condom but will only release it to people who call an AIDS hotline and to some health professionals. James Brown, a department spokesperson defended this murderous decision by saying, "Obviously the federal government does not tell local communities what to teach their children. We're telling them it's available. It's up to them to decide to use it." But if you were to substitute any other disease for AIDS in this situation, do you think it would be so socially acceptable for government to just leave it up to a handful of individuals to decide whether they educate anyone about a deadly epidemic or not.

At the moment, we have more of these bozos in the senate, such as Jesse Helms and William Dannemayer, who are trying to dismantle the NEA because a few public coins have supported images of diverse sexuality, as well as examinations of organized religion. Their hysteria gives the impression that these few images will cause the foundations of civilization to crumble and family structures to implode. The reality is that the NEA already has a terrible track record in funding minorities' expressions. It also ignores the fact that our tax dollars are paying for bigots in the churches to open their quivering yaps and get their agendas spread all over the media. These are agendas which adversely affect all people of all religions and nonreligions in this time of the AIDS epidemic. Our tax monies are being used to support the catholic church in its hiring of lobbyists to intimidate politicians on issues such as condom use and abortion.

Helms is the man who introduced and helped pass legislation that cut all federal funding for safer-sex information and AIDS education designed for lesbians and homosexuals. Why doesn't any reporter or colleague ask Helms whether he believes in capital punishment for homosexuality? His actions amount to the same thing where death is delivered in a crap-shoot created by state-enforced ignorance. Why don't they ask him why he is obsessed with homosexuality? Why don't they ask him at what age he might have first experienced same-sex attractions and what in his environment caused such a strong, murderous reaction?

In early January of 1990 I heard a story from a journalist concerning a bunch of videotapes that were seized by american troops during the invasion of panama. Apparently Noriega had been secretly videotaping visiting politicians and north american public figures who made trips down to panama over the years for what they may have considered fun, rest and relaxation, away from the eyes of the u.s.a. The journalist thought that Helms' name had surfaced among those rumored to be implicated on the tapes. In researching this story, the rumor that his name was connected to others on the tapes proved to be unfounded. He may not have ever gone to panama. What a pity.

The tapes were discovered in the ransacking of one of Noriega's houses. They were quickly cataloged by members of the C.I.A. along with slathers of other videos, sculptures, baggies of suspicious white powder, and photographs and then were "disappeared" into government top-secret archives where the tools that could topple governments and regimes and political careers usually find their dark sleeping finales.

At the time every major news station carried stories of PORNOGRAPHY and COCAINE and STATUES OF HITLER found in Noriega's house. This information was bandied about on our television sets as if this were the moral excuse for invading and ransacking a foreign country and killing hundreds of poor people who happened to live in the vicinity of one of the Noriega strongholds. The cocaine turned out to be flour or plaster dust; dummy coke props. The laughability of using pornography as a moral reason for invading panama can only be measured against the fact that pornography is a multi-billion-dollar industry in the corn-fields and alleyways of america. The reporters who stared at the studio cameras and gave horrified accounts of statues of Hitler being found in Noriega's house forgot to tell you that they also found statues of american presidents as well. Or maybe the C.I.A. just "forgot" to include these facts on their log-in sheets.

But what if Mr. Helms had been to panama and he were included on one of the surreptitious videotapes documenting the desires of visiting politicians—what could his desire possibly consist of? I spent long afternoons reading copies of the congressional record and could only surmise one thing— Giant Roosters. I could imagine him somewhere in the rolling hills of summertime panama, inside a specially constructed sanitized chicken coop, naked with a hen's feather Scotch-taped to his ass, wearing giant red plastic chicken's feet and hopping around in a room full of roosters making gobble gobble noises.

Someday our curiosity may quenched and we'll actu-ally find out what Mr. Helms' desires consist of. Until then, Helms joins the ranks of characters sliming around the contours of the great petri-dish of washington, William

Buckley, William Dannemayer, and John Cardinal O'Connor: Sexually insecure men who make it their lives' work to create policies that contribute heavily to the state-condoned violence and murder toward Lesbians and Gays.

What exactly is Helms afraid of? What image of sexuality can be so disturbing in the tail end of the twentieth century? How do you consider the images of death and murder on the evening news in comparison to an image of someone's desire or sexuality? Why are paintings of rape any more or any less scandalous compared to an image of two men kissing or fucking? Helms, by the way, had more of a problem with the fact that the two men on "a marble tabletop" happened to be a black man and a white man than with the idea that they were engaged in an act of sexuality. What is that all about? Another crackerjack racist is going to legislate what our desires should be?

What some people call "pornography" is simply a rich historical record of sexual diversity that has been made invisible in this world for centuries by organized religions. Control their bodies and you can control their minds. The u.s. supreme court has decided that the state can determine who you can make love with and how. They may soon determine whether women can decide for themselves whether or not to give birth to a baby. If Helms can make a determination on whether or not I can make love to the person who has consented to make love with me, then I **DEMAND THE IMMEDIATE RELEASE OF WHAT I CALL THE PANAMANIAN ROOSTER VIDEO SO WE CAN DETERMINE WHETHER HE HAS A RIGHT TO HIS SEXUALITY.**

Bottom line, only a person with a twisted and repressed sexuality would think it *their right* to tell consenting adults that they cannot explore their own bodies. Boneheads such as

Phyllis Schlafly and Pat Buchanan have represented Helms in the media, whining that public funds should not be used for art or educational materials that reflect the true diversity of sexuality in this country. If they truly believe this then I propose we change the electoral process—put *everything* on the ballot—make election day into election week. Make the voting process a three-hour process for each person with information printed in every language, as well as having interpreters on hand. Make it a paid holiday as well. Let us all decide how and where and for whom and for what our tax dollars are spent. Let us truly decide without the bogus representation we are presently stuck with in our antiquated electoral process. Let us decide, in our communities, in our cities, in our states how our taxes will be spent. Of course this has little chance of ever taking place because the government will not have enough to buy the left wing of a stealth bomber.

———

Each painting, film, sculpture or page of writing I make represents to me a particular moment in the history of my body on this planet, in america. Therefore each photograph, film, sculpture and page of writing I make has built into it a particular frame of mind that only *I* can be sure of knowing, given that I have always felt alienated in this country, and thus have lived with the sensation of being an observer of my own life as it occurs. I have had this feeling ever since I can remember—beginning with a childhood when instead of Heads of State or Politicians, there were Heads of Family: Mom and Dad. Once outside the home, Mom and Dad were replaced with Teacher or Policeman or Store Owner or Land Owner or Neighbor or Priest or God or Arresting Officer or Detective or Psychiatrist or Politician or President. It always felt to me that most people in this country feel a sense of relief when Heads of Family are replaced with Heads of State. I have felt and believe this to be true because most people never indicate otherwise. But maybe it isn't true. As times goes on, I have come to believe that all things are not necessarily what they appear if you judge them only by their silence or invisibility.

———

If I say I am homosexual, or "queer," does it make you nervous? I have experienced various reactions to that simple disclosure in the course of life. I often wonder whether my being a queer who asserts his sexual identity publicly makes some people see the word "QUEER" somehow written across my forehead in capital letters. And I wonder whether or not that revelation prevents some from hearing anything else I say, or whether or not it automatically *discounts* anything else I might say. Dismissal is policy in america. Our elected "representatives" have come up with a fail-safe system of symbols based on a prehistoric moral code built by other humans years, decades or even many centuries ago. The moral code is chameleonic in nature. Its design changes and twists on whim by those who wield it. In this country the elected representative has only to attach one of these symbols from the moral code to any social problem and people who are not immediately affected by that problem feel safe and distanced. If there is homelessness in our streets it is the fault of those who have no homes—they *chose* to live that way. If there is a disease such as AIDS it is somehow the fault of those who contract that disease—they *chose* to have that disease. If three black men are shot by a white man on a subway train—somehow they *chose* to be shot by that man.

And life goes on and on and on. Most people tend to accept, at least outwardly, this system of the moral code and thus feel quite safe from any terrible event or problem such as homelessness or AIDS or nonexistent medical care or rampant crime or hunger or unemployment or racism or sexism simply because they go to sleep every night in a house or apartment or dormitory whose clean rooms or smooth walls or regular structures of repeated daily routines provide them with a feeling of safety that never gets intruded upon by the events outside. There are scores of the population who either feel safe for the same reasons or else are too exhausted from trying to survive in this society by working dehumanizing jobs to keep a roof over their heads. Or else they feel safe because they are part of the structure that keeps the moral code intact. Or they feel safe only because once in a great while they can enter the illusion of the ONE-TRIBE NATION by stepping into a tiny curtained cubicle and pulling a metal lever that elects a twelve-inch-tall man or woman they saw for a short period of time transmitted across the boundaries of space into the antennae of their television screens.

———

I grew up in a tiny version of hell called the suburbs and experienced the Universe of the Neatly Clipped Lawn. This is a place where anything and everything can and does take place—and events such as torture, starvation, humiliation, physical and psychic violence can take place uncontested by others, as long as it doesn't stray across the boundaries and borders as formed by the deed-holder inhabiting the house on the neatly clipped lawn. If the violence is contained within the borders of the lawn and does not mess up the real estate in any way that would cause the surrounding properties devaluation, anything is possible and everything permissible.

I had a father who brutalized his first and second wives with physical violence. Any signs of life from the family he supported with his paycheck from his job as a sailor was met with extreme violence. In my home one could not laugh, one could not express boredom, one could not cry, one could not play, one could not explore, one could not engage in any activity that showed development or growth that was independent. I remember the first time I discovered the forests that grew in the distances from my neighbor's houses. Once I discovered the universe of the forests and lakes, I went there whenever possible. In the universe of the forest I didn't think about the Universe of the Neatly Clipped Lawn. I didn't think of what it felt like as a five- or six-year old being dragged down the basement stairs and having my head and body hit with a dog chain or a sawed-off chunk of two-by-four. I didn't think of my father picking up my sister and slamming her down on a sidewalk in front of our home in one neighborhood and I didn't think of the brown stuff that came out of my sister's ears and mouth and I didn't think of the neighbors mowing their lawns and watering their flower gardens without missing a beat when my father did these things. In the forests I made human forms out of mud and sticks. When they dried they fell apart or I would throw them against tree trunks. I climbed trees and smoked pilfered cigarettes until I got so dizzy I would almost fall out of the branches. I found giant birds' nests I could only assume were made by eagles. Or maybe it's just a matter of perspective. When one is small, many things look relatively monumental. As one grows older, things tend to look less monumental, and things looking less monumental doesn't always have to do with vision. It can be affected by thought processes and analysis. As I grow older, my father looks less monumental, both because he is dead now—he hung himself in the basement of his home about fourteen years ago—and because I can see and understand a little better his humanity and his demons. And he looks less monumental because I speak of him and bring the fear-charged memories of him outside of my head and make them public. Sound is so interesting in this way. Words are so interesting this way. Words can strip the power from a memory or an event. Words can cut the ropes of an experience. Breaking silence about an experience can break the chains of the code of silence. Describing the once indescribable can dismantle the power of taboo. To speak about the once unspeakable can make the **INVISIBLE** familiar if repeated often enough in clear and loud tones. To speak of ourselves—while living in a country that considers us or our thoughts taboo—is to shake the boundaries of the illusion of the **ONE-TRIBE NATION.** To keep silent is to deny the fact that there are millions of separate tribes in this illusion called **AMERICA.** To keep silent even when our individual existence contradicts the illusory ONE-TRIBE NATION is to lose our own identities. **BOTTOM LINE, IF PEOPLE DON'T SAY WHAT THEY BELIEVE, THOSE IDEAS AND FEELINGS GET LOST. IF THEY ARE LOST OFTEN ENOUGH, THOSE IDEAS AND FEELINGS NEVER RE-TURN.** This was what my father hoped would happen with his actions toward any display of individuality. And this is the hope of certain government officials and religious leaders as well. When I make statements like this I do not make them lightly. I make them from a position of experience—the experience of what it is to be homosexual in this country.

What it is to be a man who is capable of loving men, physically and emotionally.

Judge Jack Hampton is a judge from Houston, Texas, and although I live in New York I know who this man is because about a year ago an eighteen-year-old guy was convicted of shooting to death two men who happened to be homosexuals. He was given a life sentence in prison for these shootings. Judge Jack Hampton of Houston, Texas, reduced this guy's life sentence to 30 years solely because his victims were homosexual. Judge Jack Hampton said he didn't think homosexuals should be on the streets and that he also didn't think it would hurt his chances for reelection as judge if he said that he believed two men's lives were worth a whole lot less because they loved men. He asked only that the journalist he spoke to that day spell his name right. J.A.C.K. H.A.M.P.T.O.N. He also said he would be hard put to convict someone who dragged prostitutes into the woods and shot them dead. Judge Jack Hampton of Houston, Texas, is just a pimple on the face of a society that suffers from what I consider to be an extreme disease. A disease that shows itself in the prevalence of **FEAR OF DIVERSITY** and is characterized by various symptoms. Among them are sweating palms, angry outbursts, hysteria, the discharging of handguns, the passing of certain legislation, the invasion of foreign countries, the burning down of homes, the running out of town, and ultimately the legalized murder of those who are diverse in their natures.

———

In the last four years, homosexuals lost their constitutional right against the government's invasion of their privacy. And unless one is homosexual and happened to read that piece of information in the daily newspaper, no one would know. There certainly hasn't been any huge public outcry about this supreme court decision. But life goes on and any time I assert my individual right to explore my feelings of love or desire toward men, I do so at risk of jail. I wonder how many people understand what it is to grow up in a society where one is invisible. I wake up every day and if I turn on the television set or look through a magazine or look at billboards or look at political candidates or go to the movies, I see *no* representation of my sexuality. I see heterosexual plots and subtexts in every media form and it is enraging to feel homosexual longing toward another person in this context. A federal study of suicide shows that *thirty percent* of *all* suicides in the united states of america are gay and lesbian teenagers. **TEENAGERS.** And a congressman from california named William Dannemayer asked president Bush to denounce the results of this study in order to protect traditional family values. **TEENAGERS!** President Bush has not yet made a decision about this request. **TEENAGERS!!** Republican senators have tried to block the passing of an antiviolence bill because it contains the category "sexual orientation." Given the climate and silence of a *large* percentage of citizens in this country, I can leave this room and step outside and be shot dead by a person who believes in the moral code as set down by politicians and the various organized religions in this country and all the person has to do is say I tried to touch them and the courts will probably set that person free. That act of murder could easily be applauded.

———

I never have had what could be described as an ART EDUCATION. I am not even sure what an ART EDUCATION entails. As a kid, I loved the places where one could get lost while engaging in the act of creativity, the places inside one's head. Even in the face of wrath that generally came from my father, I would experiment with tracing images out of science books or books about life under the sea, or trace one-liner comics from magazines I could barely read and then color them in and present them as my own. I discovered that making things meant leaving evidence of life behind when I moved on. Making things was like leaving historical records of my existence behind when I left the room, or building, or neighborhood, the state and possibly the earth . . . as in mortality, as in death. When I was a kid I discovered that making an object, whether it was a drawing or a story, meant making something that spoke even if I was silent. As an adult, I realize if I make something and leave it in public for any period of time, I can create an environment where that object or writing acts as a magnet and draws others with a similar frame of reference out of silence or invisibility. Or that object or piece of writing can give me comfort as well as others. To place an object or writing that contains what is invisible because of legislation or social taboo into an environment outside myself makes me feel not so alone; it keeps me company by virtue of its existence. It is kind of like a ventriloquist's dummy—the only difference is that the work can speak by itself or act like that "magnet" to attract others who carried this enforced silence. It also could act as a magnet for those with opposing frames of reference, as in the recent case of the NEA and Artists Space.

I remember reading Archie Comics when I was a kid and being bored because they dealt with a world that had no correlation with my own. I remember having curiosity about sex and wondering why there was no sex in the world of Archie—the world of Riverdale. I remember taking a razor and cutting apart some Archie comics and gluing pieces of their bodies in different places so that Archie and Veronica and Reggie and Betty were fucking each other. A close-up profile of Jughead's nose on page five made a wild-looking penis when glued on Reggie's pants on page seven. After hours of cutting and pasting I had a comic that reflected a whole range of human experience that was usually invisible to me. But at the first sound of the key in the front door I'd throw everything away. I was curious, but I wasn't stupid.

What I'm trying to say here is that all of my life I've made things that are like fragmented mirrors of what I perceive to be the world. As far as I'm concerned the fact that in 1990 the human body is still a taboo subject is unbelievably ridiculous. What exactly is frightening about the human body? What is it about this society which supports the premature death of so many of us solely because of the fact that we are denied information about our own bodies in the time of an AIDS epidemic. Why can't *every* woman who wants an abortion get one in this country? If a woman who desires an abortion has to travel miles away to get one because of restrictions imposed by the state, can we assume this woman can afford to make that trip? Why is it men who make the decisions that affect these women's bodies? Why is it any other person but myself can make a determination that affects the health or safety of my body? Why are so many people silent in the face of this? Is it because the sky is blue that most people feel safe from this disease called AIDS? To be quite frank, most heterosexuals I know do not use condoms when fucking. Is this because they believe this virus has a sexual orientation and a moral code? Do they think that because they sleep in a comfortable place that this disease will stop outside their walls? Do they think that because the person they make love to is kind and sweet and sexy that he or she could not have this virus? Do they believe that the virus stays within the boundaries of large urban centers even though this is a country of trains and planes and automobiles and this virus travels wherever people travel? Did you know that the *New England Journal of Medicine* recently reported eleven women—middle class and well educated who didn't think they were in a high-risk category because they limited themselves to just one or two sexual partners who were neither bisexual nor intravenous drug-users—contracted HIV from the same guy who didn't know he had the virus and recently died from AIDS? One doesn't have to adopt the stupid line invented by those bozos in the government or media or churches—the JUST SAY NO TO SEXUALITY CAMPAIGN— you can fuck in a healthy and safe way with the right information. Does everyone have access to the right information? How many people understand how to use a condom in the correct way so that it doesn't break or tear? How many people know that lubricants that are oil or grease based can cause ninety percent of all condoms to have microscopic tears and that one must use water-based lubricants in order to avoid this? Or that just because a lubricant washes off with water doesn't mean it's a water-based lubricant? How many people know how to negotiate the use of condoms with their lover? Why isn't this information provided on television or in all newspapers? And how many know that penicillin-resistant venereal diseases are reported nationwide as being on the rise again? That this is prevalent among heterosexuals? How often has anyone heard the fact that people with AIDS can and do have sex without spreading the disease? Who has heard the story of the woman in Reno, Nevada, who, right this moment, is serving a twenty-years-to-life prison sentence because she is HIV positive and agreed to have sex with an undercover cop, even though it was on the condition that he wear two condoms, one on top of the other? I believe this woman was incredibly responsible in her actions but the courts decided that she should be charged with attempted murder. Should she be charged with any crime at all? How are one's responses to this formed? If there were a disease that appeared to strike only politicians and religious leaders, would the president hesitate for more than twenty-four hours to allocate more funds for research and health care? Would the president hesitate to shift the entire $350 billion defense budget toward research and health care? How many people believe those who give you information on the evening news? What is the economic class of the people who speak to us every night on the evening news? Do some politicians have a direct communication with god? Do those people on the evening news really believe the version of the world they report on? Should one person's interpretation of god determine whether another person lives or dies? How many members of minorities are afraid to speak? How many are afraid to speak if they think they are the only ones who feel the way they do? If the president's god said that one couldn't feed his or her brother daughter sister mother father aunt uncle grandparents or good friends when they were starving, who would sit by and allow that? Does the denial of information that causes people to become ill and die a permissible thing? What if that denial of information ended up killing hundreds of thousands, even millions—is that still okay? Would it be a crime if that denial of information only killed people that you didn't feel comfortable with? Would it be a crime if that denial of information only killed people of color? If that denial of information only killed people who frightened you? People with strange ideas? Strange because they didn't show these ideas on the tv or the evening news? What does one make of government policies if those policies let people die by saying those people die because they want to? What if those people are screaming for help as they die? Is the government telling the truth in the face of massive deaths that are caused in this fashion? Even if one essentially trusts the government, who would dispute publicly this thing they call truth? Would you? Who knows that the vatican and the catholic archdiocese have issued statements that "it is a more terrible think to use a condom than to contract AIDS." Should people pick up guns to stop the casual murder of other people? If that casual murder is only of one other person? Ten other people? A thousand others? A million? More? Do laws reflect the diversity in our society? Or do they only enforce the "morality" of a select few? How many people stop to get to know the person he or she sits or walks next to? Does he or she make it comfortable for that person to express ideas that might change his or her ideas? Who cares about these things? Does the fact that one cares or does not care reflect a feeling or position of power?

"If I had a dollar for health care I'd rather spend it on a baby or innocent person with some defect or illness not of their own responsibility; not some person with AIDS" says the health-care official on national television and this is in the middle of an hour-long video of people dying on camera because they can't afford the limited drugs available that might extend their lives and I can't even remember what this official looked like because I reached in through the tv screen and ripped his face in half and I was diagnosed with AIDS recently and this was after the last few years of losing count of the friends and neighbors who have been dying slow vicious and unnecessary deaths because fags and dykes and junkies are expendable in this country. "If you want to stop AIDS shoot the queers . . ." says a politician in Texas on the radio and his press secretary later claims that the politician was only joking and didn't know the microphone was turned on and besides they didn't think it would hurt his chances for reelection anyways and I wake up every morning in this killing machine called america and I'm carrying this rage like a blood-filled egg and there's a thin line between the inside and the outside a thin line between thought and action and that line is simply made up of blood and muscle and bone and I'm waking up more and more from daydreams of tipping amazonian blow darts in "infected blood" and spitting them at the exposed necklines of certain politicians or government health-care officials or those thinly disguised walking swastikas that wear religious garments over their murderous intentions or those rabid strangers parading against AIDS clinics in the nightly news suburbs there's a thin line a very thin line between the inside and the outside and I've been looking all my life at the signs surrounding us in the media or on peoples' lips; the religious types outside st. patrick's cathedral shouting to the men and women in the gay parade, "You won't be here next year—you'll get AIDS and die ha ha . . ." and the areas of the u.s.a. where it is possible to murder a man and when brought to trial one only has to say that the victim was a queer and that he tried to touch you and the courts will set you free and the difficulties that a bunch of republican senators have in albany with supporting an antiviolence bill that includes "sexual orientation" as a category of crime victims there's a thin line a very thin line and as each T-cell disappears from my body it's replaced by ten pounds of pressure ten pounds of rage and I focus that rage into nonviolent resistance but that focus is starting to slip my hands are beginning to move independent of self-restraint and the egg is starting to crack america america america seems to understand and accept murder as a self-defense against those who would murder other people and it's been murder on a daily basis for nine count then nine long years and we're expected to pay taxes to support this public and social murder and we're expected to quietly and politely make house in this windstorm of murder but I say there's certain politicians that had better increase their security forces and there's religious leaders and health-care officials that had better get bigger fucking dogs and higher fucking fences and more complex security alarms for their homes and queer-bashers better start doing their work from inside howitzer tanks because the thin line between the inside and the outside is beginning to erode and at the moment I'm a thirty-seven-foot-tall one-thousand-one-hundred-and-seventy-two-pound man inside this six-foot body and all I can feel is the pressure all I can feel is the pressure and the need for release.

AUTHOR'S NOTE

In the following pages, I originally included segments of letters I'd received over the years from the guy named Dakota. They were letters filled with a terrible beauty outlining in words a fierce attempt to experience freedom and that elusive thing we call *life* in all its diversity and variousness. They were letters pertaining to his sexuality in early morning dreams, his desires for a structure of his own choosing, descriptions of standing in tornado winds and rain on the texas plains, baring his body to the elements, scenes of pushing the gas pedal to the floor along abandoned roads in the gulf coast countryside in order to experience the closest thing to flight the human body might possible attain outside of death, and sweet descriptions of melancholy interactions with a dying parent, as well as notes from an asylum that he'd checked himself into in order to detox. The notes from the asylum were chilling stories of families that psychically killed their children in the name of God and Society and Morality. I chose these letters because they were the only surviving pieces of evidence that allowed Dakota to speak on his own behalf about his humanity, his animal grace, his own spirituality. An interpretation of the copyright law brought about by a case (among others) involving J. D. Salinger prevents me from using any of these letters, despite the fact that the last letter I received from Dakota says that I was the only person who ever found use for his creative gestures. In tracking down a member of his family in order to see if I could get permission to use these letters from the legal owners of his estate (in this case, since he died in texas, texas law states that in the absence of a legal will, Dakota's belongings and estate, including the contents of his letters written to others, belong to his surviving parents), I spoke to his brother, who told me that Dakota's life work—his writing, screenplays, drawings, paintings, collages, photographs, and musical recordings—were destroyed by the parents. I was told there was absolutely no chance to get permission from them to publish the letters Dakota had written to me.

I believe that the copyright permissions law is valuable in terms of protection for living people who desire the type of privacy afforded by this law. But I also believe the law is terrible in the event of the death of the letter writer, because it creates a whitewash of personal histories. In the case of Dakota, his entire identity has been murdered by his folks. What fragments of his existence survive, in letters received by friends, are made invisible by the State in the form of this law. Dakota's surviving brother understood something essential about Dakota's life. He offered to write a letter of permission for me, but Texas law makes that letter useless. I would hope that in my recollections of Dakota, as well as the recollections of his friends, some sense of the guy comes through in a benevolent way, as it is very emotional for me to have to participate in the process of denying him a voice by editing from this manuscript his personal words to me.

Names have been changed and in certain instances some composite identities were formed in order to protect the people involved in the following story. Given the hysterical nature of the times we live in, I have taken this precaution.
—D. W. 1991

THE SUICIDE OF A GUY WHO ONCE BUILT AN ELABORATE SHRINE OVER A MOUSE HOLE

Death comes in small doses. Some days this room becomes an architecture of fear when the sun goes down. The night comes down between the buildings and presses itself around the moldings of the windowframes, spreading itself across and through the glass. It becomes thick and textural. What I feel is the momentary shock of realizing that most of the wood, metal and plastic fixtures, the sinks, lampshades, the shower stall, and even the drinking cups will all outlive me if my body follows the progression that this tiny, invisible-to-the-eye virus has initiated. Time reveals itself to be a childlike notion of false structure. The social landscape

I have grown to be comforted by is being exploded and is disappearing. There are dozens of faces I hardly know but who have become familiar over time; I have been reassured by the fact that those people are somewhere walking the face of the earth, pushing air around and *thinking*. Each one of them is a receptable for some belief or projection of beliefs and each one of them carries a piece of myself; and in the last month each time I pick up the phone it is to learn that another of them has died. Piece by piece the landscape is eroding and in its place I am building a monument made of fragments of love and hate, sadness and feelings of murder. This monument serves as a shrine where innocence is slowly having its belly slit open, its heart removed, its eyes plucked out, its tongue severed, its fingers broken, its legs torn off. At the base of this shrine I place the various elements that define each person who has died or is dying.

It becomes too much after a while. Seeing so much death, hearing of so much death, *feeling* so much loss. I wondered recently if I was becoming numb to the idea of death itself. What was in the mid-eighties a recognition of loss so profound upon hearing about the first person I knew who had just died of AIDS, has slowly become so familiar that I wince upon hearing that someone new has died and then tuck it somewhere in my psyche and try and refocus my thoughts to something simple like paying the rent or buying the food for my evening meal. A month ago someone called from out of state to inform me that a guy I knew from ten years ago had died. I'd had a fight with this guy and thought he was an asshole up until the moment when I'd heard he was ill. He then become perfectly human in my eyes. I'd been comforted seeing him on the street since then; something about his being alive and occupying space meant that my life was not threatened by this virus. Now he's dead and I feel more vulnerable, like I'm standing on a conveyor belt leading into an enormous killing machine.

There is one homely queen I used to see years ago on the streets of the west village on nights when I was on the prowl. He had coke bottle thick glasses and long straggly hair. Sometimes he was alone, sometimes on the arm of a tough-looking street hustler or borderline homeless type. Our eyes have met for twelve years and we have never spoken a word, not even a nod, but we have had whole conversations in that brief contact. I have always been amazed at his regal bearing and the enormous sense of intelligence that lay in his eyes, the rest of him buried under that cultivated surface of salvation army cast-offs. In the last few years I have taken comfort when rounding a corner east or west and suddenly coming upon this familiar stranger and seeing that he'd changed very little; he was still looking healthy in the midst of a terrible epidemic. There was the familiar rosy flush of his cheeks and the same searching movements of his eyes behind the now-yellowing lenses of his eyeglasses, and each time I'd seen him since the mid-eighties I'd think: "Good for you—you're still around, still alive, still healthy."

Yesterday I was walking down first avenue and was crossing the street from one corner to the next when I came upon him walking in the opposite direction. I saw him at the last second just as our bodies passed among turning cars and the first thing I recognized were his eyes, only now they were wild with misery and panic and it was only then that I realized his face and neck were blurred with Kaposi lesions like a school of burgundy-colored fish upturning around the contours of his jaw.

My heart is a vacuum of horror; I want to run amok but I am too civilized. Instead I lay his thick yellowing glasses at the shrine in the back of my head and buy some take-out soup from the counter in the nearby restaurant, surrounded by this unbelievable noise made by the living and the unconscious with various silverware against plates and bowls, and I think of what a shit planet this is these days. I think about the seven other people I know who have died this month from AIDS. I think of one guy in particular who was a junkie for years and who ran every scam imaginable on his friends, and all his past routines and games and delusions have become charming because they all boil down to survival and survival is such a lovely thing, such a transient thing.

———

Why does this one die and that one not? What does all this mean? How do I map all this down? I respect just about every attempt at survival I witness these days. But every person will eventually lose his struggle just as I will one day, and that makes each attempt more filled with life; that means sadness at the loss, but more sweetness in the attempts. That means maybe fewer hours on the face of this disorderly planet, but less shit I'll have to deal with and anyway here I am in the back seat of this taxicab waiting for the light to turn green so that I can arrive at my home, because I feel too sick to walk or wait for a bus and isn't it lovely this pattern of sunlight drifting through the side window across the back of my hand, laying at rest on my thigh. Isn't it beautiful, the fact that I can *see* this light? One day I won't. One day you won't either. Sometimes I watch the leaders of this country on television and think, at least "nature" will reach where assassins are unable to tread. Maybe they'll die of massive

coronaries from all their cannibal banquets, or maybe brain
tumors from the radiation in their environment. Education
is, and will always be, a generational thing and because of
that I lose hope sometimes in the idea that the shape of what
we have to live in might change. I have always viewed my
friends as checkpoints in a series of motions of resistance to
the flood of hyenas in state or religious drag. If we all die off
what will happen to those we leave behind who are just this
moment being born? I realize that cretins have roamed, and
always will roam, this planet, whether I am here or not;
there's one born every minute—this is a jarring drift; this
perspective makes my heart and soul sway. I want relief from
this tired yap yapping of my brain. I wish I could pluck it
out and throw it into the corner where it can chatter away
while I go out for the evening.

———

There was a period of time immediately after getting
off the streets that I could barely talk. I lived in a halfway
house with a group of ex-cons. There was a high rate of
recidivism for the guys I hung around with. Someone in the
old neighborhood kills a distant cousin; you get a gun and
shoot the guy who killed him and then tap into the old family
network and take a series of trains to the south—honor is
upheld, revenge extracted, and nobody gives a shit in the
overloaded law enforcement agencies. I kept going back and
hanging around on the streets every chance I could. It was
the only place where I felt comfortable and surrounded by
people with a similar frame of reference. In the halfway
house, guys were provided with the minimal structure of
Other World existence: how to do your laundry, how to wash
dishes, how to keep a bank account for part of your meager

earnings, how to make a bed, how to impress a boss when asking for a janitor job. No one spoke my language except for the hustlers back on 42nd street or the occasional John who'd picked me up for some cash and wild times. I learned how to appear in such a way as to never give an indication of my past when walking through the structures of daily life and work. But in order to not go crazy, I planned robberies of electronics shops in Herald Square and I planned robberies I never committed of banks and some individuals on the streets or at the fund-raising parties given by city politicians for kids in the halfway house. We were invited to upper park avenue co-ops to eat meals with shrunken rich people, sitting at banquet tables attended by servants in uniforms. Hours afterwards I'd be in a midtown hotel bathroom, fucking some businessman in a quiet toilet stall for twenty dollars. Death was a corporate type wearing an oversized death-skull mask and gesticulating at me from the horizon. My fear was based on understanding the social structure that beckoned to me and promised a life of security and support to me if I would just embrace its illusion and lies. If I let this illusion wrap is stinking arms around me I knew I'd suffer a death more terrifying than physical death: an emotional and intellectual strangulation. The life that the man in the grinning death mask waved like a banner from the edge of the horizon was one in an activity that I cared nothing about but one that I would repeat endlessly until the day my teeth fell out, all in order to be able to eat and sleep inside a tiny wood and plaster structure he'd allow me to call: home.

I did what I could to pull away from the certain demise I'd been facing on the street and at the same time threw myself into situations that suggested a possibility of looking into the eye of death which was disguised in a more attractive form. I crawled through the walls of every social taboo I could come across. I wanted to celebrate everything we are denied through structure of laws or physical force. I just did it quietly and anonymously. As a homosexual in america I couldn't openly explore my expressions of loving. Expressions of loving are never an acceptable thing publicly in this society—even straight loving, let alone homosexuality. Just look at television. We can look at the latest body count in close-up and yet the human body is still taboo. So if I couldn't express my sexuality I could at least subvert it within forms of violence which could pass through the streets without resistance. The circle of friends I interacted with publicly shifted and was replaced over and over until one day the violence of my street life finally arrived at a point where it was indistinguishable from aspects of my public social life. The vietnam war and its daily tv displays of faces numbed with horror, the repeats of slow-motion videos of burst flesh and dead babies and ravaged exploding villages, slowly came to an end. I saw photographs of necklaces of human fingers and ears. I saw album pictures of guys my own age standing in a field littered with human heads. I saw the caved-in faces of people whose skulls had been literally popped out of their heads by mortar fragments, looking like obscene balloons left over from a distant celebration. The youth of the urban centers of america, as well as their dislocated counterparts in the suburbs, began slowly warming up for a dance of social death by first quietly and then publicly tracing all the outlines of taboo and violent activities and forms of nihilism they came across. They began to push everything they could to see how far they could go before they exploded it, or it exploded them. By the time these activities went public, nobody outside of those social activities seemed to notice, or maybe they thought that by having bought the illusion of security, or having money and food, it wouldn't touch them. Maybe it was that the violence they'd witnessed on television during wartime had gotten completely confused with the seductive commercials that surrounded those images. I felt the whole landscape surrounded by media faces expounding how normal things were and how thoroughly wonderful life in america was and how well we all were doing and yet all my friends were doing a death dance in front of these surreal propped-up facades: little jerking physical movements suggesting suffocation in the asphalt streets of slums and imploding neighborhoods. Whole neighborhoods of youth entered a period of superficial communication masked in the black clothes of mourning. Most of them were in their early twenties and in a nation gone numb they didn't want people to know who they were or how sensitive they were and how much they suffered. Drugging gave them the salve for the schizophrenic nightmare they were living in and literally gave their brains a television quality of unconsciousness so that they could survive a walk from one side of town to the other. The people in power knew their own physical deaths were well within striking range, so they cared about nothing more than strengthening their secret accounts and their control forces and the height of their security fences. They invested more in the design of manipulative sound-bites than they did in any form of moral food and social answers.

———

For a period of time I entered a circle of people who were attracted to forms and expressions of violence and bloodletting because these things contained some unarguable truth when viewed or experienced against a backdrop of america. In a country where an actor becomes the only acceptable president, a country where fewer than half of those eligible to vote even bother to do so—and when they do they elect for two terms a man whose vocation is to persuade with words and actions an audience who wants to believe whatever he tells them—in this context, violence presents a truth that can't be distorted like words and images. Living in america during the Reagan years had the same disorientation as a texture dream; that sense you get at times lying with your face against the sheets with your eye open, millimeters away from the microscopic weave of the linen, and suddenly your body freezes up and your eye is locked into the universe of textures and threads and weaves, and for an extended moment you can't shake yourself from the hallucination. Instead of a piece of linen, it was a television set in the corner of the room and on the tv was a series of carefully choreographed gestures, winks, fake warm smiles, hand motions, and feigned deafness beneath the roar of helicopter blades. The criminal tidbit that Nixon got booted out of office for was a joke in comparison to the Iran-Contra affair alone. During the Reagan years, outright starvation or murder by assassination of the competition or opposition became public and commonplace, yet an entire country was plugged into an accelerated decomposition of the bogus morality america had come to define as its purpose for existence, and almost nobody blinked. And it was televised. And it continues.

It became a time in which one had to choose one's tribe; choose one's *reality*. Some of us felt like the incredible shrinking man on the late night television movie; he realized that no matter how small he shrinks (how invisible to the eye of government he becomes), he is still alive, just his environmental references have changed. It is the moment where you understand the con that you bought by being born into this pre-invented existence and speaking your first word in imitation of your family, how that word supports and continues a structure that is basically about death of the soul, of the emotion and the intellect. Sure, one could practice voting and maybe rearrange a few of the threads, but in the end it is just the same old fabric covering the pillow that covers one's face. An act of violence spoke with an implicit truth. Drugs provided a psychic rearrangement of a physical landscape that is totally owned by white people with money, power and all methods of communication and control. We understood the message from our elected representatives in government: who could go for the ride and who couldn't. Some of us chose our own transportation, some of us got on the national roller coaster to hell our own way. As the ride through the 1980s came to an end, we look around and realize that some of us are still surviving while others fell to the wayside along the route. The television still blinks out its increasingly accelerating display of the variousness of the con routine—the sawdust pouring out of Reagan's head on the landscape of television did nothing to wake very many people up, and thus we have a former cia director as our current death god. The streets have become our sacrificial temples, with millions of homeless and millions more entering that status. What form will the death dance take in the next decade?

———

"This is life—let's swim in it."—(dream conversation)

———

One night I ate a bunch of mushrooms and walked out into the psychedelic streets and headed uptown to see Johnny. He lived in a building up on third avenue that would be the first building in new york to fall if an earthquake struck the city. It swayed in the breeze and like most people's apartments it had floors that slanted at extreme angles. In ten minutes' time I was beginning to feel amphibian-like; my arms felt twice as long as they should have and I kept trying to stuff my hands in my pockets so that no one else would notice. It took me an hour to find my way through the thick paranoid atmosphere of the Jell-O streets and traffic to the front door of his building. It was a trip through the fun house. I kicked the front door until it cracked open on its bent hinges and a swarm of particles rushed at me: the smell of sushi gone bad mixing with a scattering of grime and dust like billions of tiny demons came screaming through the yellowing haze of cheap fluorescent hall lights, flying into my nostrils and face. It was a topsy-turvy mix of darknesses and lights which gradually formed the vague outlines of hallways and rickety staircases. He lived four flights up. On the second floor I interrupted a sale of dope between the resident dealer and a white boy with pimply face and biceps. The dealer was a skeletal apparition that forever stood in the shadowy depths of the darkened hallway, and every time I visited the building he made me for the heat and would spin aroung pocketing the dope and mutter something about how he's tired from walking up the stiars and just in the hall taking a breather blah blah blah. The next flight up reveals a short huge-bellied middle-aged guy leaning across the hallway windowsill with his head over the traffic. He had an operation the year before and they took out one of his lungs and leaning over the sill on a beach towel was the only way he could stop the sense of suffocation, so this was his prime activity for eighteen hours a day. I thought of beached whales as he breathed-wheezed hello, at my passing to get to the next flight. Standing next to him in the shadows is this prematurely-aged alcoholic woman whose boyfriend is in rikers prison and whose kids are sometimes referred to as the demon kids; they're up the next flight of stairs heading towards Johnny's place. They stop mid-flight and break into a rap routine and attempt to break-dance on the staircase. They're ten and eleven years old and usually found sitting on or around Jimmy's easy chair. They come up so they can smoke Jimmy's cigarettes when he's out in the streets foraging. Jimmy is the guy who lives in the hallway outside Johnnys' front door; he's got the chair and a radio and an ashtray stand and some current hardcover novel he's been reading and he's a sweet guy. Jimmy stopped drinking recently and was almost stabbed to death by his best friend not long ago. Five days after getting out of the hospital he let his best friend sleep with him in the hallway because he had no other place to go and the kids in the building woke him up saying: "Now's your chance Jimmy—he's asleep. You can cut his throat while you got the chance." Jimmy said sweetly: "No no he's my best friend, I can't do that." The demon kids plop down in his easy chair, big enough for both of them, and light up one of his cigarettes. They have the eyes of forty-year-olds. Downstairs their mom screams: "COME DOWN HERE THIS MINUTE BOTH OF YOU." The kids ask: "For what?" and the mom goes: "WHATTAYA MEAN, FOR WHAT—IT'S CHRISTMAS —THAT'S WHAT. NOW GET DOWN HERE," and the kids hop up and down in the slimy july heat saying: "Oh

goody— it's christmas, it's christmas!" and I wearily reach
the front door of Johnny's place and bang bang bang bang
he's not home.

———

I met Johnny in a rock and roll bar where he was a
bartender and I was a busboy. It was a club that traded on
the memory of Chubby Checker and was run by the sleazy
grade-B–level mafia. The creeps that counted the money also
managed some of the hustler bars on eighth avenue and one
or two of the drag queen bars in the times square area. For
minimum wage I had to pick up bottles and puking drunks
off the floor as well as unload hot merchandise from the backs
of hastily driven midnight trucks. I unloaded stolen comput-
ers and various weird cargo and lived on the tips the
bartenders kindly threw my way.

Johnny was a geneticist at a respected uptown laboratory. He also put out a xerox magazine called *MURDER*,
which concerned itself solely with murder. It contained found
clippings from newspapers, photographs of both real and
staged murders, drawings of mayhem such as Elmer Fudd
standing with a shotgun outside of a california McDonalds
saying: "Where's dat silly wabbit." He culled most of the
material from daily newspapers. When he compiled enough
pages he would run them off on the hospital copy machine,
putting out a couple hundred copies of the magazine. One day
a security guard found him photocopying the magazine and
hauled him up to the head of the lab, who told him the
magazine was obscene and eventually fired him. It amazed me
that this guy could walk through rooms of cages filled with
mice heavily laden with intentionally introduced cancer tumors, past tables of beheaded rats, slit open and splayed out

past the stench of death and the refrigerators filled with vials containing every horrendous disease, past lead boxes of highly radioactive materials—even worse was the fact that this lab, according to Johnny, obtained hundreds of thousands of dollars in AIDS research grants with no intention of using the monies for that purpose—and yet he could pale before the photocopies of news murder stories that his co-workers poured over every lunchtime while eating their sandwiches. I remember asking Johnny at the time why he made the magazine. He talked about the thin line people contain, which they can instantaneously cross to become windmills of slaughter. He talked about the hypocrisy people embody when they can step over the dying alcoholic sprawled outside their front door on their way to the newsstand where they buy a paper and become horrified at a printed photograph of a starving ethiopian. He said: "It's the separation people feel from those who commit acts of violence or murder. The way they feel that a person who murders belongs to the *other*. But then a guy murders thirty people and seven million people line up to buy the book about those murders.

"Look at what we live in, the violence evident in the scores of people dying in the streets of starvation. It is the result of growing up in the techno age; people are unable to respond emotionally to reality unless it is translated through media images."

————

JOURNAL EXCERPT:
Two centimeters beneath Johnny's curiosity about murder exists one of the sweetest heterosexual guys I've ever come into contact with. His intelligence and his fearless: "Yes" to everything reminds me of the intense friendships I

had as a kid, when you think you'll know each other the rest
of your life and there is no such thing as death or danger.
The world we create in a day's adventure exists outside the
rest of the world. Or else, it seems as if the outside world
participates in the adventure we're creating with our own
actions and gestures and ideas but somehow a transparent
envelope of protection has opened up and we're traveling
through it and doing what we want and the world is
surrounding the envelope, frozen and witnessing us for
fractions of time but unable to interfere or step through the
invisible walls of the envelope except to give us pizza or drive
the subway train we're on. I love feeling invisible to the
world when I want to walk through it, or examine it.

Some mornings, after getting out of the club at 5:00
A.M., Johnny and I stop at the place he shares with Sylvia and
maybe do some coke and then walk into alphabetland and
start climbing the fire escapes of the burnt-out buildings. All
the doors are blocked up with cinderblocks or are chained
and bolted steel doors and the fire escapes are the only way
to get inside. In the night hours it's all drug dealers and guns
in people's faces and heads being blown to bits and a sudden
hand comes up out of darkness and street movement and a
gun is in your chest and, blam, down on your back, blood
shooting out like ole faithful geysers and multiple slapping
of feet heading away fast in all directions and cinderblocked
doorways to abandoned buildings are opened up and a small
hole where, walking by at night, you see somebody's legs for
a second, hanging out the hole, then sliding inside and then
they're gone or someone huddling next to a wall and a
cinderblock disappears by their shoulder and a hand reaches
out like Thing on Addams Family and takes your cash and
hands back a small envelope of cut dope. One night, walking

through there at 4:30 A.M., a little dog wearing a plaid winter overcoat and tiny plastic galoshes came running out of a hole in the wall and skittered down the street lost and frightened. But everybody and everything clears out as the sky grows light and we spend hours climbing through the burnt-out slum tenements examining the evidence of lives in the melted junk hastily left behind when sirens once wailed through the winter streets.

One weekend we did peyote and went out to spend the day in the country. For us the country is taking the tram out to roosevelt island and kicking around in the weeds and trees surrounding the abandoned insane asylum. We climbed what was left of the broken and decaying buildings, taking pictures of weird discards of civilization in the light of the chemical sunset. When it got too dark and silent we headed back to the tram and then took the subway to times square. This is where it gets really weird. Saturday night on 42nd street is a fishtank sensation of glittering streets swimming with what feels like too many people, but somehow it all fits together strangely: angry drug dealers appearing out of the soup with magnified hands blurring in front of my face and I can see each drop of sweat on this guy's forehead even in shadows and the video trail of faces belonging to frozen ticket sellers in the dirty glass booths of moviehouse lobbies, with numbers relating to times of the slasher flicks and grade-B science fiction movies playing double bill. I see my feet and they're rising and falling on the dark sidewalks and then the jiggling motion of orange crush sloshing around in the plastic tanks on the counter of some hot-dog joint and the wipe of a napkin over a tourist's face, looking kind of panicked at the rollercoaster of flesh sliding by and around him, and there's some spastic preacher screaming through a microphone plugged into a tiny screechy pig-amp and my camera comes up periodically to my eye and the whole scene is chopped down to a little rectangle and the rectangle is filled with arms and legs and shiny pieces of automobiles. The traffic is heavy and constant and there is a gray-faced pederast lurking in an entranceway to the sporting goods shop, trying to look nonchalant next to a deep-sea skin diver with a fucked-up manikin face behind the snorkel glass mask; its nose all chipped off and lips broken and the rectangle is moving and faces loom up to it 'til I just see an eyeball and there's breaking glass and some wino is having a fit and throwing empty bottles at his demons. All the world is a sliding sensation filled with things to buy and things bought and groups of kids armed with carton cutters are spontaneously exploding away from an invisible radius spilling through the traffic and cars are screeching and bus exhaust spitting in short bursts and these kids are going to get something, what with the frightened tourist waving his hands in traffic running up the middle dotted white line— the spinal cord of every road and the rectangle comes down and I realized I was so moved by the details I forgot to take a picture; my hand feels like it is independent of me anyway. I wish I could pick up that guy's arm and examine the elaborate tattoos on his biceps and fingers and I'm thinking of sex in the dirty sheets of the ten-dollar hotel rooms. It's a one-way ride to my childhood and it is touched off by that group of sailors, three of them, and I never did figure what ship they got off of; it's definitely a foreign country because nobody in america in their right mind would wear a hat like that with a dumb red pom-pom waving in the breeze and they walk through all this like an integral part of the picture. The rectangle is up and surrounding everything, even the spit and tin cans underfoot and the fragments of moving arms and legs and the face of a prostitute in the biggest wig I ever seen all flamed red and there's something in her eyes: it can only be a guy with all that thick make-up and I can recognize something like anger in those eyeballs: "DON'T YOU TAKE NO PICTURE OF ME" and of course I won't, I'm just part of the scenery drifting by through a tiny window and I see long legs and spiky boots and elegant high heels and three prostitutes suddenly surround a business man from the waldorf and they're saying: "Come on honey" and rubbing his dick, rubbing his chest, kissing his neck leaning in front of his face murmuring sweet things and his wallet appears behind his back in the hands of one of them and they all drop away as he continues to giggle like a sex-mortified five-year-old and I remember the drugged kids I saw being sold in that subway staircase and what is all the racket? It's an ambulance stuck in the traffic wailing away, my fucking ears hurt and the psychedelic stuttering of light bulbs surrounding doorways and peep show entrances are tapping into my spine and my belly and we're turning a corner. I keep getting frozen fragments of faces. An eye with all the language one could hear casting over its surface and a neck I'd like to put my tongue to and I'm amazed at how many different styles of shirts and pants and jackets and coats there are in the world. A hustler nods out against a wall among the huge rush of people exiting from the three-dollar movie and he's squeezing his dick absentmindedly and I'm taking pictures which will never come out because of the light quality and the speed of the film but the visions are so intense that 'til the day I die I will always have these photographs in my brain and suddenly a face fills the rectangle and it's so filled with hate and larceny: "Let me hold that camera," that somewhere in the back of my etch-a-sketch brain I realize there is danger, but the effects of the drugs make me feel that if the guy whips out a knife or throws a punch, it will take his arms an hour to travel the hundreds of miles of distance in order to connect with my belly or face. The drug-induced sensation of distance helps my body language emanate total fearlessness which no one will bother to challenge.

———

Through Johnny I met Dakota one evening in the club. I remember a skinny guy in a trashed out white t-shirt looking like it was awash with perspiration and floor grime, and black pants and a long turkey-like neck with a hawk head; a flesh covered skull set on top of that neck. He was variously a writer, artist, musician, scientist, and actor in super-8 films, but I felt instantly drawn and connected to him because of his physical look and energy. I always considered myself either anonymous or odd looking and there is an unspoken bond between people in the world that don't fit in or are not attractive in the general societal sense. That's why you have whole retirement villages in Florida filled with "freak show" castoffs. You immediately feel warmth with each other's presence. I remember his face when I first laid eyes on him sitting on a stool at the bar; he had a las vegas cardshark's smile that literally wrapped around his head and he wore dark highway-cop sunglasses. He was bouncing off the walls with roped-in energy.

He lived in a welfare hotel uptown that I visited once and, walking through the stinking halls, it was a shock to step inside a single room that had all the subdued air of a cathedral on a mountainside. Vague remnants of incense and various shrines to deities I wasn't familiar with. He lent me a drawing for something I was writing about violence: image, physical, and psychic violence. It was a mandala-like drawing of a man and a woman fucking each other in a yin-yang pose; at the same time the woman was shooting the guy in the head with a revolver and the guy was stabbing the woman with a hunting knife. It was a marriage of conception and death. I wanted to place it next to a photograph that Johnny took of a lab rat, decapitated, slit open and splayed out for research. I was trying to uncover something in people's responses to images of violence: how a drawing of violence seemed to some people to contain more of a repellent *intent* than a photograph of violence, possibly because the photograph suggested that the image was merely witnessed— its intent was buried in the medium.

Dakota lent me a film script he had written that took certain myths and a historical treatment of voodoo deities and created a narrative out of the information, making use of the psychological properties of light. He researched and understood the effects of light on the human eye and constructed a script that would use segments of film made at dawn and dusk as well as in brilliant ocean sunlight and the dark shadows of afternoon cities. The film promised to produce unconscious and physical sensations in the viewer while battles of power took place through the various centuries between practitioners of certain spiritual beliefs.

I remember two lamps in his room that were covered in meticulously cut out pieces of construction paper that had been previously folded in the ways we folded paper as kindergarten students to make chains of dolls. Only his dolls were intricate mandalas of spiritual figures from voodoo history, hearts and skulls, jagged frenetic energy explosions,

bodies in lotus positions with enormous hard-ons, jeweled
crowns, buddhas, interconnected figures, and even his own
profile repeating in mirror-like smiles. He also made long
cut-up prose poems using fragments of newspaper headlines
and sub-headlines and pieces of type from advertisements.
He was fucking with the validation implied in media. He was
tugging at the trust people have for information when it is
disseminated through cold type in a daily newspaper, a
paper propped up by millions of advertising dollars. When
you buy a newspaper you are being bought. Dakota used
dime-store scissors and glue to turn the WORD in on itself like
a psychic snake swallowing its own tail.

———————

TAPE RECORDING:

DAVID: When was the first time you met Dakota and what do
you remember?

JOHNNY: The first time I met him I was living with Sylvia.
Nancy, who I think was our roommate, brought me over to
his house on the west side, which he called the Palacial
Mansion. I'd read a bunch of his cut-up pieces in one of Joe's
magazines, and I think he was going to help me with my fruit
fly experiment. It was around 1979–1980.

D.: What was the experiment?

J.: It was just classic genetic stuff; growing fruit flies and—

D.: Did he help you collect? He always had that reptilian
quality about him.

J.: No, man . . . heheheh . . . I don't have clear memories of my
first meeting—what I remember was that I was kind of awed
by him, by his house. He had these huge windows that were
covered in hundreds of xeroxes of planes crashing, one after
the other filling up the entire window like a shade. The plane

was a passenger airliner and it was positioned at a 45-degree angle and the light came through them at certain times of the day. He had monstrous xeroxes all over the place and a bunch of Frankenstein models with their monster hands out, all lined up in rows like they were worshipping. He had tons of small electronic machines; keyboards and synthesizers and children's electronic musical toys.

My first impression of him physically was that he was a strange-looking guy. He used to call himself an ectomorph—he wanted to start an ectomorph club. He wanted to print up and hand out cards to people. He was very attracted to skinny people. His ribs were sticking through his skin and he had a jutting chin. He had an appearance like nobody else. I remember making a death mask of his face—he was originally going to be the devil in the film you and I were making. We had made a whole bunch of death masks of different people and death masks never usually look like the person you really are—Dakota's mask was the only one that looked like him; you could not mistake that thing. I still have it in my house.

He made my life change. I learned so much from him spiritually—he pulled me up from the bottom of the ladder. It was the information he gave me which affected the way I think. When I first met him and hung around with him I was pretty intimidated because he was so fucking sharp; nothing slipped by him—he would turn a word you said, or something that happened; he would relate it to all these other things. There were so many connections going on in his brain that it was amazing. He could give value to experiences or devalue them—he could see through all the bullshit like just watching tv or dealing with newspapers; with his scissors he could take something we live with every day and turn it into something very powerful. He'd turn the mundane into something with meaning and power; into something relevant. He brought me up to a level of awareness where I could see the truth in things within the structure of the world.

———

JOURNAL ENTRY:

Down in the piers around sunset, gray lines of the river are easing towards the dusk. There are times I see myself from a distance entering the torn, ribbed, garage-like doors of this place from the highway—I step away from myself for a moment and watch myself climbing around and I wonder, what keeps me going? Why is it these motions continue over and over, animal sexual energy? The smell of shit and piss is overwhelming; everybody uses this place as an outdoor toilet, getting fucked in the ass and then letting it loose in some spare corner. Undershirts and socks people used to wipe their asses months ago, after sex, mix with cast-off clothes and pools of urine. To get further into the warehouse I have to breathe lightly and stay near the openings in the walls and walk quickly way back into the darkness to the farthest point, where the walls open out to the river, and a concrete platform that seems to ride the waves, every so often crumbling and sinking as if into raging seas. Deep in the back of my head I wish it would all burn down, explode in some screaming torrent of wind and flame, pier walls collapsing and hissing into the waters. It might set us free from our past histories. Once it was all beautiful rooms that permitted living films to unwind with a stationary silence that didn't betray the punctuations of breathing, the rustle of shirts and pants sliding.

Somehow I got drugged. I barely remember the motions

of it, a hand with a cloth and another hand with a bottle and a quiet shaking motion and I turned away to fish a cigarette out of my pocket and the guy's arm appeared around the side of my head saying, "Try this," and it had a clinical stink to it and I was in slow motion, falling to my knees. I felt the weight of his body in darkness, hovering over me, seeing his face half in shadows, everything grainy and foreign. A quiet claustrophobia entered my body beneath my skin, mixing with the bloodstream to form a sense of fear, not grounded, not severe, but more like a passing notion of vulnerability, wondering at his hands as they reach out of the darkness and slide warmly beneath my neck, over the sides of my neck, palms across my cheeks, then over my eyes. Thinking at that moment of him as a murderer, then slowly falling deep inside pleasure sensations; first the shock of his warm hands slowly tightening for a moment around my neck and then sliding down to my waist freeing the buckle on my belt, then the buttons of my overalls and his face following his hands as they peel back my pants. He gathered saliva in his palms and spit some on my chest, rubbing it in with his hands and I realized it was just the stranger in him that I was feeling cautious about . . .

———

One night, when I was feeling depressed from too much speed, I met Joe. Johnny called me over to the bar to introduce me to him. All I remember now is this sexy apparition in a goofy winter hat with two earflaps that stuck out at angles. He was a dark-haired guy with a corruptible face; I turned to Johnny and fanned my face with my fingers as if I were swooning. I guess coming off the speed made me horny that night. I asked Johnny if Joe was straight and he shrugged and then snickered, "I don't know. Why don't you find out."

Joe wrote stories about white-trash teens in southern states drugging and fucking and shooting off handguns. He wrote about killer cars and boredom. He showed me a story about a power junkie who invents a machine or system that allows him to suck the brains of other people and ingest all their knowledge. The guy becomes the smartest man in the world. I forget the ending of the story but it left me with a slight gnawing doubt about my proximity to Joe. When I met him he was putting out a xerox magazine that had a rotating title that reflected all the various possible addictions. He published writings by Dakota, stories and photographs by Johnny, anonymous ramblings by mental patients dropped into the streets of the city by the medical system, and one time used one of my Archie and Mr. Weatherbee cut-ups, where the two of them have anal and oral sex in Mr. Weatherbee's office. The comic ended when Archie caught a bad case of crabs.

Joe was also making photographs and super-8 films. His films stripped all the tedious buildup from hollywood movies whose essential draw for the ticket-buying public was five minutes of graphic violence. His films *were* the five minutes of blood-letting and mayhem. He also explored the power plays embedded in the sexual act. In one film I played a character who was obsessed with an older man. My character was so obsessed with the other guy that whenever he rejected my pitiful advances my neck would explode unleashing torrents of blood or my arm would blast off my body bouncing off a wall. I loved the film because it made the intensity of emotions become an external physicality. Dakota played a lascivious derelict who made goo-goo eyes at my love object one day as we were entering our apartment across from the Bowery Mission. My brains almost exploded out my ears in jealousy. I'll never forget Dakota's face in the rushes, licking his lips, with his zomboid eyeballs projecting detailed scenes of sexual romp positions at me. His eyes exhausted me with their energy.

Another film Joe made showed in grainy black and white scenes a young guy sitting in a chair in his house brooding. Suddenly the guy gets up and begins methodically smashing the entire house apart and the camera follows along as each piece of furniture explodes into toothpicks and a television set with the knob turned on and commercials playing on the screen gets imploded by a series of well-aimed kicks. A mirror gets smashed into thousands of glittering pieces and, thus, they reflect our psychic environments.

––––––––

TAPE RECORDING:

DAVID: When did you meet Dakota and what do you remember?

JOE: The very first? It was around 1980 and I was living in Philadelphia and putting out the Addict Magazines and Dakota wrote me a letter. He was already in New York City. The letter was so fucking weird I thought it was a joke. After a second letter I wrote him back, then I moved to New York and he was the first person I met. I hooked up with him because he told me if I ever needed any printing done for free, he would do it for me. He worked for a big foundation. He was an assistant to a doctor. From what I've heard the doctor was a pretty eccentric dude, in his forties, and he hung out on 42nd street all the time going to peep shows and talking to weirdos. I guess he was sort of Dakota's father figure, because he always supported anything Dakota did and he lent him money when he was broke.

So I remember calling Dakota and hooking up with him. We had a common bond, being that we were both from the south, plus, he was a punker and I fancied myself a punker. I remember going and visiting him in this huge fucking apartment on the west side. He had a printing press called DAKOTAPRINNERZ, which was basically the copy machine at the foundation he worked for, the best xerox machine made at the time. We'd go in there at night and the magazine I did, which had a circulation of 200 copies, went up to 2,000 copies overnight. He also did free mailing out of there with their postage meter.

D.: What was your first impression of him?

JOE: He liked to smoke pot; he liked to drink rum. He seemed real perverse; he seemed to be really into death and stuff—more than I was anyways.

D.: What do you mean, "into death?"

JOE: It means: when you can't have what you want, you want everyone to die. Hahaha . . . and I know that feeling myself; I felt the same way. I have a fascination with anything out of the ordinary because daily life is so mundane. What I used to tell people was that, when I die, I want the whole world to end at the same time. If I have to die, I want everyone else to die; I want it all to cease at the same time. Everyone says, "Oh, that's a very selfish outlook." But then again it's from a feeling of not feeling fulfilled—feeling that you've been denied your due, which I still feel all the time. We grow up having these lofty ideals, which we're taught to expect by society, but then we don't get it. We didn't *want* to get it the way we're told to—by working for it—we wanted a shortcut.

D.: Do you remember what you wanted?

JOE: Yeah. Happiness. At that age it boiled down to wanting someone to love us . . .

———

"Our society desperately needs monsters to reclaim its own moral virginity."   —Sylvere Lotringer

———

There is some part of me that has never cared if I died. So what. I know these feelings aren't genetic or because of chemical imbalances. They were obviously born somewhere, from something. I have always experienced *fear* living in the world; sometimes it is hidden for periods of time. Maybe it was daddy, maybe it was mommy, maybe it was the american dream. Maybe it was the fact that the american dream bombed out for the parents of our generation. When we rolled around out of the shifting layers of childhood and our teens, we found ourselves reflecting on the national blank spot of the '70s. At least in the '60s some of our parents had a momentary idealism they shared as a reference point. They tore down parts of the psychic screens to reveal something a tiny bit more real; something that approximated a *freedom* for them, however ridiculous some sections of its framework turned out to be. The communes had the same stupid hierarchies as government institutions. Fake jesus-types wandered the dead highways and interstates flashing peace signs even until as late as 1979. Adults from the 60s pushed at the boundaries and borderlines of prescribed social toler- ance and acceptance until the boundaries acknowledged and included them to some degree. Then the boundaries snapped in around them like rubberbands around a stack of pencils. Immediately, the interior masses, collected as they were around the illusory core of "government" and "ideals," began their amoebic dance of consumption and assimilation. The Black Panthers at least instituted breakfast programs that were for a time picked up by the State for kids in the slums. The country was at the height of industrialization, so government could afford to buy off poor whites, blacks, and hispanics—in the form of welfare—in order to keep them from organizing as extensively as they appeared to be doing. What does this have to do with the price of milk and eggs? During the Carter years, urban centers started being gentrified, rents tripled, driving up the numbers of homeless, inflation went nuts, and by the time Reagan got lowered into power the agenda was the smashing of unionization, cutting of social programs, and the elevation of the media sound bite. The middle class was so brain dead from the intoxicating effects of its brief affluence that it was a conservative takeover that rivals *Invasion of the Body Snatchers*.

When kids of my generation hit their twenties and began to reach out to tear down the screens, in the same way that every generation before us exercised as a prerogative (reflecting their states of mind and need for psychic room), we found that our preliminary efforts revealed a black hole and it wasn't in outer space. It was right here on the surface of North America. The mummified assholes in power could only be imaginative enough to fill it full of propped-up cardboard images portraying the "spectrum" of american ideals, which beneath the two-dimensional surfaces had pieces of exploded brain matter on the lapels of their success suits. It costs millions of dollars to run for president; how much does it cost to hire a madison avenue ad agency to run a campaign? How much does it cost to make a commercial for television? This is not a democracy.

Television, when viewed from four centimeters away, was quite beautiful to us, especially if one could afford a color set. But television was what the church revealed itself to us as—nothing more than an experiment in mass hypnosis. In laboratory experiments, entomologists have discovered that they could approach a moth while it was in the middle of laying its eggs and cut its head off with a scalpel, and it would continue to lay its eggs until its genetically programmed job was done. Then it would die. I could only relate this information to the spectacle we are witnessing in the White House and its government functions.

Maybe all these things are genetic. Maybe it all boils down to the issue once raised: that we are all of different species; that like the frog or the bird world we all break down to an intense variety of forms with only our physical characteristics binding us together or distinguishing us as separate. We are cursed with an absence of varieties of bright feathers or radical pigment designs on our faces and bodies to delineate our psychic differences. Because our forms are so similar, our only defense and survival mechanism is mimicry and silence.

Some of my friends got it together enough to play *house*, so the next logical step in this environment was to learn to play *doctor*. Ever since my late teens I have fought the urge to go to sleep for a thousand years. Then I discovered that Johnny had been doing heroin for a period of time. During that period of my life I always tended to do the exact opposite of what I emphatically stated as something I wouldn't ever do. I would try it at least once, just to see what I was afraid of.

———

JOURNAL ENTRY:

ANDROGYNOUS BLACK WOMAN LYING ON MATTRESS IN DEALER'S HOUSE:
"You know all these (Operation Pressure Point) busts have
to do with the economy. See, it's a plan of Reagan's, see,
where the cops are told to allow all these junkies to get in and
buy their dope and then when all the money is in the hands
of the dealer, then the cops bust the dealer and take the
money and put it back into the economy. This way the
economy is gonna get better, and they only got until septem-
ber to get the economy back in shape. You watch, if septem-
ber comes around and the economy isn't fixed up—all hell's
gonna break loose."

———

TAPE RECORDING:

DAVID: What was it about "dark" things that attracted people
back then?
SYLVIA: Well, if you're afraid, then you dive in and you want
to get inside it so it's just not a separate thing. My nature, the
nature of how I see things is I can barely look at some of
those things.
DAVID: I find myself at times sliding towards depression in
confronting some materials—my attraction for a moment
might be more of: why are they attracted to it—I mean;
medical deformities, nazi regalia, videotapes of that politician upstate shooting himself in the mouth . . .
SYLVIA: Exactly . . . it's once more removed. I think we're
observing *that*—because all these people had specific things;
it's: why did all these people have these specific attractions.
The attractions themselves are arbitrary.
D.: Well, what was the attraction to drugs?
SYLVIA: I'll tell you—talk about a generation. Whatever it is

that's there when you are in your twenties—I could put
things down to age; before you're deciding, you just do
whatever is there. I don't ever remember saying, "I need
drugs. I'm going to do drugs." It wasn't really a decision,
they were just there. If they weren't there, it would have been
something else. I think drugs themselves are their own issue.
I didn't do them to explore or anything, I did them for fun.
I did coke to get to work—it was just there. I didn't really
think about why I did it. It was only in my marriage that
drugs became an issue, when I did heroin with my husband
because life was so miserable and I would go down with him
and I definitely did it to try and hide, which never worked
for me anyway. I can never fake myself out. Eventually I
was doing them just so I wouldn't be sick. You don't use
drugs—they always end up using you. I did them for the
buzz, to take the edge off, to go through all the motions and
go through it with a smile. To get through the everydayness,
the pointlessness, the two dimensionalness of everyday life,
which is sort of ironic because all we do is look underneath it
all the time—I don't exist on the two-dimensional sphere; I
see way beyond it. So why are we taking a drug to help us to
do that? I think we do the drug because we do see so much
more, but we want, on some level to keep things two-
dimensional. It's a dichotomy; you can't stand things because
they are so superficial so you take drugs to stop seeing
further.

D.: Yeah . . . You have a headache, you take aspirin. You have
a *normal* life, you take drugs. Is that what it boils down to?

SYLVIA: Well, like I said, I took them just to get rid of the
mundane aspect of everything I am seeing, but I've never
seen anything mundane in anything, so I must be taking it to
eliminate the depth, to get through the everyday and *see* it

that way. You talk about this nation of zombies, what do *they*
do? I know they don't question things but how do they do it?
I don't think I'm special—

D.: I think we are. We see something about the structure that
others take for granted or seem blind to; the structure
consumes them and all they know is to get that job, get that
food, get that comfort and, hopefully, get that retirement.

SYLVIA: I've always envied people like that on some level,
people who knew what they wanted to do, what they had to
do, didn't question it. And they don't want you around;
they'll fuck you so bad if you say, "Excuse me, stop and lets
talk about all this for a minute. Why are you doing this?"
They'll fucking kill you.

Last night I called my mother. I said, *"I'm really
fucking smart."* Everyone has been saying I'm too smart for
my own good. I say, "Get the fuck away from me—that's
right, I'm too smart, that's all I have."

D.: I've been told all my life that I'm "too sensitive," as if you
could just turn the tap off and feel a little less sensitive for
the rest of your life and everything will be okay.

SYLVIA: "Too sensitive"—oh, definitely. Too smart, too sensitive, intuitive. It is *"much sensitive,"* not "too sensitive," as if
it were derogatory. Excuse me, that is what I am. I'll spend
my whole life trying to maintain this rather than trying to
turn it off. That's why it is hard. I want to be as smart and
as sensitive as I am and see things the way I do. I want to be
strong enough to stay that way. I don't want to dull that. I
did drugs to dull these feelings, to avoid paying bills I
couldn't pay. On the other hand I can face shit head-on. I'm
even stronger than I want to be. No matter what happens
technically, no matter what kinds of jobs I've worked—it's all
incidental to thinking. That's all that is important is the

thinking. I don't know how to make money from it. It would be great to pay the rent. And I don't want a million bucks and then just sit around thinking all day—I also have to be in the middle of it, I don't care what it is. I'm not justifying the horror of the last five years—that's *mine*; that's my *choice*, that's my *reason*—I'll move on from here. None of that is going to set me back because I've been thinking all along through it; I cared about it. It doesn't matter what's happening, it's how you look at it. I'll never let anyone take that away from me with, "You're too sensitive." Fuck you— you're lucky there's people out here thinking about why we're doing anything. But *one* is not good without the *other*. Even if someone can go through the motions and not know it, they're not getting anything out of it. They are just getting through it. We can't be alive and questioning it without doing a little of that "maintaining."

———

TAPE RECORDING:

JOE: . . . I know a lot more about what I was feeling back then than I did at the time. Someone asked me recently about the movies I made, and I said, "My only intent is to destroy sex." They said, "What do you mean?" It occurred to me that whatever we are denied or whatever we do not get in the way that we want, we want to smash it. I could never understand romance and shit—it never seemed to work out like in the picture books or the movies, so, naturally, I wanted to destroy it. It is just that in your twenties you don't realize that you don't necessarily want that which you cannot have—it just seems that way. It is *states of life* that end up being attractive; things where other people seem to be content. Like—I wish I had a wife. And a house. And a car. But my desire for that makes me hate it. Such as, seeing a couple kissing; I hate it. It makes me sick. Just because I don't have it.

DAVID: Do you mean media images of *happiness*?

JOE: Yeah. But that's all we have to go on, especially if you don't have a strong family environment. I mean we all come from fucked-up homes. Most of our fucking input is from fairy tales, from the movies, tv, magazines, and from all that shit. It took me *forever* to figure out that that's all definitely a bunch of fairy tales. I feel like an idiot for not seeing that when I was a kid . . .

———

Q. Why did the monkey fall out of the tree?

A. Because it was dead.

———

JOURNAL EXCERPT:

I was sitting in Joe's house trying to figure out where I am and where I am going. That question was solved when he took out a syringe and started uncapping a hit of ecstasy. I joined him in the kitchen and talked him into letting me use the needle after him. It was the only needle he had. He resisted at first, something to do with me being queer and all. I felt insulted and then he remembered bleach could kill the virus if I had it. When he was fixing he dropped the cotton ball out of the spoon onto the dirty floor, cursed and picked it up saying, "Oh what the fuck," and rolling it around between his filthy paint-covered fingers. After he hit up I cleaned the needle with Clorox and spring water a few times. When I hit the vein and pushed in the depressor it was like a golfball of heat and light blew through my heart and sped up into my brain. An inaudible pop behind the chest and skull and the world was instantly beautiful. I left and walked downstairs and pushed through the group of people waiting on line to score from the old lady on the third floor. The streets were emptying out with the falling of the sun.

Later tonight I was walking around like a loaded pistol, out and around the streets where the air is so thick with pollution and death. The streetlamps burn dim and over in the dusk above the buildings there's a blimp hovering in a torturous drift, with "McDonalds" written on its side. I wish someone would take an elephant gun and blow it out of the sky. Over on Avenue A, near 11th street, three little puerto rican kids are beating the shit out of a giant Snoopy doll with nail-studded boards. They beat its head until the white guts of cotton stuffing were completely emptied. An insulting vision appeared in the burnt-out streets, in the poverty of the block, the broken tenements and doomed kids; the little park filled with broken glass and shacks made of cardboard; and the o.d. sleepers and the puke and shit and the stains of yesterday evening's bloody knifing and the hungry stray dogs and the old man they sleep with in winter to keep from freezing in the abandoned building; and the little brats waiting to grow old enough to sell dope and shoot other kids that step on their turf and the people with disease selling their used hypodermics—into the middle of all this walks a stupid boy cop fresh from queens and pale with fear trying to twirl his baton like a seasoned pro.

I get back to Joe's house and he's still going strong with the needle. I got no other place to live and all the rents are up because the rich people decided the suburbs are really hell and are moving back to the cities. Joe informs me that people die of heart attacks all the time from one i.v. shot of ecstasy. It's the last time I do it. The darkness that comes

from this shit is so pervasive that it taps into the dark tone
of american structure. Everything that is horror-filled and
powerfully ugly about the american dream and its resulting
nightmare descends like a twenty-mile-wide blanket over
this part of the city. I wish I was travelling in a disposable
body through the landscape of the u.s.a. map and I was like
a blinking light moving from state to state. I could be a killer
stalking a president or I could be engaging in some sordid
and tender sexuality with a stranger I've yet to meet in the
folds of landscape or among the monoliths of foreign city
canyons. I could be on a warm current of air drifting towards
the wet and smelly center of someone's butt in the turning of
dirty sheets and summer humidity and neon shop glow and
breaking bottles and fistfights down in the streets and
abandoned lots and I could live forever in this drift; my body
could last a hundred centuries or my brain could last a
thousand more without benefit of my body's weight and it's
all possible and it's all false and it's every which way and its
all edgy and surreal and maybe I just want to scream a bit
right here and even if I were to scream it would do nothing;
everything is blowing out sideways: this elliptical stretch of
flesh and mortality, the death implied in a refrigerated
existence, the mounting and piling up of these words; these
fragmented shapes called letters, the piling up of words in
the pages of this book and the reader's eyeball at the
voyeuristic microscope or telescope pouring over these
sound-images and rattlings and bursts of thoughts and fuck
you maybe I should be in some ratty ballerina outfit wearing
the mask of a salivating mad dog twirling like some psychotic
diva in a circular spot light all for your edification, for your
discreet voyeuristic pleasure, and I should make a wild
pirouette through the frameworks of my social death; a wild

pirouette and a leap through the air to land at your feet only
to throw up on your shoes. jerk.

———

TAPE RECORDING:

D.: What attracts you to the "dark" things: murder, medical
deformities, and other stuff like that?

J.: It just shows the difference between "normal" and "abnor-
mal." People walk around and everyone thinks they're
normal—like people in suburbia—and anybody could have
stuff like that happen to them, like a genetic defect—it's
possible, it's in everybody's genes. There are recessive chro-
mosomes for all kinds of unfamiliar stuff. It always fascinated me; the things that determine what the world is made
up of or what defines "normal." Some of the stuff is dark and
upsets me but I just can't stop looking at it—I'm drawn to it.
Like murder, I can really see . . . well, sometimes I can and
sometimes I can't. I'm just fascinated by what makes some
guy climb up a fucking tower and start shooting at a
McDonalds. The fact that somebody can lead a "normal" life
like Son of Sam—working in a post office for years and years,
carrying on this regular life while he's killing all these
people. Everyone else thought he was a regular joe. There's
all this stuff hidden inside of people. I'm attracted to what's
hidden. That's why I'm into the occult too. Things that you
don't see everyday. It breaks up the boredom. When I was
making that magazine, *MURDER*, I was dealing with the
imposed line that people put up inside themselves, where
they think they are different from those who commit murders
or violent acts. Part of my fascination is bringing up these
things and putting them in the faces of snobs to see their
reactions and make them think about it. I think death is a

part of life; death is the end of life, the end of the circle—it's
a new beginning. The mystery of death is seductive. I want
people to think about the fact that death is in *front* of us as
well as around us. It's something we have to look forward to.
Also the fact that "normal, everyday people" do go out and
cut somebody's arm off and kill their children, and this
happens all the time. There are people who are snobs about it
and think that nothing like that could ever happen to them
and they're full of shit. It can happen to anybody. Look at
Donald Manes. He fucking cut his heart out. It's in everybody. The possibilities of violence to themselves or to others.
People still believe that cops don't kill innocent people. Let's
do an experiment: you go kill a cop on the corner and let's see
what people say about it. My work is an outlet for these
feelings. I've thought about killing, like when I got ripped
off—I used to have a gun but I got rid of it because I felt I
would end up using it—like Dakota ended up killing someone. I remember I'd be dopesick and I'd have forty dollars
left and somebody'd go and take it from me and I'd end up
going nuts and want to kill somebody. The drugs are part of
that feeling but even without the drugs I get pretty emotional
when somebody is taking away my liberty. Dealing with this
material is a catharsis. A lot of people say that after they
punch a wall they feel a lot better, but their hand is broken.
I've done that too. It helps to get it out. Some people say that
doing this stuff, or obsessing with this stuff or handling it,
that you're adding to the violence in the world. But most
people *aren't* living peacefully and happy, especially in a
city like this with millions of people stacked up on top of each
other. I came across one of the letters Dakota sent me, where
he said he had been sleeping in Central Park during this one
winter in 1984 and he said he was getting really tempted to

just give away everything he owned and just duke it out with nature. He said, "I just can't think of anything else to do. Can you?"

D.: I've had those feelings—why just help maintain the structure you're surrounded by; why try and struggle and survive in it? Why not just drop everything and go out and do things that are absolutely raw and without boundaries and laws and deal with survival on a real level, not one surrounded by all these fucking illusions? That was my impulse for years.

J.: Yeah. It's giving up on the world and the imposed structure of everyday life; it gets really frustrating—like living where I am now, living in an apartment where there's been a fire and there's soot everywhere and I got a kid and I still have to pay the landlord money to live there and there's this fucking killer; this guy John who's killed a bunch of people—I found him stripping my bicycle and I came out in the hall with my sword and was going nuts. This guy is friends with and lives with the woman downstairs with all those kids. He's been hanging out there and he told me when I came out with the knife, "Don't pull a knife on me. You don't know how many people I've killed for doing that." He recently came out on parole after years in prison for killing people. I told him that if he keeps fucking with me, something's gonna happen. I'm trying to deal with this guy and he's a scary guy; all muscular and bigger than me . . .

———

My arm was turning green and black. All I can remember from my flirting with heroin is the problem I had keeping myself from throwing up each time I did it. Normally after a week or two of doing it on a daily basis I'd imagined that I wouldn't be wasting what little money I had on bending over the curb between parked cars and trying to discreetly empty out my guts onto the asphalt, which appeared in some sort of magnified state with each fragment of garbage and wrapper and dog shit and scraping and bottle cap. Somebody had given me a number of fresh hypodermics and for a while they made me happy and focused on something outside the black cloud of depression that seemed to swallow the streets outside my door every time I left the house to go do the meaningless work routine or buy food. I lived in a shitty one-room apartment in the back of a building on east fourth street. My back window had a view of the shower room of the firehouse on 3rd street, where occasionally I would watch some sexy fireman step out of a shower stall and dry his body off and put on each article of civilian clothing he kept in a neatly folded pile on a ledge behind the window. There were a couple of weed trees that were about four stories tall that waved between the brick walls of my building and the firehouse. I literally felt I was at the end of my life; existence seemed like a bad series of routines that led to nothing I cared about. Ever since I was a kid I couldn't shake the realization that life was essentially a series of activities designed so that one could pay out money to keep from dying; if one stopped paying, one died; whether from exposure, starvation, lack of medical care or invisibility.

I fixed myself a shot and went out for a walk and got about seven blocks when I started puking. I had to stop about five times on each block to spew out water between parked autos. My eyes were tearing up and the city streets expanded and contracted 'til they became tunnel-like and brilliant with sunlight bouncing off the edges. I went home and laid down on the mattress. It was like a cave, all dark and cool, while outside the brick wall was glowing with sunlight and the whispering shadows of a breeze-tossed tree. I saw a series of transparent images appear in the air halfway between my face and the windows, almost like a slide projector carousel clicking away. First a series of physics equations and then a donald duck no more than five inches tall looking at me with his quacky smile. I leaned over the side of the bed and threw up into the wastepaper can I'd placed there. Then I felt warm, like my bones were resting in a bathtub full of almost hot water. Then I went unconscious.

Later, in a restaurant with Peter Hujar, having a cup of coffee, I showed him my arm. It felt foreign to me, like an arm out of a monster movie that belonged to somebody else. I felt like a long distance scientist showing another scientist a weird animal relic. I was almost completely disassociated from myself. Peter looked at me with an odd look in his eyes and said, "Don't ever come over my house again. I won't be friends with you if you're going to do that." I burst into tears. "I just feel so terrible about living," I said. "I feel too self-conscious about living and it's driving me crazy." He reached over and rubbed my arm. I went home later and never did it again. It took a number of months for the grainy black pall to lift from the surfaces and activities around me. It never lifted completely, but I realized that would never happen unless the entire society stopped dead in its tracks and the direction it was speeding in got erased.

———

Sometime in the mid-80s, I was working on a filmscript, with Johnny, called *Teenage Satan*. We based it on a true story of a group of kids out in Long Island that followed an

older kid through a series of motions that embraced black
magic and mescaline and any other drug they could lay their
hands on. The leader of the group ended up killing one of the
other guys in an acid laden hallucination of communication
with lucifer. None of the thirty or more kids who learned
about the murder said anything to their folks or the authorities. Some kids even went back to the local park where the
body was lying under a pile of dead leaves to look at the
states of decomposition. The leader of the group said if he got
picked up by the cops he'd kill himself and chase the dead
kid's soul to hell. Some girl eventually heard about the
murder at a pool party and called the police. The leader got
arrested and killed himself in jail. We were using the script
to talk about relationships of power: how the leader was
given power by the other kids and even though he was kind
of stupid, the other kids' adulation and respect kept him
propped up there in control. It's kind of like Ronald Reagan.

We planned to shoot scenes involving the constant
hallucinations of the leader and use those hallucinations to
outline a series of power structures in american society. We
understood the kids' use of drugs and their kind of ignorant
understanding of the basics of black magic to be nothing
more than the only available tools with which to rearrange
the imposed hell of the suburbs for brief periods of time. We
wrote the part of lucifer for Dakota. The leader of the gang
was constantly hallucinating conversations with lucifer. An
independent tv group had filmed the leader in an interview
that was later played on television. We figured that even if
the leader was delusional, the power of media helped validate
his sense of power among the peer group and helped add a bit
of rocket fuel to the murder that ultimately came about. We
planned to film the suicide from the leader's perspective—

after he dies from hanging himself in the jail cell, he tries to get into heaven. Shooting from his point of view, heaven was an ultra-fancy restaurant with a maitre d' that refuses him entrance. Jesus was played by a myopic overweight guy with frankenstein stitches evident around his neck and temples, bad teeth, and a penchant for gluttony. He sloshes wine around and chomps into a roast chicken, throwing half-eaten legs into the air where the camera would follow their slow-motion descent through the floor into hell, and starving wretches would scramble for it. Muzak played in the background and a soundtrack of a man's voice periodically announced, "ATTENTION SHOPPERS ... THERE IS A SPECIAL SALE ON HOLY WATER IN AISLE THREE. ..." Tapes of Jimmy Swaggert were recorded backwards and mixed in the soundtrack to reflect the practice of the church to plant subliminal messages in our environment.

During the making of this film, Johnny was getting yanked around by his addiction. There is nothing worse to me than witnessing a friend's addiction to dope accelerate. It leaves me with the feeling of standing in the distance watching a person I like and respect slowly twitch around and disintegrate into fragments, quietly becoming a shell of his former self. It feels like something related to body-snatchers films on late-night tv, and nothing you say, no gesture you make, stops the unravelling of it. I remember at the time that his addiction brought a quality of energy to the filming. Even though I'd get pissed off and depressed with all the kinetic fragmentary whirls of darkness, it seeped into the scenes and the constant odd occurrences that seemed more than chance. Things would happen that gave us an impression that our environment was fucking with our

minds and adding spice to the proceedings once the cameras
were rolling.

I don't remember what happened to Dakota. There
were times leading up to the beginning of filming when he
disappeared for long periods. I remember people wondering
if he had committed suicide. I heard that he had a crush on
Joe. Then he'd surface again. I heard he was addicted to
dope. I heard he stabbed somebody and it wasn't sure if the
guy died or not. I felt a disjointed kind of sadness for him;
everything was too erratic in my daily life and if I thought
long enough about it I could only think that there wasn't
anything I could do. I didn't know him well enough and I
didn't think it would have mattered—he was blasting
towards something in another neighborhood and though he
was familiar to me in terms of something he carried, some
similar code and energy, I felt like my own life was twisting
and rushing just out of my grasp. I was waiting for
something to drop like a mile-long boulder on top of me or
on top of my life. I wanted a radical shift to occur so I could
have a few minutes' peace or experience the silencing of my
brain. I wanted to be another person living a quiet farm
life in a foreign culture. I wanted to wake up and find
that I was five years old and my parents and neighbors
would say, "My, my, what an imagination." I wanted to be
physically erased and start over again. I didn't want to
be here. I didn't want to be there. I guess I wanted to be
nowhere, I wanted to listen to my brain talk inside of
nothingness. I wanted to be untouchable and have no *need*.
I figured if Dakota stabbed and killed somebody, it was for
a reason that only made sense to him. The stranger he
stabbed was one-dimensional in my mind. I knew Dakota
wasn't dangerous; he was simply skidding through the

grainy black pall that surrounds addiction and life in america.

––––––––

TAPE RECORDING:

DAVID: What was the first time Dakota tried to kill himself?
JOE: It must have around '84 or '85. See, I hung out with Dakota just about every day for a long time. He was like my best friend. I had various girlfriends around this time and I could never understand why he hated them so much. Then I found out he was attracted to me. This was around '84 and I was moving into a different circle. Things were changing around me. It was because I was tall and attractive and Dakota was short and ugly—let's be blunt here—people were more willing to talk to me than they were to him. I think his suicide had a lot to do with him seeing his circle—Johnny was also very attractive; we seemed to have no trouble getting laid and Dakota did; he'd always be telling me about these weird encounters and shit. He'd always be meeting these weird guys who were all kinked out and he'd have sex with them. Anyways it seemed we were going places that seemed closed to him, and when I look back I was always asking all these people to be in films and I'd only ask him to help with them. Now why was this? I don't know—we were moving around in all these circles and he resented the fuck out of it. He tried to kill himself. He wrote me this letter saying, "By the time you get this I will be dead. Come up to my apartment and you can have my synthesizer. I'll leave the door unlocked and I want you to take pictures of me dead." I got this letter on a monday morning. He'd shot ten bags of heroin. So, I called up his job and there he was at his job and I said, "Hey . . . this is *real funny.*" Stuff like that just tended

to alienate me even more. It got to a point where I just wished
he'd go and do it—he tried it again. I think he was reacting to
seeing his support group just peel away. He did tell me a *lot*
that he just couldn't find anyone to be in a relationship with;
just could not find anyone. When he went to texas he wrote me
and told me he did find someone—he found a girl *and* a guy.
See, I'd black all this shit out cause I wasn't interested in it.
I remember him telling me once that he met some guy who he
had sex with in doorways—he'd just bump into him; no names
exchanged or nothing like that. Dakota also told me, as have
some other gay people, his curse was that the guys he was
attracted to were straight . . . which . . . I mean . . . why not give
yourself two headaches . . .

D.: . . . When you got that note did he really try and kill
himself?

JOE: Yeah. He shot ten bags of dope but it didn't work—he
just woke up two days later.

D.: Did he explain that he was infatuated with you?

JOE: Yeah. Of course. But I blocked it out—didn't think
about it; didn't want to think about it because then it would
make me question my own self; my own closetedness . . .
these are things we macho dudes want to keep down . . . you
know? I have the same taste for the bizarre that anyone else
does but I fight to keep it in check . . . y'know? 'Cause I got
enough cans of worms . . . hahaha. You know I went through
my bisexual period—that's probably what freaked Dakota
out; because I went out with some other dude. Me and this
guy would start sharing these girlfriends; we'd start having
these threesomes—I knew why I was doing it . . . because I
was having doubts about what I was into. But that might've
sent him over the edge. I also noticed that—see, we were
drifting apart and this happened to me before; this just

happened to me recently—this girl I was with, I told her, "I can't see you any more"; we'd already had this agreement that we wouldn't get serious, anyway, "I can't see you any more." So, "Oh, I'm pregnant." It's like, "Oh, I'm gonna kill myself."

———

I was entering a state of mind where I saw the outline of my life as far as the direction it was moving. I could see the outline, the content, and the back wall of it. I knew I didn't want to touch the back wall because there was no coming back for me. I kept having the recurring sensation of standing a block away, watching this familiar but transparent version of myself pacing around in small circles next to a line of self-destruction. Every so often the figure would stop, turn to face the line and lift one foot in the air as if to step over. The foot remained in that position while I got in a car and left for a trip around the states. I met up with Johnny, Joe, and Sammy some months later in Nashville and we headed southeast through tobacco fields and southern floods, hits of acid and shopping-mall movies. One night, in some dying coastal town with a pitiful amusement park, we did some acid and walked the beach until we found a building containing a pool that glowed from underwater lights. Jumping off the diving board seated in easy chairs, we threw all the pool furniture into the water. We had a box of fireworks in the form of large gunpowder-filled Space Rockets. Down on the dark, wet sands of the beach we opened the box. We snapped the wings and air blades that determined flight direction off the sides of each rocket before lighting the fuses. What resulted at the moment of launch sometimes had us throwing ourselves to the ground covering our heads or

else running towards the midnight waves with a flaming
projectile close at our heels.

TAPE RECORDING:

DAVID: What happened the second time Dakota tried to kill
himself?

JOE: The other time Dakota did it was really funny. It got to
the point where Dakota would disappear for ages and—this
is typical dopefiend activity—somebody's ignoring you so
you try to kill yourself or get into big trouble just to get their
attention; 'cause that's the only way you can get it. Its like
when you're in a relationship with your parents where they
always beat you. You almost welcome the beatings because
it's a show of some kind of affection—you'll take anything
when you can't get nothin'. The second time he tried it was
really funny—he'd disappeared for days and we'd call all the
people who knew him: "What happened to Dakota—oh, I
hope he didn't kill himself again. I wonder where he is?" and
this would go on and on and I'd keep going to his house
trying to get in and he didn't have a phone, so you'd go out
there and scream from the fuckin' street or try and get in the
building. And I went up there all the time anyway and just
sat up there and smoked pot with him—it was during a
period when I'd quit smack. Then this next time he just
disappears for a *long* time and finally I find him—I seen him
walking down the street—that became the only way I could
contact him anyway, 'cause he wouldn't show up at his job.
I'd say, "Where you been man?" and he'd say, "Oh I just got
out of the hospital. I tried to kill myself," and I go up to his
apartment and the whole place is covered with blood, man.
He lived in this little room about ten by ten and one side's all

newspapers up the wall cause he saved every newspaper and the other side's all garbage 'cause he had to save all his garbage and all these rows of bottles filled with piss—there was a bathroom right there but he had to save all this shit—and there was a whole wall of synthesizers and stuff. That was his apartment, with two windows and this little tiny, yuck, bed. He had a green shower outside in the hall—green from scum—and he was always infatuated with this suicide shit. All his poetry and shit would have stuff about suicide and "the young prince kills himself . . ." and all that stuff; he was really into Harry Crosby, you know—the Black Sun and all that shit. But you know, since the last way didn't work, he decided he would cut his veins 'cause cuttin' your wrists never works, 'cause your blood always clots up, you know. If you had seen Caligula you know you had to keep your open wound in the water to keep it from clotting— so he said that since he knew he could stick needles in his arm and it didn't hurt he figured the best way he could do it was to cut these big hunks of his veins out up on his . . . what do ya call it? Triceps? Biceps? Biceps! So he cut these big hunks of his veins out with an Exacto knife. But the funny part of the story was: well, first he'd like done all this buddhist stuff—he was way into buddhism; he'd done all this alter shit and he put these two big buckets of hot water in front of the altar and then he cuts out the vein on this side and he said the blood just starts shooting all over the place—I'm rolling on the floor when he's telling me this. He said the funniest thing was when he was trying to cut his other arm the blood from his first arm kept shooting up into his face and it took him forever to get the second one and he runs over and sticks his elbows into the water—he puts one in each bucket to keep them from clotting—and he's just sitting there in front of the

altar like this and blood's shootin' everywhere, but then the
water starts getting cold and he's going: "oh fuck I'm clotting
up!" and he cut these huge hunks cause he figured it'd be too
big to clot up and then he goes over to this little sink and he's
trying to fill up the buckets again and take 'em back over to
the altar and blood's still shooting out everywhere. He puts
the buckets down and goes: "goddamn, man I am tired . . .",
y'know he was starting to get all cold and dreamy and shit
and he just leans against the wall there near his sink, slid
down the wall and fell face forward over the bed and passed
out and since he didn't have his arms in the water, they
clotted up. But he said he lost so much blood he felt this huge
tourniquet was twisting around his chest; like all his vessels
were collapsing and he said he'd never try it this way again,
by the way. He said he was lying there passed out and he's
groaning—his body's there passed out, totally unaware of
groaning— oh oohhh. His fuckin' neighbor heard him groaning, comes and knocks on the door, opens the door and sees
him laying there and the blood everywhere and calls the
cops. So then the paramedics came and got him and they
said, "We can arrest you for attempted murder," or else they
were gonna put him in the psycho ward, and they sentenced
him to go to the psycho ward every day and he said, "Yeah
. . . I'll do that, I'll do that." Of course he didn't do that after
the first day. And . . . uh . . . that was his second time . . . that
was around '85 and this was the time when we were into the
bigger, the more outrageous something is, the better. And
this was about as outrageous as you could get, y'know.

D.: WHAT DID YOU SAY TO HIM? HOW DID THAT MAKE YOU FEEL?
JOE: I was laughing my head off. Because I couldn't believe
it—he was laughing too. I just thought it was such an
incredible story.

D.: But what did it bring up in your own head about yourself?

JOE: Nothing. But then after that point ... It brought up nothing because ...

D.: Were you doing dope at that point?

JOE: Yeah, yeah—I think ... maybe not. But it made me want to ... um ... I was getting tired of it, y'know? Because it was gettin' obvious what he was doing ... um ... he was fascinated with suicide ...

D.: Yeah, but earlier you said he had all this desire for connection with somebody ...

JOE: Yeah, but he was fascinated with anybody that killed themselves, y'know? After that second attempt he would disappear all the time and after that I just wished he would either do it or split because it was something I just didn't want to think about. I just wanted my old friend who was into doing stuff, see—I had moved into my own things and I assumed he would move on into another direction; it's just that when I didn't take him along with me into my direction ... I wanted to see everyone flourish but when people stopped flourishing and just got suicidal I didn't want to see it anymore. He was shooting a lot of coke at that time.

———

Death was everywhere, especially in my apartment, a gentrified space right above Joe's place. In my depression I kept thinking it was Joe's fragmented state of mind that was pumping death vibes up through the floor. Later I found out a woman with three kids had occupied my apartment before I got there. She apparently died a slow, vicious death from AIDS. I felt like the connection between me and this circle of friends was getting buried in veils of disintegration; drug addiction creates this vortex of psychological and physical fragmentation that is impossible to spotlight or put a finger on. Joe was wrestling with it and at the same time seemed unconscious of it. I thought he was becoming a creep, sliding into a pimp mentality. Whenever I ran into him he was babbling about Charles Manson and all the girls that were throwing themselves at him in nightclubs. Johnny was getting more erratic and transparent in his addiction. I kept seeing those visions of myself, transparent with one foot lifted in the air, frozen in mid-step over the line. Everything in the environment was a huge soup of contradictory and confusing energies. Most people I knew had never been there and I couldn't even bring it up. I couldn't talk about it until I knew what I wanted. Having come out of a violent background as a kid, living on the streets until I almost died of malnutrition and exposure, having wrestled with thoughts of suicide because of the idea of living in a social structure that would rather I disappear or remain invisible or die, because of my sexuality and mental framework, I felt myself at a point where I needed to either define certain boundaries for myself or get away from my life as it was. The seductiveness of everything the State finds repellant or threatening to its structure always draws me back to examine it, at least until I see its shape. But how can one understand something about *death* unless they actually die?

Dakota was leaving town to head back to Texas. It was a murky time and I'd heard that he was completely broke and fighting withdrawals, and also there was a pall of gray from the stabbing incident surrounding him. I could feel the heaviness in him; I don't think there was even a fragment of judgment coming from those he knew. The line was always there to cross—we recognized that. I mean we were "americans" and in america you have cardinals preaching bloodlust from the pulpit during times of war. The fake moral screens are unfurled by the State whenever they decide to send troops into another country to protect their corporate interests. You have the concentration camps set up by the State in the form of ghettos. Aside from the insane, anyone who lives in america carries a rage and an impulse to shred the screens of physicality and the fake moral codings that fence that rage in.

I saw Dakota walking down the street the day before he left town. I was in a car I owned at the time, that cost me forty bucks. I opened the passenger door and invited him in. All I remember is wanting to place my body on top of his. Instead I told him that I always felt a strong connection to him, like I've known him for twenty years and that I was sorry he was leaving and that we'd never had the chance to uncover the connection. I told him to take care of himself and be sure and write me from texas. I might have given him some cash. A month later I received a letter from him, but I was in the midst of a serious depression and never answered it.

———

TAPE RECORDING:

JOHNNY: Dakota's and my relationship was so weird at the end, I just wanted to make it up to him and make him feel better because I had long gotten over him ripping me off for all that money. He had been out of a job and I had given him the key so he could use my phone to call around for jobs, and all this money I had, that I was spending on films, I kept in drawers and it kept disappearing little by little. I couldn't believe it was Dakota, but he was the only person who could've done it, and it went on and on and I just kept thinking, "I misplaced it," because here was this guy in that Palacial Mansion—he built a *shrine* over a mouse hole. He wouldn't kill a cockroach and here he had totally turned around and was ripping me off and I just couldn't believe that this person I was so close to and that I was spiritually connected to could be ripping off a blood brother. I set a trap and I caught him; I went down to the street and I was so pissed off I wanted to punch him. He was waiting to buy drugs with my money and I was so hurt, I was like, "Give me my money back and don't come around me anymore." I started to cry; I was so upset. I just never expected somebody I was so close to to do something like that. If he had just asked—I'd told him if you ever need money—I'd have given it to him. Even if it were for drugs I'd have given it to him. Even if it were for drugs I'd have given it to him or helped him to stop or something. When I first met Dakota, I asked him if he ever did dope and he said, "No. I don't want to start ripping off my friends." An old lover of his had ripped him off. I think he was on his way down with the whole deathtrip and stuff.

It blew me away when he stabbed someone. The reason he did that, I think, was because he was feeling intensely all his shortcomings; like the way he felt picked on, the way he's so skinny and he couldn't fight back, and I think this was just a statement to these drug dealers because he said he stabbed the guy over a ten-dollar bag of pot. This guy ripped him off for pot and Dakota said he wasn't gonna take it anymore and he said, "I've been pushed over the line." He practiced with a knife on a coat that was padded and stuff to see how far he could stick it in. For two days he practiced, and then he went back to buy pot and he dressed differently so that the guy wouldn't recognize him and he reached around behind him and stuck a knife into his kidney. He said the guy just went paralyzed, and he heard a day later that they found a body, so he assumed that he killed the guy. It all ties together: he was numbing himself with drugs and he stabbed somebody and he ripped somebody off and all that at the end, where he changed and had different values; but it all came from that powerlessness that comes from being a human being, something we all feel like when they raise taxes and the landlord raises rent and there's nothing you can do about it and you got a baby—he just got fed up and started lashing out.

———

"It takes an entire village to raise one child."—African Proverb

———

TAPE RECORDING:
DAVID: When was the first time you thought about killing yourself?
JOE: Me?
D.: Yeah.
JOE.: ME?
D.: Yeah. You.
JOE: Only when I was doing drugs; when I saw no other way out. Only when I did drugs ... or when I was a kid. Now, when I was doing drugs I thought about it very seriously— you gotta apply this to Dakota too, because he was doing drugs and drinkin' like a fish. And when you're in that state everything looks totally fucking bleak all the time. When you're caught in the maw of heroin or alcohol, in particular, you try to imagine your life going on and you can't think of

any way to stop doing whatever abuse you're doing and it just looks like this endless progression of: I get high, I work, I get depressed, I get high, I get depressed, I get high and it looks pretty fucking bleak; and you just think: well this is pretty hard to take, why don't I just end it now. I can only say this 'cause *now* I can see the way out and I can look down the road and it doesn't look so bleak. I can totally sympathize with Dakota.

After he did the stabbing thing I'd hooked up with Audrey and I kept telling her, "You gotta meet this guy Dakota, you gotta meet this guy, he's so fucking nuts—he wasn't really nuts, he was just a really nice guy and I'd been looking for him all over the fucking place and he'd disappeared again and I thought maybe he killed himself again and so I kept going up to his apartment trying to find him . . . I'd get up there and keep banging on the door. I was up there with Audrey and I ran into him on the street and I said, "Where you been man? I've been looking for you for like three fucking weeks?" He told me about stabbing that guy and he'd been hiding out—and this time he didn't like want to shout it from the rooftops like when he tried to off himself or something. And he told me it was the first time the suicide urge ever left him was when he stabbed that guy. He said he saw that movie *Network* and the guy says, "I'm not gonna take it anymore, not gonna take it any more." So he just picked out this guy, and he really researched the whole method of how to stab somebody and do the most damage and get away with it and then he carried it out.

D.: What was that method?

JOE: Well, he was always real into medical texts and all that shit and he found out the best way to get somebody was in the kidneys; y'know, instant paralysis even if you don't kill them. And this drug dealer had ripped him off for some pot. A guy had taken Dakota's money and sold him something and this other guy came up and said, "Hey man, he ripped you off, he ripped you off. If you give it back to me I'll go back and make him give you the right amount. And Dakota, always wanting to be friends with whomever, finally relented and gave it to him and the guy split and never came back. So this really pissed Dakota off because he always got beat all the fucking time. So he researched it, found out the kidneys are the best place, took that switchblade I gave him and he was like practicing on his bed and his pillows and stabbing through different kinds of fabrics just to make sure he could do it. Then he went back down there at two in the morning after practicing for a couple of weeks and went up to this guy and said, "Hey man, I want you to get me some pot. Here's twenty bucks—you can do that can't ya?" And the guy goes, "Sure, sure, sure," and he knew the guy was gonna try and rip him off again and he says, "Well I don't want to pass it to you on the street here—lets walk down this side street a little bit" and Dakota says he put his arm around the guy and said, "Man, y'know you're O.K." and he pulled the guy towards him like in an embrace and pulled out the switchblade and just stabs him in the kidneys and just left the guy laying there and he told me all these things, like he was wearing tennis shoes and he was afraid they'd find footprints so he went all over the town and like put one tennis shoe over here and one tennis shoe over there and he buried everything— got rid of the switchblade and all that shit and ... um ... pretty sure the guy died because he read a thing—I saw this thing in the paper about them finding this dead junkie type in a dumpster up there. He didn't put him in the dumpster; maybe the guy climbed in there or something. So that was the first time his obsession to kill himself ever left him. He finally felt free of all that weight; he finally stood up to it all.

JOE: He always wanted to pay back all these people he felt were oppressing him, and a drug dealer—what more perfect candidate for somebody who oppresses people. Another important thing that happened at that time was he had this crummy little apartment on 36th street and it was a corner place; a tiny fucking apartment but he had these two windows—it's a proven fact that you need a certain amount of eye room to keep from going crazy, and from this room you could see a building on one side, a building on the other side, but right straight down the middle you could see all the way to the river. You know we all hated fucking rich people and we still do ... make a little note there ... and they started building this fucking condo co-op thing right on the river, right in his view and he'd sit there and say, "Look at that—that motherfucker's gonna put it right in my fucking view and then I ain't gonna be able to see nothing but buildings," and that building would go up and up and up and finally it was just like a fucking door shuts, y'know? That kind of shit really affects you.

JOE: Well, after he killed somebody he seemed to be trying to get his shit together and he started talking about leaving town. Johnny can tell you all kinds of weird stories because I was losing track of him ... like I was trying to break the connection. Johnny lived right down the street from him and Johnny was hanging out with him and I was breaking connection there too. It's all fuzzy, y'know ... like if Dakota was more attractive ... (TAPE RUNS OUT)

... Dakota was broke and I was giving him pot to sell and he would just never have the money and he was getting way in debt and it was starting to look like a bad scene and, naturally, I would move away from that scene, I mean—who wouldn't? But it's funny because since I got straight I've been wanting to talk to people that I broke connection with because the straighter you get—like if Dakota had stayed straight—the more you realize how much you really like that person; how much you really love that person . . .

D.: Yeah, I find that with increased mortality it shows me how much I like people—which is the exact opposite.

————

Peter was dying from AIDS and I was helping to take care of him with a handful of other friends of his. I barely spent time at my apartment above Joe's place and had little contact with him or Johnny. I had been at the bedside of Keith David when he died, and watching his body grow still after the doctor removed him from the life-support system turned something around in my head. Johnny was moving around in california and for periods of time flying between the two coasts. I'd heard that at the latest count he'd died three times but was revived. One always hears that an addict of any sort has to reach bottom before they can come back swinging. I talked to him once or twice on the phone and he told me he was running packages of ecstasy from the west to the east coast. His physical condition was deteriorating; I didn't understand why any cop in sight didn't turn him upside down and shake the obvious drugs or money out of his pockets. He seemed to lead a charmed life, or else maybe some part of him wasn't ready to die yet. One flight he was preparing to board in san francisco almost tripped him up. He had a pound of ecstasy in his carry-on bag and I think the X-ray technician spotted something weird. The agent reached into the bag and lifted the pound of ecstasy into the

air, saying, "What's this?" while combing through the bag
with his other hand. The X-ray machine was six feet away
from the door to the airport police station and cops were
exiting every few seconds. The agent said, "Tell me the truth
now." Johnny told him it was ecstasy but that it was for his
own consumption. The agent stood there for an extended
moment and then placed it back in the bag and said, "Okay
. . . go ahead."

I was getting weird about all the shit in my life. I told
Johnny I couldn't hang out with him anymore because,
emotionally, it was too ugly to be taking care of a guy who
was battling to live and then hang out with people that were
jamming shit in their arms or throwing themselves into the
varied arms of death. I had previously tried to help him get
off heroin by paying his way on a trip to mexico, stupidly
thinking that the mere physical separation from the drug
contacts would help erase his addiction. We went down south
of the border to mexico city and he went through withdrawals
on the train ride. The energy that came out of his brain and
body for days afterwards was like some psychic kinetic
hydraulicism. I saw in the air of the hotel room a transparent
multi-armed creature devouring the heads of tiny humans. I
gave Johnny some cash to get him to the yucatan and told
him we had to separate. After he split I made friends with a
taxi driver who took me through the slums on the outskirts of
town, where a gas storage tank had exploded, demolishing an
entire town. "Right over there on that hillside," said the guy,
"there was a horse standing there made entirely of charcoal."
The gas company had completely rebuilt the town as well as
adding a new playground. Just above the playground on the
hillside were two brand-new gas storage tanks. When I
returned to new york city I saw Johnny about two weeks

later. He was in town a couple days and his eyes were heavily lidded from dope. I started avoiding him after that.

———

DREAM:

In this sleep I unlock the front door of an apartment and enter a small studio with one partial wall separating the windowed room from the front door and hallway. I lie down on a small white bed, suddenly wondering if I've locked the front door, when I hear the sound of some thing or person push open the door and enter the apartment. I turn over onto my back and stretch my head back in the direction of the dividing wall—no one there—and I feel a slight shiver of fear and get up from the bed. It is night and this isn't my apartment. I had come through the streets of a foreign city and somebody was allowing me to stay in this studio. Tom, my boyfriend, lives downstairs, directly below, in an identical place.

Suddenly this guy rushes around the corner of the wall and pushes me backwards onto the bed. I am pushing him away with my arms but he is too strong, there's too much weight behind his movements. His silhouette is muscular, like a weight lifter, and as light casts over him from the window I realize he is covered in Kaposi's lesions. He is naked from the waist up and his head is shaved. He lowers himself onto me and opens his mouth in a kind of grin. His mouth looks wet. He leans close to my face to kiss me, saying, "You would have thought I was very sexy and cute if you had seen me before I got ill." I am upset at everything that is happening but I give him a kiss because he is so sad. I feel sorry for him, briefly, but then I push him off me and rush out the door into the hall and down the staircase. I get to the door of Tom's place and push the buzzer, wondering if it is loud and will it alert the guy upstairs as to where I am. A loud quick burst of buzzer and I push it again and again until it no longer works. I'm frightened and I start banging on the door. Tom opens it up and I'm crying, "Oh god . . . you won't believe what just happened."

———

Peter was dead. I felt the landscape shifting beneath my feet. I felt disoriented from lack of sleep for periods of time. When I was in the street walking, it didn't feel like walking; it was simply the body being jerkily propelled forward on blind legs. I was preoccupied with the sense of disease and death in the environment. I was involved with a guy who I loved as far as I could ever let myself be loved, but the grainy black pall had drifted down from nowhere, without the benefit of drugs, and settled over the landscape. Nothing seemed to relieve it. I wanted to take the abstraction of death and look it in the eye and snap its weary neck. I isolated myself and spoke to hardly anyone.

Joe had sold the lease to his apartment to his landlord and left town. I got occasional cards from san francisco. It seemed every time I spoke to someone from there they were cranked up on speed. When Joe showed up for brief periods of time I ignored his messages on the phone machine until invariably he'd appear on the street as I was exiting the front door. I'd go sit and have coffee with him in a nearby restaurant. He was trying to kick heroin but seemed to be falling into amphetamine use. Maybe it was the discordant jitters he was having from being away from dope, but I remember a last meeting at a restaurant table before he split again and it was a disjointed monologue spilling out of him about his new "positivist attitude" that was changing his life around. I recall fragmented sentences and images about a motorcycle garage he lived in, or maybe it was a garage where motorcycles would appear and get chopped up and some girl was having a baby and he was running with a gang that was stealing telephone booths and *everything was really fucking great* and this motherfucker was trying to fuck his girlfriend and that motherfucker was saying that and he was looking for someone to do some "real jobs" with and he was going to buy guns in arizona and everything was fucking cool and in the midst of all his frenetic wordspills I felt like I could have been just a mirror above his sink at home. I felt like I didn't exist for him even though he had searched me out to speak about all this. He also had some terrible skin ailment, that spread just by touch, which he was absentmindedly picking at.

I realized later that it didn't matter if he did know I was there or not; it was me who was lost. I was in the midst of a dark tunnel that I still feel traces of today. I was feeling something similar to a sensation I experienced in my teens when I first came off the streets. I had almost died three times at the hands of people I'd sold my body to in those days and after coming off the street and adapting to familiar routines of working and living under a roof, I could barely speak when in the company of other people. There was never a point in conversations at work, parties or gatherings where I could reveal what I'd seen. That weight of image and sensation wouldn't come out until I picked up a pencil and started putting it down on paper. Here it was more than ten years later and I was having the same experience again. I felt like I was in the midst of wartime and the fucking explosions and heat were getting closer and closer; in fact I could see the bodies flying through the air just mere inches away and every fucking minute of every fucking day I felt like I could do nothing more than wait for that moment where I'd hear the whistling sound and feel the presence of the bomb tracking me. I was diagnosed not long after that.

————

As a kid I thought I would die amidst a tumbling of horse legs in the dust; I wanted to live in 1800s cowboy country and see my end tilting off a cliff with arrows piercing my body, or slow-motion hurling backwards under a fusillade of bullets in some self-styled bank robbery. These were the only possibilities of death and, aside from that, I would only think of death when I reached age eighty or ninety. To be losing one's friends at a relatively young age leaves one with what I imagine a concentration camp survivor might feel—to be the repository of so many voices and memories and gestures of those who haven't made it; *those who have died from the way this disease was handled by those in positions of power*; the fact that our mental structures are shifting at this early age to reveal our mortality for more than just a few seconds. A friend of mine recently said, "I remember my first feeling of fear—it was around age twenty-five or twenty-six," and that statement approximates something about the odd feelings I have if I substitute the word *death* for "fear" in that statement.

I've come down with a case of shingles and it is so scary, I don't even want to write about it. I don't want to always think about death or the virus or illness. I don't want to see in people's eyes that *witnessing* of my or others', silent decline. I don't want the burden of *acceptance* of the idea of death, departure, of becoming fly food, as my friend Kiki would say. I don't want to cease to exist. I don't want my mobility to cease to exist. One can't affect things in one's death, other than momentarily. One cannot change one's socks or tuck the sheets or covers around one's own body in death. One cannot be vocal or witness the lies of time. I don't want to witness the silencing of my own body. I don't want to be polite and crawl into the media grave of "AIDS" and disappear quietly. I don't want my death to have the pressured earmarks of *courage* or *strength*, which are usually catchphrases for the idea of politeness. I also cannot scream continuously without losing my voice. I wonder if it was the mid-'80s realization of the AIDS epidemic that woke me up and helped me draw back from the self-destruction that these other friends found themselves spinning into uncontrollably. I also marvel at how death can be so relentless and constant and how such enormous sections of the social landscape can be viciously exploded by a handful of rich white people, with an entire population's approval and participation. And I am amazed to discover that I have been building a suit of armor in response to the extensive amount of death overtaking members of my social landscape. That suit of armor consists of making more of an attempt to *continue* each time I hear of a new death. The grief hardens and is added to the armor. The armor takes the shape of wanting to see an accountability taken by those responsible. I know I'm not going to die merely because I got fucked in the ass without a condom or because I swallowed a stranger's semen. If I die it is because a handful of people in power, in organized religions and political institutions, believe that I am expendable. And with that knowledge I lie down among the folds of my sheets and dream of the day when I cross an interior line. That line is made of a quota of strength and a limit of pain. I know those

institutions are simply made of stones and those people are
simply made of blood and muscle and bone, and I know how
easily they can go, how easily I can take them with me. My
thoughts consist of wondering if the earth will spin a little
faster when my thoughts become action.

————

PHONE CALL:

"David . . . you know that friend of mine in Kentucky?
Well I got a call from a friend of mine who just got back from
being down there. She said he was getting way out of it . . . I
mean, like . . . he had lost about fifty to seventy-five percent
of his body weight and they were having to transfuse him
once a week. He was down; he couldn't walk at all. He was
being carried around by his family, in a wheelchair and he
had to go to the hospital every day, also, because of DHPG
transfusions, because he was becoming blind from C.M.V.
retinitis. So . . . uh . . . he would spend most of the mornings
in the hospital and then the afternoons he would spend
resting at this house that they had. Then he had a grand-mal
seizure . . . and he was just like . . . you know—convulsing
like crazy . . . I never seen one of those; I only heard . . . and
uh . . . you know—he became all different colors . . . and . . .
uh . . . was just gasping for breath and finally they were able
to sedate him somehow so that the seizure ended . . . and . . .
uh . . . this friend of mine who was very close to him went
down to visit because his family had called and said, "It
doesn't look that great." And . . . uh . . . I think, after being
there just one or two nights, he was deteriorating—his fever
went up very high and he was really kind of delirious all the
time. They were giving him a lot of morphine. They had sent
him home from the hospital; they stopped all the treatments

and everything like that because they felt that this was just like ... "Why torture him any more?" And ... uh ... at one point—finally, these two people—a friend and a family member—after he had had a small seizure and was in a semicoma—they just decided to put a pillow over his face ... you know ... do that ... and there was no resistance or anything that they could tell ... and ... uh ... I think they made a very courageous decision ..."

———

I found myself in the midst of a media spectacle concerning an essay I wrote for an exhibition at a publicly funded space downtown. The show concerned AIDS in a community of friends. The government agency that partially funded the show stepped in and yanked the funding because I called a notorious bigot in st. patrick's cathedral a "fat cannibal." I regret that I didn't take the time to go public and apologize to the cardinal for calling him "fat"—thereby inadvertently insulting people with weight problems. Being that this cardinal is such a media ham and has secret martyr fantasies, it didn't take him long to pull his skirts up and reveal his psychotic intentions in the AIDS epidemic. Within a week, the vatican and the cardinal put forth their opinion that, "It is a much more terrible thing to use condoms than it is to contract AIDS."

A number of letters arrived in my name at the exhibition space and a person who worked there put them in a large envelope and mailed them to my home address. The envelope was lost for a month and a half in the new york city postal system. I finally received the package about two months ago. There were a few letters from born-again christians wondering about the state of my soul. I never bothered to read them

once I got to the first mention of "jesus"—besides the fact
that there were no tape recorders in those days and the guy
they call jesus was wildly misquoted—born-again christians
are worse than reformed smokers.

One of the other letters was from a married lawyer in
another state who had once been of essential help to me in
getting off the streets as a teenager. He and I had had a
relationship that started out as sexual, with money changing
hands, and ended in a real communication that helped me
take the steps to get off the conveyor belt of 42nd street that
gave a one-way ride into the mouth of a giant grinning
deathskull. I'd met guys this society would incarcerate or kill
who gave me more than any government official, state
agency, or christian outfit like the salvation army ever did or
could.

The other letter was from Dakota.

TAPE RECORDING:

JOE: Once you recognize the shape of something, the thrill of
it is gone—well, the death appeal, I realized for me is: I
recognize the mechanics of what I'm doing and then it loses
its appeal and I look at the fact that this is gonna be my life
forever, doing the same thing—and I ain't just talking about
drugs. I'm talking about *everything*. This is what made me
leave North Carolina and come to New York. It's looking
down the line and realizing that this is the way it is until I
die and most of the time the dissatisfaction with that outlook
makes me essentially know what my life is gonna be like.
Here is death down here at the end and you're up here
looking down this line, then you say, just like in the tv
commercial where they go like, "Take a Certs," and then you

go swoosh, and you say, "Let's just move *death* right up *here*," and skip all this shit because it's gonna be the same thing over and over again . . . it makes death seem appealing. I just had that feeling the other day, it's like, "Oh. *Great!* This goes on *forever.*" Why don't I just move it up and get it over with. I'm sure that that's what was happening to Dakota, especially when you come off drugs; I've said this over and over again, I mean, you look at the sum total of your life and it's usually in a pretty big wreck behind you and it's almost impossible to see ahead of you to see the changes. Only when you can get some real distance on it can you see that the future can be just as exciting as the past was, because you have no idea what's gonna happen. So then it makes it more appealing to live.

D.: That's what I'm trying to get at. The grainy kind of dark shit that's already there in the psychic landscape of america, in the structure of things we're trying to survive in—but then, when you add the drugs to it, it exacerbates it in a way so subtle that you don't even realize it and it's so consuming that there's no point in stopping the drugs. Plus, once addiction sets in even if you can magically get to a place where you could get perspective on it, you're already caught in its gears. I mean, in the midst of the fake moral screens of government and organized religion that chews up life rather than supporting life, all the structure we're told to assume in the midst of heavy control and manipulation—even the violent act that Dakota created—it's totally recognizable what that anger is: the desire to tear through what is outlined for you to follow, and you know it's not true to you. There's nothing about the government's actions or the actions of rich white people in power that can convince us that that outline is true. We're told not to cross certain lines, and yet those lines are crossed every day by those in power, in the guise of protecting interests or whatever. What I understand about the things you make and the things Dakota made is that if the government and institutions want to play this game called "freedom" and they want to speak at political rallies and say, "Yes. yes. yes. We have freedom in this society," then people are going to push at these invisible boundaries to see if it's true. But what is the attraction to death images? Is the attraction based on the idea that death is coming anyway? So why not speed up the process because we're just exhausting ourselves waiting?

JOE: Not so much that it's coming, it's just that in society we have such a high thrill index, due to the way everything is assimilated so fast with the media, especially with tv. We have a desire for a quick end, y'know people, I think this is a common thread in all people, not just us. Once you recognize the void, how do you fill it? Most people fill it with money, fill it with romance, with thrills—but most people are afraid to carry it out to it's logical end, to where they really want it to carry them, so as a result we have tv shows that show people getting caught by the cops and doing all these crimes because it's *real* people doing *real* crimes that *we* wish *we* could do. Or it's people loving to see someone get seriously murdered just because they don't do it themselves. It's no secret that people have a big fascination for the Manson cult or Patty Hearst or the S.L.A. or something like that, because they do what people wish *they* could, because all people feel these same things about society. Well, I think all people feel this inside, but a lot of them just bury these feelings under a lot of other stuff.

D.: It's true. I feel that only the "insane" may not feel this impulse to shred these screens.

JOE: Only the people who don't *accept* it—that's the dividing line. There are people who accept the way things are and the way things are gonna be and then there are those who don't. Dakota was one of the ones who didn't accept the way things are gonna be—so he did something about it. You and I see the same things he did but we have chosen to accept the way things are. That's a real challenge—to keep doing things in spite of the way things are. I still have these very violent fantasies. A good example: Joe Stark, or Donald Westlake, as he's known, wrote this whole series of books about this guy Parker. They came out during the Vietnam war and during the Nixon years and they were all methodical accounts of this guy Parker planning these bank jobs or these big heists and never getting caught, and he was totally emotionless. The national attitude was: we hate Nixon and what he's done, what he did was all wrong, and yet these books were totally popular because people still had these fantasies of doing these totally anonymous crimes against the system. I have a real problem with that *still*—when I went out to california I was looking for somebody who wanted to do *real* jobs, that was the thing and I could never figure it out. I just didn't give a fuck at that point, and that was right when I came off drugs. I still have these fantasies: I try and think of places I can just go in and rob. Who knows? Maybe I will someday, and if I do nobody'll ever fucking hear about it . . .

———

JOURNAL ENTRY:

I wrote Dakota and haven't heard back from him. I included my telephone number and asked him to call collect. Nada. I've been starting to obsess about seeing him. I know he carries something that I recognized when I first met him

years ago and maybe with him being clean for the first time
in years I can touch that with him. Maybe he can show me
something in myself, some essential tool that will connect all
these fragments I've seen. I feel like I am half stationary and
half seated on a weird carnival ride, being flipped up and
down and all around, but really it is nothing more than
going through the paces of each day. Maybe it's the information coming through electronic instruments: this person
died, that person's dying, so and so died, on tv. I'm still
hearing "fag" jokes, president Bush holds a press conference
to tell the world he hates broccoli, Jeane Kirkpatrick sits on
television talking about the glorious state of the u.s.a., and all
I can think of is gallons of human blood. Nixon is telling
everyone it never happened, Ryan White has died and
already the media has replaced him with a ten-year-old from
portland who says, "It ain't a bad disease . . ." while Ted
Koppel, the announcer, says, "Why do you think adults act so
silly about it?"—*Silly?*—do you poke a microphone in the
face of a ten-year-old and suggest that Hitler was being *silly?*

I wrote Dakota another postcard, telling him I wanted
to try to go down to texas and hang out with him and maybe
ride the back roads together. I'd heard about some legendary
swimming holes where, among the moccasins and alligators,
country boys play naked country boy games in the shore
reeds. I tell him that Joe is clean and in N.A., that Johnny is
on methadone and he and Laura have a kid—a sweet
big-headed little guy with huge eyes filled with amazement
or confusion. I don't know what I think anymore. I feel like
some terribly important question is left hanging in the air. I
ask Dakota why he isn't answering my letters.

PHONE CALL:

"Hi David. Remember at the beginning of February . . . I looked down at my leg and saw this purple spot and everybody's trying to convince me it wasn't a purple spot? Uh, uh—no mole here. I knew it was a K. lesion. I decided to go to Berlin to the film festival, had a great time, came back and had an appointment with the ophthalmologist. I've never gone to see an ophthalmologist, but everybody is talking about C.M.V. retinitis—it's the latest dance craze . . . I decided to check it out, you know—me and my nineteen T-cells—I have to be aware of these things before any symptoms appear. So she didn't find any C.M.V. retinitis, thank god, but she did find P.C.P. in my eyes, which is the pneumonia thing, and this is very very unusual—she said she's seen only three or four cases . . . whatever . . . and I didn't have any symptoms or anything. She called up my doctor right away, and he took the phone call, which is very unusual in and of itself. He gave me a thorough examination without an appointment, which is even more unusual. He told me I had to go to the hospital right away and start treatments. I thought: What is going on here? I went, in one month, from being asymptomatic to having one little K. lesion and now to having P.C.P. It was that nightmare of moving from stage to stage in the disease's progression that everybody fears . . . and . . . uh . . . alright. I didn't have a place to live at this point; everything was upside down. I felt very out of place in the world. So I went into the hospital. I've never been hospitalized in my adult life. I went into co-op care. My doctor comes in and puts in this heparin lock, which is an intravenous line, and they started my treatments and I stayed there for fourteen days. By the end of my stay there the pentamidine started overwhelming me to the point where I became anorexic, and I couldn't eat anything. Everything tasted like it had a chromium edge to it. They took chest X rays and found P.C.P. in my lungs even though I'd been doing the aerosol pentamidine treatments. Then it was over. I moved into a new apartment and thought things were more or less in order and I went to the doctor to get a blood test and my red blood cell count went all the way down. I was white as a ghost. I don't know if you know that feeling of looking at yourself in the mirror and going: "Oh my god—there is definitely something *wrong*." They took me off all medication—I'd been doing D.D.I. That was frightening, too, because there is some sort of psychological dependency where you go: "well, I'm doing this stuff, so, good things have a chance of happening." The doctor thought, maybe it's just a transient anemia, we'll wash the pentamidine out of your body and maybe it will just have been a drug reaction. He didn't want to give me a transfusion because that's dangerous for people with AIDS because you never know what kind of infection you'll pick up from other people's blood. I mean, if you can do without it—fine. So I said okay. For three weeks in a row I went to the doctor, but the red blood cell count didn't go up much. He told me that he really wanted me to have a bone marrow biopsy. That frightened the shit out of me. They come at you with a needle that is quite long, quite sharp, and they put it in a spot that is quite painful. I'm getting really anxious—I've never been this scared. My parents came into the office while the procedure was being done. They shot the whole area up with Novacaine, which really burns, and while the whole thing was happening I knew what was going on—that the doctor was going into my body with a giant needle and taking out part of my bone. It wasn't that painful. It was sore for a couple of days afterward—I couldn't walk around that well. I haven't heard back on the results yet and I'm in the middle of an anxiety attack over what that will be . . ."

———

JOURNAL ENTRY:

I picked up an envelope from the staircase where all the mail gets pushed through the slot. It was simply addressed to David W.—Why is it we know when something is up? I stepped into the street with my arms full of packages trying to get this envelope open. Rain clouds are covering the whole earth and the construction workers are standing around eating baloney sandwiches and ogling women. Kiki once said she wished she could raise her hand and their dicks would wither and fall off. I'm trying to get this fucking envelope open with cold fingers and the paper is fibrous and I couldn't get the letter out, so in impatience I bent back the top fold in the letter and read:

". . . . committed suicide around january . . ."

and I stopped in shock. I'd built the armor well, I thought. I learned how to freeze out death and the intensity of reactions to it. But the death I was freezing out was the death of people who were fighting to live and, despite that, were killed by a microscopic virus and a conservative agenda. Suicide slipped through a minuscule chink in the armor. I thought of my friend in Philadelphia and wondered if he didn't really die of AIDS-related pancreatic cancer like I'd been told. Then I thought of Johnny and Joe; I thought of bodies with blank faces waiting to be filled in with identity. I yanked the letter out. It was from his father. It was unsigned and had no return address and informed me that Dakota had committed suicide in January.

I felt like my soul was slammed against a stone wall. I started crying, something I haven't done in months. There was something about the last half year, about all the deaths in the air. I'd been wondering if death has become so constant that I will never feel anything again. I fear losing the ability to feel the weight and depth of each life that folds up, sinks, and disappears from our sight. I thought of whether anyone will be able to feel anything about my death if it takes place. Is it all becoming the sensation one feels when they pass a dead bird in the street and all you can do is acknowledge it and move on. I thought of the late night tv announcer's voice saying, "In the Insect World, after the attack, the slaughter, and the massive loss of life in the colony is over, life simply goes on. Each insect goes back about its job without any thought towards fortification or defense . . ." Dakota's suicide left me with a sensation that there was something that was so irretrievable. Suicide is a form of death that contains a period of time before it to which my mind can walk back into and imagine a gesture or word that might tie an invisible rope around that person's foot to prevent them from floating free of the surface of the earth. I keep going back there and I am on a jet plane that is arriving in texas and I am seeing his dogs and his pickup truck and I am seeing him and he is vanishing and his dogs are sitting lonely in the yard. All I see is his absence, a void, a dark smudge in the air where he previously occupied space: "Man, why did you do it? Why didn't you wait for the possibilities to reveal themselves in this shit country, on this planet? Why didn't you fucking go swimming in the cold gray ocean instead? Why didn't you call?"

———

TAPE RECORDING:

DAVID: What was familiar to you in terms of his desire to kill himself?

SYLVIA: I just think it's a constant struggle. It could be a daily thing, I mean for me—I know I'll always be here—its probably the *vision*; just the idea of having to go through this for fifty more years; whatever it is, or just being aware that life is something that we have to *get through*, and you have to work so hard to make sense of it. It makes me mad when someone kills themselves, it makes me feel bad that I wasn't there, and what could I do? Besides that, I don't blame him, for him to stay alive; it was probably easier for him to kill himself rather than sit around thinking of it and try not to. It seems as if your life is trying to stay alive as opposed to just living. Just looking at things from the negative side and trying to make it positive *wears on you*. How do you maintain an element where you're happy; how do you find a little scope that you're the center of—you can't stay in the center of it—there's too much other life coming in.

D.: What creates that pressure or that feeling of struggling to survive rather than just living?

SYLVIA: I think the problem is not so much that there's something that *we can't fit into*, because I don't think the society or the situation is sitting there waiting to reject people; I don't think it's aware enough to say, "You don't fit in." I don't think it's that aware—I think that's what the problem is. So I think of who makes it and who doesn't and the pressure; a lot of it comes from us. We set a standard that we can't even live up to. We expect too much of a society that is probably going to reject us—it's probably not even thinking of us. I don't want to have that struggle that's trying to knock on the door and get in, and just sort of be invisible and

float so you can do your own thing—I think that's the part
that comes from us; I don't think that was set up; that's the
part that is hard to maintain. I mean, I want to *adapt*. I don't
think I'll be giving anything up. I don't care if I don't value
the thing I want to adapt to; it's there—it's a structure. I
want to adapt to it; I don't care if it's something I don't
revere. I think the fact of *wanting to adapt* is what makes a
difference whether we stick around or not. Some of us can't.
I wouldn't think Dakota killed himself because he couldn't
stand the structure that was there and because he didn't
believe in anything it stood for and just would have no part
of it, because if he felt that way, he'd just go and design his
own. I think it was just not being *able* to fit into it no matter
what it stood for.

D.: Can the bigger structure make room for the smaller
structure you design?

SYLVIA: If you measure it against anything else, then you will
always be susceptible to the other structure. You have to first
get a little place inside the larger structure and then make
your own. That's the problem. If you want to stay separate
completely you can't, because you will always end up measuring it against the larger structure . . .

———

PHONE INTERVIEW:
BETH: I've known a lot of friends who've killed themselves
but for some reason with Dakota I feel okay. I think he knew
what he was doing. He was pretty reclusive—he lived only
two miles away from me and we never saw each other, and he
explained that he didn't want to see anybody because he felt
his personality was too absorbed in other people and he
needed to be his own self. He had just recently got fired from

his job because he got caught—he wrote his friend in Dallas and they found the letter, it came back to work—he wrote in full detail how he lied to his boss about his grandfather being sick and how he stayed home and got drunk every day. He got off drugs when he came to Houston. He was going to an asylum during the day but he didn't think he was going to stay there at night. He killed himself with gas and a plastic bag. It sounded pretty painless. I feel like he comes in and out. I wish he could have left a book of his mind behind. I think he was too kind for this world. It kind of makes me cry to remember the sad parts of it, but with Dakota, more than anyone else who's done it, I can understand it more. Sometimes I wonder if when people kill themselves they don't leave as quickly; they circle around a bit longer. I told his brother to call me when he came to town, I was real anxious to get his ashes scattered. They're in an urn at his parents' house. I don't think it really matters, but for a while I was anxious to get him beyond that spot. I hope his family doesn't burn his stuff.

————

TAPE RECORDING:

DAVID: What was the first thing you felt when you heard he killed himself?

JOHNNY: I was really upset that I never resolved my relationship with him—like when he ripped me off and then he moved away. He had a lot of guilt; he kept writing me all these letters saying: can you ever forgive me? Every time he called me he'd be really drunk. I have this feeling of being responsible in a way, but not really. So, one part of me, I feel awful that I never got to finish something with him and also help him get the burden off his back. The other side of me feels almost relieved for him because he tried to kill himself so many times. He was just a very unhappy person. Almost the entire time I knew him, he was that way. One thing was that he thought he was really ugly. He had a big crush on Joe and at one time maybe on me. He hung around people like us and we weren't gay or anything but he would always hang around us. He hung around people he couldn't have relationships with and I think that that was part of it. I think he'd had enough. In death you know *you* can't come back but you know what you come back for. Some people believe in reincarnation and I'm sure some people commit suicide so that they can pop into another life. It doesn't work like that but . . .

DAVID: As far as I'm concerned, if there is reincarnation, I'm refusing to come back. Once is enough. If there is somebody you appear before who determines where and when you'll come back—I'll punch them in the face. Maybe that will put me on the end of a *very* long line for the return flight.

JOHNNY: That's the way I feel too.

D: Why do you think he killed himself?

J: A person like Dakota couldn't live for too long in a place like texas. He couldn't be satisfied. Did you hear how he'd amuse himself down there? One thing I'd heard that he was doing was breaking into people's houses and putting on these cowboys' cowboy hats and like putting on their gun belt and walking around the house naked and fantasizing about being involved in these people's lives, I guess, and jerking off into their beds. I mean, if those people found him they probably would have shot him, y'know, like he was just going to great lengths to amuse himself in texas. I think in general he was a brilliant guy and who was he going to find in texas, I mean, as his peers—where could he find people that think like him,

I mean nobody thought like Dakota anyways, at least no one I ever met. I think the boredom was too great.

D: Yeah, but in New York he apparently tried to kill himself a few times.

J: Yeah. I think that he was a beautiful person inside but he had this insecurity—as superior as he was spiritually I think he felt very alone and unable to connect with anybody and have a relationship including sex. He was great because he could just make things out of nothing; his music and drawings and cut-outs and writings.

D: What do you feel about death?

J: I have mixed feelings about it. While I'm here I want to make what I can out of it but sometimes I feel a desperation ... death would be an end to the boredom ... but ... death is an escape, an alternative—I'm sure it's a great experience, I mean all the experiences you hear about people who've died and come back—immediate peace and, depending on their spiritual beliefs, some people see their god or angels or choirs or buddha or whatever. I don't know what *I'm* going to see, but people seem to get their ultimate spiritual fantasy when they die—mine would be ...hahaha.

D: I'd heard that you died a number of times.

J: Three times that I can remember.

D: So you might be dead now. ALRIGHT DAKOTA, YOU CAN COME OUT OF THE BACK ROOM NOW.

J: Hahaha.

D: Do you remember anything from when you died?

J: I never had any mystical experiences. I was so drugged up that I couldn't—although I guess if your spirit came out of your body it wouldn't be drugged. I have no recollections at all. I was out for over a day at one time and I was in a coma. I stopped breathing and my heart was beating irregularly

and they thought it was gonna stop and I was on a respirator.
I remember waking up and they had everything—I was in
intensive care and they had every function, like, they had a
catheter in my dick and they had tubes in my nose; they had
tubes everywhere, and when I first came out of it I had all
these wires attached to my body to monitor my pulse and
wires on my lungs to monitor my breathing and all this
high-tech equipment like graphs behind me and the doctors
told Laura, "Ask him if he knows where he is," and I looked
over one shoulder and then looked over the other shoulder
and I said; "I'm on Star Trek." Thats all I remember. It was
too many combinations of alcohol and chemicals.

D: What was the last thing you remember before blacking
out?

J: Breaking a mirror.

———

TAPE RECORDING:

D: What did you feel about Dakota possibly murdering that
guy?

JOE: I thought it was great because I've wanted to do it a
million times. I still have fantasies. My friend Keith has an
AK-47; y'know, it's a real accurate sniper rifle, and many
times I've sat there in my apartment when the dealers are out
there yelling and I wonder if I shot my little pistol out the
window if I could hit them. And the AK-47 was there and I
thought out every single way; I even wrote it out so I know
what I'm doing—try to think of every single way I could do
it and get away with it: shoot those drug dealers standing
across the street. I figured if I could just shoot one or two of
them standing in the doorway out there yelling, that the
other ones would get the idea and quit, y'know? Dakota did

it—I wish I could do it. My big problem with justifying killing drug dealers is that I once sold drugs. I would like to see my fantasies become real. I mean, look at all these killers—they have a tremendous fascination, depending on who they're killing. I have a fascination for the S.L.A., even though it was a totally bogus organization, just because I can't *believe* people actually carried it out—like the Weathermen, they actually did things like that. It's about having a purpose; quitting drugs gave me a purpose ...

... Another thing I was thinking about is that thing where—say, with Dakota killing somebody—well, if somebody says to Dakota, "That's crazy ... that's insane that you did that," or if somebody kills someone else or somebody robs someone else and a person says, "How can you do that? That's crazy, that's insane, because that doesn't fit into the rules of society as we know it." If that's the case, then how come not everybody who does a violent act can come up on an insanity plea? How come the rules change when it's a thought or you verbalize it. Then people say, "That's crazy," if you *do* it, then it's a crime. *Then* you're not crazy; it's a crime and you must be punished for it.

You know, in theory, you can't punish somebody who is crazy. Because nobody knows what they're doing until they do it ... and then they might have ... I mean, premeditation is a very gray area that gets interpreted by the powers that be.

———

TAPE RECORDING:

DAVID: Okay—so, this guy killed somebody. What did you feel?

JOHNNY: I felt really sad that he could do that. I knew what a breach of his own morals that was, and the fact that he went that far—I just saw it as a point of no return from that point on. I knew he'd be living in a lot of guilt. Some people can kill somebody and not have those feelings, not have that guilt. The ability to do violence is there to some extent in everybody unless you're insane. But in somebody like Dakota, who was, on one level, super-rational—I could just imagine what he was living with. When he grew up he was the school geek and then later he was completely miserable doing drugs and feeling unsatisfied with his life because he had all these gifts and there was no place in the world, in the society, for people to embrace that. Not having any relationships, not being touched—it's a terrible weight to carry. The thing about being attracted to examine violence and murder and stuff like that is partly the frustration of dealing with this structure imposed on us and feeling sick of all of it, and the other part is actually an intellectual and spiritual curiosity. Death is curious; it's the ultimate ending. You have to look at Dakota's writings to understand what he thought about death.

TAPE RECORDING:

JOE: ... The people who were horrified; I'm sure if they were walking down the streets and saw somebody getting the fuck beat out of them they'd just keep right on walking. They wouldn't run up and just start pulling people off. It's primitive instinct—there's killers inside us and that information's suppressed by society. Say, if you were in the old west, and somebody stole your horse—you could hang them. It depends on how high in the hierarchy you are; whether you get away with it or are allowed to do it or not. In the south it was justifiable homicide if you shot your wife's lover; or in France if a woman killed her husband you could get off with "crime of passion." The rules always reflect the protection of the powers that be. That's the way it's always been.

D.: Do you think Dakota killed himself because of guilt over stabbing that guy?

JOE: No way.

D: Other people I've talked to say they didn't think Dakota could shoulder the weight of crossing that line.

JOE: No way. Maybe ... I—

D: People are telling me all these stories of him not killing roaches and this kind of reverence for life and it seems like this schism between those descriptions and then this thing where he researches how to stab somebody the correct way—well maybe there isn't really a schism, I mean all things contain their opposites within them. People who feel worthless all the time sometimes have a moment where they feel a great sense of power or self-worth; it's just a spectrum between opposites. Plus, he had ripped off Johnny and he was getting paranoid and had to leave town. Johnny showed me these endless letters where the guilt for ripping him off was unbelievable; it was to the point where he wrote this one letter saying—I don't know if it was something in his magic or what—but he said that judgment had been passed; the sentence had been passed and that they weren't going to give him the chinese rope or something. From what I understood he wasn't going to have to commit suicide but that the only way he could resolve having ripped off his best friend was that Johnny would have to stab him and everything would be okay. I don't know if Johnny answered him but there were other letters saying please forgive me.

JOE: I think I blew it, too, when I wrote him that letter

saying, "Lay off all this homo shit." That might've just slammed the door in his face, too.

... My last contact with him was when I'd write him all these letters and he'd send me all this stuff from texas, so it was when I was doing all this speed; I was high all the time and doing all this kinko sex and I had all these fucking sicko pictures of me with all these various people, and me naked and various people doing weird sex and shit and I sent him this great big stack of porno pictures—lots of nude pictures of me, and the response from him was he started writing me all this homo stuff, all about this obsessive homo stuff he wanted to do with me. My head was like—I don't wanna hear about it; I wrote him a letter saying, "Man I really love ya but stop writing me all this obsessive sex stuff because I don't want to do it with you and it ain't ever gonna happen"—and all I got back from him was this letter that said, "Sheeesh. What a grouch." That was the last I'd heard from him. I can't believe it, I just can't fuckin' believe it. This letter makes it more real; I don't know ... I start crying ...

D: So you don't think his suicide had anything to do with remorse or guilt?

JOE: I think it was more about looking down the line at endless remorse, and not waiting long enough for that remorse to go away ...

DREAM:

I woke up and stepped out of a room into a second floor hallway dark with morning. All along the hall, ending at the top of the staircase that leads down, are all these street people: poor people lying in beat-up sleeping bags or under old frayed and dirty blankets. Some of them stir slightly as

I pass them, walking towards the stairs. I stop halfway down
the curved staircase. It's a mansion with huge ceiling-to-floor
windows and behind the windows there is the clearest
wintery kind of light I have ever seen, and it is coming
through the bare branches of large trees growing just
outside. The light comes through the windows, and as I turn
to follow its path into the enormous room, I see a grizzled and
filthy vagrant. Under the large chandeliers he is dancing this
odd waltz-like dance, his arms upraised in a classical ele-
gance, slowly turning in the rays of light.

POSTSCRIPT

Late morning winter light bathes everything in the
landscape, giving it an apparition of warmth. I'm sitting at
a second-story table of a restaurant, behind the plate glass
windows of some crummy piece of architecture, feeling dark.
Maybe it's what we call "sadness," maybe it is darker than
that, and all I can think about is the end of my life.

In the far distance, at the edge of the runways, is a thin
wedge of horizon made up of dead brush, maybe trees—it is
formless, other than the enormous rusted oil refinery thing
and the couple of odd buildings made up of blond concrete
and shadows. What does it all mean? What's going on in this
head of mine? What's going on in this body, in these hands
that want to wander that guy's legs over there?

I just had a fight with my boyfriend in the middle of
the airport, twenty minutes before boarding a plane to
Mexico. I console myself with the sight of the construction
crew in the fenced-off area of the runway asphalt. I can count
eight or nine of them in winter drag and helmets, and I feel
like shit; years ago I could start thinking of what the
interiors of those construction trailers look like, filled with
drafting tables or cheap oak furniture and calendars and
ringing phones; I would have had fantasies of one of the crew
taking me inside and locking the door, a ratty couch over to
the side, and him removing his sweater and thermal under-
shirt all in one move, so I could reach over and put his sweat
on my palms—but that is a drift of thought that takes a lot
of effort right now and I don't care about making that effort.
What does it mean, what for and why? The red tail-fins of

some of the planes parked nearby have white crosses on their sides, and I think of ambulances—oh, love is wounding me and I'm afraid death is making me lose touch with the faces of those I love; I'm losing touch with the current of timelessness that drove me through all my life 'til now. Maybe I won't grow old with a fattening belly and some old dog toothless and tongue hanging. I won't grow old and maybe I want to. Maybe nothing can save me despite all my dreams as a kid and all my dreams as a young guy having fallen to their knees inside my head.

I wished for years and years that I could separate into ten versions of myself in order to give each person I loved a part of myself forever, and have some left over to drift across landscapes and maybe even to go into death or areas which were deadly, and have enough of me to survive the deaths of one or two of me. I thought this was appropriate for all of my desires but I never figured out how to manage it and now I am in danger of losing the only one of me around. I'm in danger of losing my life and what gesture can convey or stop this possibility? What gesture of hands or mind can shut it down in its invisible tracks? Nothing. And that saddens me.

———

I can't let go of Dakota's suicide; he followed me on the flight to Miami, and now light turns to dusk and I'm sitting in a replica of the earlier waiting room until the next plane begins to board. My boyfriend Tom is wandering the billions of airport shops and I am smoking a cigarette and thinking about death. A man on the balcony takes a Kodak picture of the sunset and uses a flash—what does he hope to illuminate? If I could, I'd descend the stairs and run with my eyes closed across those runways to the far horizon and break through the screen of dusk as if it were a large piece of paper held vertically, and enter a whole other century or life. If I could, I'd jump into a warm ocean and swim until I disappeared like a cartoon dot on the horizon.

Once, years ago, in a warehouse along the hudson river, I wrote on an abandoned wall about a man who flew a single-prop airplane out over the ocean until it ran out of gas, and I envied the man so much it hurt. That was years ago; does that mean up until now I have been living on borrowed time? Should I count backwards like the Mayans so that I never get older? Will the moon in the sky listen to my whispers as I count away?

———

I sat on a bench in the park in Merida wondering how much heterosexuals really love each other. Everyone I know has come from a childhood where they suffered some element of abuse at the hands of their parents. They watched the marriages of their parents turn into ugly battlegrounds whose parameters were defined by the four sides of a house.

In the streets of Merida there are hundreds of poverty-stricken kids selling handfuls of wild roses to the tourists for the equivalent of mere nickels and dimes. At dusk, someone saw these kids sitting on the benches in the park eating the petals of the flowers they hadn't managed to sell. The murderous jerk they call the pope is on his way to town in the next ten days for a tour. Another press agent for god who will in all likelihood tour the garbage dumps on the outskirts of the city, where groups of seven-year-old kids and their families comb the hills of putrid garbage looking for a handful of rotted food to fill their stomachs. Buzzards lift and descend on the stinking landscapes, in competition with hundreds of stray dogs for a mouthful of food. I went walking there with Tom once and the flies that poured through the air around us had us running in fear of what the marriage of insect and fucked-up immune systems might produce in us. A woman in the dumps, seven months pregnant and with four kids by her side, was asked on tv if she ever thought of using birth control, and she replied, "I heard that birth control causes cancer." There is no doubt that the church has spread that information among these people. Back in the states, the archdiocese, with the blessings of the vatican, says that condoms and clean needles are lies in the face of the AIDS epidemic. The lovely mexican queens who sit in the shadows of this park at dusk can't afford to buy rubbers when they sleep with the north american and european queers and straights who come here for vacations. It is left in the hands of visitors to provide protection. With the advent of acrylics, the rope this city was once famous for is no longer needed, and the economic problems extend even into the tourism industry. I went to a local zoo and most of the animals were laying in dazed pools of urine and diarrhea in the cages. Those animals that had died were taxidermied and placed back in the original jail-like homes. Thinking about all this and the constant sighting of Dakota in the labyrinthine streets makes me feel like tipping over sideways off the bench I am sitting on, or else buying a gun.

———

I felt something in my mouth—like a sensation you get when you're in a car or on a bicycle or just walking down a nighttime country road under the breezy trees and something flies into your mouth, like an airborne insect caught in the flow of currents. I pulled it out and laid it down on the white porcelain edge of a sink. I also may have found the thing floating in a puddle of water, not in my mouth: the two possibilities of discovery converge or at least intersect. It looked like a tangled body of a thin long mosquito or spider from a distance, but looking closer I saw it was a young mermaid, tiny and perfectly formed, no longer than three quarter inches long, and she was unconscious in the tiny pool of water that surrounded her on the porcelain surface. I thought if I picked her up and dried her off with a piece of tissue, or else put her on a dry surface, she might expel the water in her mouth and survive. I found a pair of cuticle scissors. I planned to use the thin closed blades to lift her up by the waist because my fingers were too large and clumsy to pick her up without squashing her. I made a delicate attempt to slide the scissors beneath her body in the tiny pool of water, and she separated at the waist. Her upper body was a quarter inch away from the rest of her body. I felt a subtle shiver of horror and kind of wiped away at her with my fingers—trying to send her lifeless body into the emptiness of the room. I felt embarrassed and self-conscious. I woke up glad to be dreaming again after months of emptiness

———

Tom found a poster on a distant corner, advertising bullfights. I felt sluggish in the intensified light and heat of the day and didn't really feel like going to a bullfight. I couldn't shake the transparent sense of death inside of every minute and every image and every movement of my body among the sheets of the hotel room, in the slow turning blades of the ceiling fan, or in the curves of stone and concrete making up the streets and buildings. At the last minute I shook the exhaustion and went with him, hoping the sight of blood would shake me up and wake me up to all that which had no words.

———

It's a hot day to kill a bull. The bullring is in a part of the city that looks like an incidental suburb made up of dying buildings reflecting the bright hot light of an unbearable noon. We're seated in the coliseum-style bleachers made of rough concrete with small numbers traced into dollops of cement that delineate each seat. There are crowded groupings of spectators, bunched into certain sections of the stadium, under portable umbrellas, behind dark sunglasses; all wearing hats or fishing caps. People are still arriving and the stadium is only half filled. Six large megaphone-style loudspeakers begin to blare a scratchy music; bad speaker connections, harshly amplified static, buries the notes, and there are occasional lapses in electrical current so the recording slows down. When the stadium attendants seat someone in front of us, we can't move our feet. When they seat someone behind us, we can't lean back without bumping into them. Claustrophobia gives me sensations like the flu.

———

The earliest photograph I own of my mother is one of her at age fourteen or fifteen, just before she got married. She is standing on a rocky outcrop of hillside, possibly above the city of Melbourne, Australia. She is wearing a white blouse and skirt, with her arms behind her head holding her hair against the insistent wind. At the bottom of the photograph she had inscribed the word: *Self.* At that time of her life she may have been the only person around who cared enough to ask for a portrait to be taken of herself. I barely remember what she described of her parents but it sounded as if she was unloved.

My earliest memory of my father is the glazed drunkenness of his eyes. He stole chickens for his mother during the depression so they could eat. My father was a sailor who could only describe his foreign travels in racist stories after hours of nursing a whiskey bottle. He had a tough liver that lasted fifty-four years without giving out. He loved to beat his wives and his children, in fact he made a science of it in the cinderblock basement where he kept his guns and tools, his attempts at taxidermy and making pickles. The pickles always rotted because his job kept him away for weeks and months at a time.

———

The loudspeakers of the stadium are blaring dramatic trumpet sounds. The instruments make up the sounds of an old brass band with an occasional flute buried beneath the waves of rolling music. The actual ring of the stadium is made of raked dirt and is quite small. The dirt is sunbleached and dry and surrounded by a wooden fence, chest high and painted the color of brick. There are small propped-up walls inside the edge of the ring, in various locations, for the banderilleros to scamper behind when the bull rampages. Embedded in the concrete foundation of the interior arena are small rooms with doorless entrances, marked POLICIA or SERVICIO MEDICO. On the dirt floor of the bull ring, about ten feet in from the fencing, someone has made an inscribed ring drawn in lime and inside that, yet another, smaller, ring.

———

My parents separated around the time I turned two years old. My father kidnapped my brother, sister, and me and put us up with relatives on a chicken farm outside of Detroit until he remarried with a woman from Scotland and brought her to America. He brought us back to New Jersey to live with her in a house on the outskirts of a farming town slowly being torn up for suburbs and tract housing. I remember big wet leaves in the morning trees and birds pulling worms out of the ground. I remember the first time in my life seeing a cop car scream by with red lights turning. I followed the sound of it for a number of blocks, to the front lawn of a house. The street was empty. I remember a man in a white t-shirt standing next to a woman in the front yard. I remember he had a gun to her head. I remember getting yanked away from the street by a stranger.

———

At the opposite end of the arena from where I am seated, under a cigarette advertisement painted on a wooden archway, is a half-sized double doorway. Over the top of the doors is a tunnel burrowed through the width of the stadium. I can see a gathering of men in shadows, and further back, in a strip of blazing sunlight, a couple of tan-uniformed policemen and a big white ambulance with revolving red lights.

Five rows behind us a brass band is assembled. There is a single drum. At the farthest point of the upper seats across the arena, near one of the sets of loudspeakers, the tips of a couple of healthy palm trees can be seen over the top of the wall. One bird floats in the circular sunlit hell of the cloudless blue sky.

———

With all these occurrences of death facing me, I thought
about issues of freedom. If government projects the idea that
we, as people inhabiting this particular land mass, have
freedom, then for the rest of our lives we will go out and find
what appear to be the boundaries and smack against them
like a heart against the rib cage. If we reveal boundaries in
the course of our movements, then we will expose the
inherent lie in the use of the word: freedom. I want to keep
breathing and moving until I arrive at a place where motion
and strength and relief intersect. I don't know what is ahead
of me in the course of my life and this civilization. I just don't
feel I have reached the necessary things inside my history
that would ease the pressure in my skull and in my future
and in my present. It is exhausting, living in a population
where people don't speak up if what they witness doesn't
directly threaten them.

———

The assembled brass bands starts up. It plays loudly
for about five minutes before being subdued by the intense
heat. A group of men in white cloth shirts and red berets
appears in the sundrenched part of the tunnel. The matador
appears and moves about the cops and the white-clothed
men. He glitters in a silver, black, and gold uniform. The
solitary drum starts up an irregular beat and thumps like a
breathing pattern in the uneasy temperature. The stadium
has slowly and quietly filled up.

———

My father moved all of us to another town, where
another kid and I had a gag routine that kept us amused on
boring afternoons. We would lie down on the long sloping

highway outside our doors to make the enormous trucks that came barreling over the hill hit their brakes. At the last second, before the squealing trucks would hit us, we'd jump up and run into the woods.

The only act of kindness I can remember from my father was one day when he took me into the playroom to beat me as he regularly did and, just before starting, he asked me what he should do. I replied, "Don't beat me." I remember he looked at me with a very tired and sad face, thought about it for a moment, and said, "Okay."

I remember zombie films in the local firehouse. I also remember the first times I witnessed death. One of them was in a pirate movie at the firehouse. I felt dizzy when a pirate plunged his sabre through the body of another pirate. I became the blade for a split second and couldn't picture where it went, what the interior of the other man's body looked like. I only felt helplessness because I knew it wasn't humanly possible for the other guy to survive. The second death I witnessed was when I was walking alone through a distant field and saw a brown dog tearing the brains out of the head of a rabbit. I yelled at the dog, but it paid no attention to me.

———

After being silent for a while, the band returns to song with an air of exuberance. The music sounds like roman songs mixed with Sergio Leone soundtracks. After a series of rounds it begins to sound like fusions of cabaret music and, further, like soft dreamy coastal bar music. A man in blue pants and striped shirt walks into the ring and checks out the small propped-up partitions. He pulls out and unfurls a small rectangle of red cloth. Draping it over the wood fence, he sticks his arm between its two layers and makes threading motions with a thin rod to give it support at the top. There are also mustard yellow and shocking pink banners, as well.

———

I thought of when Keith was lying in a coma in the hospital. Before he became ill he'd had a venomous relationship with his ex-lover, and some of the family gathered around his bedside continued that relationship for him at his wish. The lawyer representing Keith and his ex-lover had been battling over their loft for more than a year. Since Keith had become ill, and even then as he lay in a coma, his ex-lover hadn't seen or talked to him; the family would probably have been upset if he showed up. At least that is what I imagined when I tried to put myself in the lover's place and think his thoughts. Not long before Keith died for the third and final time, a phone call came into the room. One of his sisters answered it and it was the ex-lover. She explained the situation to him and said he could speak to Keith—if he had any last things to say, Keith could probably still hear them. She placed the phone on the pillow next to Keith's ear and left the room. I can only remember the waxen color of Keith's flesh and the slitted eyelids and the fluctuating movements of his eyes beneath them, and the dull hiss and thump of the respirator.

———

The guys in white uniforms and red berets have moved out of the sunlit part of the arena's exterior grounds into the shadowed area of the tunnel. In the sunlit area I see the fragmented movements of the picador riding back and forth on a horse that is draped with a deep blue stuffed blanket that protects it from the bull's horns.

The guys in red berets are now at the entrance gate to the dirt arena. A second picador appears at the gate. The crowd whistles and breaks into waves of applause. The band strikes up again. The red gates to the arena are pulled open. There is a drum roll. A procession of eight matadors enters the ring accompanied by picadors and banderilleros on horseback. The horses are blindfolded, with huge pieces of red cloth tied over masses of newspapers pressing against the horses' eyes. The padded coats the horses wear are deep blue, studded with red dots in a grid pattern. The drum roll repeats as the matadors doff their black hats to the crowded arena.

———

The satellite dish in the back of the hotel informs us that there has been an execution in a florida prison. Witnesses spoke of seeing flames shooting out of the sides of the prisoner's head but prison officials declared that it was not the prisoner who was burning but some faulty electrode wires. Turned out is *was* the prisoner.

———

There is another drum roll. A man prepares to release the first bull from a pen completely hidden from view by a large red plank door. The man is peeking through a slat in the door and then releases the latch and swings the door open. The bull rushes from the shadows of the pen and dashes heavily into the ring. It's got an excited look in its eyes, like a dog has when yanking and chewing on its leash. The bull stops and looks around and the banderilleros beckon with their various colored capes. The bull is tense and attempts to run each man down, and as it does each man scrambles one after the other behind the small propped-up partition walls.

———

My sister was about to give birth and I was sleeping in the guest room of her and her husband's house. Late at night I woke up from sounds of doors clacking against walls and floorboards and saw a sliver of light appear around the doorframe. I thought maybe she had to pee—the weight of the baby against her bladder, perhaps. She had called me in new york a few months before Peter died and told me she was pregnant, and in that phone call I saw Peter's death and possibly my own and everything as being cyclical. I woke up again with the sound of doors banging and thought it was odd, because her husband was usually quiet when he got ready for work. I fell asleep again. Woke up at 6:30 a.m. with an alarm clock in their room going off and I lay there slightly disoriented, waiting for him to shut it off. After three or four minutes I got up, put on my glasses and walked down the hall to their room to say something. Their bedroom door was open and the bed in disarray. I called out to them, but there was no answer in the house. It dawned on me that they had hastily left to have the baby. I burst into tears. The tears stopped as suddenly as they started.

———

The banderilleros, one after the other, attract the attention of the newly-released bull with their colored capes, goading it into charging after them, when, at the last possible moment, they throw themselves behind the propped-up partition walls. The bull is breathing hard with short breaths. Its anger, in odd moments, looks like a smile or a leer. These bulls are raised never having contact with humans until the day of the truck ride to the ring. Its stance and sudden erratic movements are purely motions of survival.

———

There was a gang of thugs in the neighborhood our parents warned us to stay away from. The oldest was a swarthy dark-haired nineteen-year-old and he built the bobby-pin guns they used to shoot the eyes out of squirrels. They also carried switchblades. Sometimes the gang would surprise a group of us in some old distant shack we'd taken over in an abandoned field for a club house. They'd show us girlie magazines and encourage some of the younger kids to stick squirt guns up each other's behinds.

One day the oldest guy caught me alone, playing in a half-built house in the construction zone. Nobody around for miles. He brought me up to the attic and had me stand on a box and tie his hands above one of the low ceiling rafters with a piece of rope. Then he told me to pull down his pants and take his large dick in my hands and pull on it. I did for a while until he began getting red in the face. I got bored and saw a box of insulation nearby, grabbed a handful of it and wrapped it around his dick and pulled. He screamed and I got scared and ran away. My father got a telephone call later and dragged me to the guy's house, where the doctor's black car sat in the driveway. After two hours of sitting on the lawn waiting for my father, he came out of the house, took me home, stripped me and beat me. At some point he took out his dick. I remember it was half-hard. He told me to play with it and when I refused he beat me some more. I remember running through the big house past a blur of faces: my brother, my sister, and my stepmother.

The matador stands inside the ring, still as camouflage. In all the excitement, the bull doesn't notice him. A picador on the blindfolded horse moves closer to the bull and stops. The bull comes out of its distraction, notices the horse and stops. It is motionless for a moment, then paws at the ground tossing clumps of earth, then charges forward. It rams the side of the horse, actually lifting the horse off the ground, planting his hind legs into the earth to better lift the horse in the air, twisting his head to drive the horns into flesh. But the padding tied around the horse protects it and it does nothing more than submit to the jostling. The man riding the horse lifts his arm in the air. He has a long wooden pole which has a sharp metal point. He plunges it into the bull between the shoulder blades and gores it with twisting motions. Hot blood pours out. The bull doesn't give up for a while, then seems to finally understand the pain and backs off. Blood is streaming in sheets down its broad shoulders into the dust and heat.

I tried to understand something about my father. I understood that he hated women. He hated children. And given that he shot or killed any animal he found me with, I guess he hated animals too. Obviously, he hated himself and I tried to find, in his limited biography, what he might have seen while looking into a mirror. It is all a terrible blank. He depended on the motions of the sea to escape, to nullify with the help of a whiskey bottle all the turning of his flesh and brain into the fields of aging. From the incidents I culled from family members about the later part of his life I learned that one day he started one brawl too many and almost killed a fellow worker. He got canned from his job after maybe thirty years of service, working the enormous boilers of various ships. (I could hear his words: "I would swell up so much from the intense heat I'd get stuck in a huge searing pipe and they would have to hose me down to get me out.") Then after months of being landlocked, working a gas pump job, he damaged and maybe killed someone in a drunk-driving accident. (One of the scariest drunken wrecks he got us into was also my favorite because of its slow-motion memory of spinning and the entire landscape becoming a vortex of indiscernible shapes until the rutted fields of corn caught the underbelly of the car and slowed us down to a gentle stop.) Being caught drunk-driving, his license was taken away for life and he was reduced to riding a mo-ped to work. A little fifteen-mile-per-hour putt-putt machine. I understand that to be landlocked was his greatest fear; it was the most brilliant mirror held up to his soul. He hung himself in the basement of his suburban home on christmas eve, leaving his still body to be found by his last son.

———

The neck muscles of the bull are pierced and maybe severed by the sharp steel tip of the picador's pole. This causes the animal's head to drop low to the ground and allows clearer aim of the matador's sword into the area of the neck and shoulders, making a truer path into the bull's heart. The primary energy with which the bull ran into the ring gives way in a short period of time to an exhausted display of the animal pawing at the earth, expelling volumes of blood

from its body and caught forever in a frozen stream of
information and stimuli so it remains from that point on in
the waves of understanding that its own death is encircling
its own pure desire for living. Smell the flowers while you
can.

————

I can pass my fingers fan-like across the front of my
eyes, making the sun's rays act like light through the spokes
of a turning wheel, and still the dust rising beneath the front
paw of the stomping bull takes on the abstract shape of
Dakota's presence. I don't, like some of his other friends, see
him waiting on street corners or among the crowds in the
subway. But I do see him. I see the reflection of his face in the
death of my father and realize that that was the last thought
to come to me. Everything else I have written to this point
was leading me into an indistinct memory of the day my
father killed himself, which triggered twenty-four hours of
me puking: off the side of the bed, into the avenue rushing
with cars and pedestrians off the corner of forty-second
street where I waited for my sister and her first husband to
pick me up for the wake, along the interstate wherever they
could pull over, and finally into the toilet on the second floor
of my father's house where I would be sleeping. I had
touched his fingers in the casket to make sure he wasn't fake.
In the middle of the night, before the next day's mass and
funeral, I woke up with a start and walked the dark hallway
to the bathroom again. When I pushed open the door I saw
streams of light coming through the floor. A light turned on
in the room below caused illumination to pour upwards
through the three or four bullet holes from the time he
emptied a gun after having pointed it at my stepmother's

head. She said, "I just continued to brush my hair, because I figured I was going to die. At the last moment he turned the gun up towards the ceiling." Smell the flowers while you can.

———

The banderillero walks to the center of the ring holding a ribboned and barbed stick in each hand. The bull notices and turns to watch with a fateful curiosity. The banderillero holds each stick delicately by the ends and crooks his arms upwards so that the barbed sticks are slightly above his own head, pointing at the bull. This action causes the banderillero to become an abstract image of a bull himself; the barbed sticks, his horns. The bull's head is down and the animal is charging. At the last moment, the banderillero runs straight at the bull in short measured steps, arches his back, and stops midflight on tiptoes and thrusts the barbed sticks into the back of the animal, simultaneously sidestepping it. The enraged bull turns, throwing a spray of dirt, and chases the banderillero to the outer wall, where the man in a vaguely comical fear throws himself over in a scrambling leap. He returns moments later to repeat the actions until three sets of sticks are embedded in the bull's back. The incessant flow of blood makes the bull gleam like a black mirror. Smell the flowers while you can.

———

The pain I feel is to see my own death in the bull's death; a projection of my own body's nerve endings and nervous system onto the body of that exhausted and enraged animal. The grief and shock Dakota's suicide produced in me was overwhelming, despite my having successfully managed to freeze out the weight of various other deaths in the last five years. I felt I stood the chance of going crazy and becoming a windmill of slaughter if I allowed myself the luxury of experiencing each of those deaths with the full weight accorded them. Dakota's manner of death opened a door to all that I've been speaking of: all these lives and their possible deaths were held in suspension by my isolation and intentional lack of contact. Now I saw my father crawling around in the dirt like in some bunuelian film, with his hands reaching for me and his eyes in magnified close-up with their pupils reflecting small films of my desire. I have always been attracted to dangerous men, men whose gestures intimated the possibilities of violence, and I have always seduced them into states of gentle grace with my hands and lips. I have loved the sweetness of their blushing long after our body fluids stopped their arcing motions and settled onto the sheets; the sweet flush of their embarrassment at the realization of the tenderness of their momentary gestures. Dakota may have killed someone in order to get permission to end his own physical life. He did what he had to do, and I respect him for it. Smell the flowers while you can.

There is a gasp and cry from the crowd. The bull in all its twists and turns before the various assaults from the banderillero has broken its front left leg. When the bull is confronted with the matador's cape, it drops its head low and paws at the ground, its leg goes floppy and obscenely doubles back on itself. After a wobbly charge, in trying to come to a stop, the bulls leg bends backwards and throws it into the dust. The crowd is caught in shocked identification. After surveying the situation, the matador shakes his head in sympathy and disgust. He arches his feet and points his sword at the bull in an affected graceful, arched motion. He takes aim with his X-ray eyes on that invisible point between the rolling curves of the bull's shoulders; the true point where the entrance of the steel blade will still the heart. Smell the flowers while you can.

————

When Tom and I first arrived at the hotel in Merida, we were given a tiny damp room that smelled of exterminator's bug spray. The porter turned on the small black and white television and took his tip from my hands and left. On the tv was a north american cartoon of a mexican mouse wearing a sombrero and chattering in dubbed spanish. The world exhausted and depressed me. I went for a brief walk to the elegant green park in the center of the city. Leaning into the contours of a wood and steel bench, I watched the fragmented images of the city spilling into the pathed entrances of the walkways. A group of street kids no older than twelve sat on the stone curb and searched each others scalps for lice. Seeing a few shreds of humanity in a person causes me to immediately love them deeply. The transparent image of Dakota has wrapped his arms slowly around the living bodies of Joe and Johnny. The last time I hung out with Joe I realized something was beginning to return to his eyes, something human. Johnny seems to me to be still caught in the flux of chemicals, only now it is state-endorsed in the form of methadone. Something much more difficult to kick than heroin. But I still have hope for him, which may not do him any good anyway. He's got to find what he needs somewhere deep in himself; some desire to again move forward. What cheers me is seeing these friends as fighters who have fallen to their knees but who are up again and returning to fighting condition before my eyes. I am glad I am alive to witness these things; giving words to this life of sensations is a relief. Smell the flowers while you can.

———

The matador distracts the bull with his red cape and executes a small series of quick steps forward. The cape moves low to the ground, the bull drops his head for the imminent charge and in one quick thrust the blade of the sword is buried up to the hilt between the animal's shoulder blades. But instead of collapsing, the bull continues to charge and is suddenly surrounded by banderilleros distracting it from every angle with various colored capes. One of the banderilleros comes up behind the bull, produces a short silver dagger and punches it into the back of the animal's skull. He then wiggles it back and forth in quick brutal motions and the bull keels over sideways, flopping against the earth among a scattering of men's legs. In a moment the bull's legs jerk out spasmodically, blood issues from its nose and mouth, and it is dead. It excretes a stream of shit from its behind into the pale dust. Smell the flowers while you can.

———

The transparent image of Dakota has placed coins onto the eyes of my father. He bends close to my mother and whispers something into her ear. I give my parents humanity, in deference to their victimization at the hands of their parents. Heads of Family; Heads of State. Whereas, I can step back from the forms of violence, psychic and physical, that I may have experienced as a child at the hands of Family—I step forward with the shield and sword to confront the State. Crimes against humanity have an unforgiv-

able weight when compared to crime against an individual.
If thirsty people demand the presence of the death penalty,
let it be reserved solely for politicians who commit crimes
against humanity. This goes for those politicians who wear
religious drag and who kill us with their fake moral codes.
The billion or more fragments of my living and my life lift
up around me in a windswell, and through that swirling wall
of snow-like images I reach way back and lay Dakota's face
at the base of the interior shrine. I also lay to rest his waiting
dogs, his idling pickup truck, his ideas and desires. Smell the
flowers while you can.

———

Three horses, two of them white, the one in the middle
black, tied together in a wooden brace, are led into the ring
by two men, one on each side of the outer horses. The stock
holding the horses in place, riding their necks, also has a
contraption attached to it through which the men thread the
rope which now binds the legs of the dead bull. Every task is
performed in utter and complete silence. I feel I am watching
a silent movie, a film silenced by the descending weight of
death. The band is playing somberly as the horses suddenly
bolt in unison, dragging the bull behind them through the
dirt. A little man in a uniform, with a crudely built
wheelbarrow, comes out into the ring and wheels up to the
spot where the bull previously lay. He takes a small shovel
out of the barrow and scoops up the blood-drenched earth
and shit and tosses it into the barrow. The band stops
playing just as the bull is pulled into the darkness of the
tunnel's shadows. The little man with the wheelbarrow filled
with evidence is left pushing his cargo through waves of
soundless heat. My body gives a gentle burp and stomach

acids well up into my throat. Smell the flowers while you
can.

In the tiny room of the hotel he removes his pants and
folds them, placing them neatly on the chair next to the bed.
He unbuttons his shirt and climbs onto the bed sitting on the
pillows with his back to the wall, his legs spread wide and
slightly bent at the knees. The biceps of his arm is rolling
softly beneath the tanned skin, mirroring the motions of his
hand as it slowly pulls up and down on the length of his dick.
He is smiling and has the same look in his eye as the bull did
when it first charged into the ring. He places the bent disk of
a rubber on the head of his dick and with the same jerking
motion he unrolls it down the length of his desire. From
where I stand at the foot of the bed, I think it's lovely the way
he pulls on his dick and then lets go of it momentarily so that
when it throbs it lifts straight up into the air, affording me
a view of his tight balls. And that relentless smile. There is a
clear joy in his eyes as I lean forward and slowly crawl over
the surface of the cool sheets with my destination firmly in
mind. Smell the flowers while you can.

We stay for two more fights and then stand up in the
dizzying heat and head towards the concrete archways of the
exit. We leave behind us the confirmed and imminent deaths
of five more bulls. Moving through the cool silence of the
shadowed passageways, we eventually step out into the sunlit
grounds of the field surrounding the arena. To our left we
notice a line of forty or more people waiting patiently for
their turn at a makeshift counter that comprises, along with

a metal-poled structure, a spontaneous meat market. Huge dripping sections of dead bulls are impaled on hooks or draped over the table. So little has been quartered that I could almost recognize which animal was which. The people waiting on line have the clothes and postures of exhausted poverty. As we stop to witness, the bulls disappear piece by piece. Behind us, far over the walls of the arena, the vague notes of the band begin again and float like thin banners across the hot sky. Meat. Blood. Memory. War. We rise to greet the State, to confront the State. Smell the flowers while you can.